the weekend Novelist

Robert J. Ray and Bret Norris

A & C Black • London

We dedicate this book to Bret's wife Charlotte and
to Bob's wife Margot. Two ladies who might think,
but who would seldom voice these words: 'It is no
picnic being married to a writer.'

First UK edition 2005
A & C Black Publishers Limited
37 Soho Square
London W1D 3QZ
www.acblack.com

© 2005, 1994 Robert J Ray
© 2005 Bret Norris

ISBN 0-7136-7143-2

A CIP catalogue record for this book is available from the British Library.

A & C Black uses paper produced with elemental chlorine-free pulp,
harvested from managed sustainable forests.

Typeset in 10/12pt ITC Garamond Book
Printed and bound in Great Britain by
Creative Print and Design (Wales), Ebbw Vale

Contents

part 1

Getting started

Introduction

The Weekend Novelist is a book of lessons. Collected, taught, refined over 30 years, these lessons teach the writer in you how to finish your novel. This book gives you a schedule, a plan of attack to release the story that swirls through your very being. *The Weekend Novelist* is a workbook to motivate you, teach you, walk you through the journey of writing a novel.

The first edition of this book started with character and moved on to plot and scene and writing. This revised edition expands the plotting section. From a dozen or so pages in the old edition, we have enlarged this focus to give you a range of choices for building your book. The basic concept you need to build a plot is architecture - the bones of the novel. By using simple diagrams - either hand-sketches or line-drawings done with a computer-graphics drawing programme that makes circles and lines - you can compress the elaborate architecture of the novel down to a single page. The compression in the sketch is followed by some quick writings - we call it 'spinning down the page' - where you go with the flow of your diagram.

As you work through the book, you'll move from a section on plot to a section on character and then, before you do your scene-work, you'll take another run at plot. Plotting early forces you to look at the 'Big Picture'; the architecture of your novel. In most published novels, the architecture shows up on the page as chapter divisions, chapter heads, or breaks made with white space. Some novels are divided into parts: Ian McEwan's *Amsterdam*, one of our model novels in this book, has five separate parts; Zadie Smith's *White Teeth* has four separate parts; Michael Chabon's *The Amazing Adventures of Kavalier and Clay* has six parts. But the real architecture - the arrangement of parts that helps the writer finish the book - lurks behind the words. So that's why you start with plot, making sketches and doing a bit of writing to bring characters into the story, and then you deepen those characters with character work.

Character work begins with a sketch, then gets deeper with back story, wardrobe, and dream. As your characters get deeper, you do more plotting. There are specific techniques to help you fashion an architecture for your novel - one that takes you all the way to the climax, the moment of resolution where one character wins and the other character loses.

With the plot contained and the characters in motion, you start writing scenes. Your novel will have a dozen or so key scenes -

moments of dramatic tension marked by weddings, funerals, birthdays, arrivals and departures, burials, executions, proposals, kisses – and this book will guide you in writing three: First Encounter (where two of your two main characters meet), Midpoint (halfway through, no going back, got to keep pushing on), and Climax.

After you write each scene, you can explore it by using our 'TWN checklist' – Time, Place, Character, Object, Dialogue, and Ritual – which pops up in the exercise sections that follow each weekend. ('TWN' is shorthand for *The Weekend Novelist*.)

We should tell you that this early work is all rough draft. In a rough draft, your stance is creative, not critical. It is intuitive and exploratory, filled with adventure, a journey open to exploration. We have several techniques to help you stay creative, but the one that works best for the large majority of writers is called 'spinning down the page'. When you spin your words down the page, using short lines, the writing looks more like poetry than prose. Freed from the paragraph, your writing generates strong verbs and useful images. Here's a quick example:

the rain beats down
her shopping bags are paper
her hair is a mess
she runs for her car
the rain stings her cheeks
her foot finds a puddle
she feels cold through her toes
she cannot find the car
a voice calls out
are you all right
she does not stop
she loses her grip on the shopping
the voice comes again
are you all right
she looks up to see

Using this book

Each section of *The Weekend Novelist*, whether it is about plotting or sculpting a character or building a scene, begins with a lesson. The lessons explore elements of narrative: the role of an antagonist, the art of dialogue, transitions from scene to scene. You will learn skills and apply them to your novel. The book is designed to build from section to section. Start small; finish big. In each section, exercises focus your writing. This is where you build the foundations for your novel. In the exercises, you work through all the extraneous details that are necessary for writing a novel but don't belong in the finished product. Throughout, you will learn about writing practice. Writing practice teaches you to put thoughts into words, tease out ideas, hone your skills. Practise your skills every day, so that when you land at the keyboard to write your masterpiece, the narrative will flow from you without distraction or diversion.

As a writer, you have a long, lonely pursuit ahead of you. Learning from the masters will shed light, open doors, connect concepts. To learn about great writing, read great books. *The Weekend Novelist* takes selections from award-winners, classics and bestsellers to show how authors succeed. These examples will teach you how to use 'helper' characters, write dialogue, and craft your plot.

Structuring your writing sessions

If you wake up ready to start right in, that's brilliant! Most times, though, you won't. Get in the habit of beginning your writing sessions with timed writing practice: this will be your saviour. Timed writing is writing for a set amount of time – no stopping, no editing, no rules – and it serves a number of purposes. First, it clears your mind and helps you lay the foundation for your novel. Second, it provides a forum for you to explore anything you want. Third, it lays the groundwork for writing a novel. The foundation, the exploration and the groundwork are critical to writing tight prose. Most novice writers wander in their novels, never catching the thread of narrative. Timed writing gives you chance to clear the air before the real task begins.

Set the kitchen timer and write. Don't stop. Don't edit. Don't think. Just write. Shatter the walls that surround you, keeping you from saying the words that excite you. Write about anything. Just get your mind working. This book provides startlines for timed writing. Begin 20 minutes of writing with, 'My protagonist is afraid of. . .' Or, 'My antagonist wants to kill. . .' As you free yourself, writing practice becomes a place to open doors and make connections. Writing practice teaches you to silence the internal editor – the one who says, 'This is rubbish. Don't waste your time.' Write through that. Misspell words. Swear. Keep the hand moving. Writing practice is freedom from error. Practise at every opportunity you can get. Hone your skill. Sharpen your edge.

Finding your workplace and writing time

You need a comfortable space in which to write; one that has positive creative energy. If you demand absolute silence, barricade yourself in the basement. If you function best in chaos, try the local coffee shop that blasts good rock music. You need a desk and chair for writing. And you need a chair to read in – somewhere you can concentrate and learn. Choose a place that brings you peace. Your surroundings melt away; you become a sponge for language and literature.

Writers battle time. You battle time in your narrative. You battle for time on the editor's or agent's desk. And you battle for time to write. *The Weekend Novelist* structures your writing, giving you a plan to follow.

There are two kinds of writers: those who write every day and produce copious stacks of material; and those who wait for creative inspiration and hoard their brilliant book ideas all to themselves. This book gives you a schedule to follow: stop talking, put those ideas down on paper, and write your masterpiece.

When making a schedule, pick a time when you won't be interrupted. During your writing time, you're a writer. Savour these moments for your mental health. Writing is your weekend job – no distractions. Mornings are best for the creative stuff: you're fresh, the air is sharp, the room is quiet, the world is sleeping. Nights are good for reading over the manuscript.

Let your family, housemates and friends know that you're unavailable during your writing time. Put up a schedule: Saturday 07:00–10:00, Sunday 08:00–11:00. Remind yourself, and pass the word to any possible intruders about when the writing space is closed to visitors. As your novel grows and you need more time, put up a new schedule. Don't answer the phone. Don't write e-mails. Don't surf the Web. This is writing time; it's sacred. Here, every minute counts.

Your writing tools

The following list is by no means exhaustive, but to become a writer you need the tools of the trade: notebook, pen, computer. Younger authors tend to include some kind of intoxicant, which is amateurish. Alcohol and dope numb you, distract you. Popular culture would have us believe that authors compose during intense highs, but good writing depends on the connection between mind and soul. Don't block that pathway.

Notebooks are the writer's canvas. Legal pads are good, but hard to organise; they break down. Spiral notebooks are the best; they're tough and easily arranged. You will need something small to carry with you as well. Steno pads are good for this purpose; they're fast and slim. On the front of your notebook, write the date you begin using it and the novel you're working on. You'll fill several notebooks writing a novel. You can even make an index or a table of contents for each notebook. Keep focused on the writing; don't let the organising – the system – distract you. Your notebooks are priceless. Notebooks are the place to confess, create, explore. They're a place for shelving ideas, images, ideas, plot points – anything and everything. In your notebooks, you teach yourself to connect with your unconscious. You figure out your story. Cherish these notebooks. Guard them.

Pens are simple. Pick something that feels good in your hand. Biros are good for pace, but leave indentations on the pages below. Felt tips are neat and crisp, but they bleed. Fountain pens are the best but expensive. Again, you will need a small pen to carry with you at all times.

Computers are essential in publishing today. You will need something that can run a good word-processing program and something to connect to the Internet. Laptops are best for portability – writing in the coffee house – but they're pricey. Desktops are easy on your eyes, but you're rooted in one spot. Software isn't an absolute concern, but Microsoft Word is the industry standard.

Documents can be translated in just about any way, but features like spelling and grammar check and track changes are very useful. New fiction writers make the mistake of experimenting with language before they command all the rules. Spelling and grammar check will help you to manage this. Track changes is a valuable software function: as you rewrite, it saves all of your edits, allowing you to see your drafts evolve. You should save each draft of your manuscript, and this function keeps each individual correction for future reference.

The Internet will be an invaluable tool – and it can be your biggest enemy. Closing your Web browser while you're writing is the best way to avoid distractions. Keeping it open, however, gives you a portal to quick research and reference. Check the spelling of a name, the definition of a word, the synonym that escapes your mind. The key is to move back to writing once you've looked up your information. When researching on the Internet, check your source, and check your source's source. *Be conscious of the vastness of the Internet*.

Adding useful books to your bookshelf

We've chosen award-winning and popular novels to serve as examples of greatness. Throughout this book, we've examined these model novels for technique, style, and method, taking them apart and giving you specific areas to look at to help improve your writing. Most great writers read constantly. Buy these books, or find them in your local library. Read, read, read.

Model novels:
The Alchemist, Paulo Coelho
The Amazing Adventures of Kavalier and Clay, Michael Chabon
Amsterdam, Ian McEwan
The Namesake, Jhumpa Lahiri
White Teeth, Zadie Smith

Books referenced:
Get Shorty, Elmore Leonard
Harry Potter and the Sorcerer's Stone, J K Rowling
Jane Eyre, Charlotte Brontë
Last Orders, Graham Swift
Leaving Las Vegas, John O'Brien
Life of Pi, Yann Martel
Madame Bovary, Gustave Flaubert
Moby-Dick, Herman Melville
The Naked Ape, Desmond Morris
The Screenwriter's Workbook, Syd Field
The Things They Carried, Tim O'Brien
Lolita, Vladimir Nabokov
All The King's Men, Robert Penn Warren
The Art of Fiction, John Gardner
The Wordsworth Book of Opera, Arthur Jacobs and Stanley Sadie
The Woman's Dictionary of Symbols and Sacred Objects, Barbara G Walker
The Woman's Encyclopedia of Myths and Secrets, Barbara G Walker
The Elements of Style, Strunk and White
The Chicago Manual of Style (Web also)

Thinking like a writer

Your big gift as a writer is creativity – images bubbling from your unconscious to become the jottings you store in your notebook. Your big weapon is tenacity; the will to keep going. Many thousands of manuscripts are landing in publishers' slush piles each year: the odds of breaking out are staggering. As a writer, your only chance of success will come on the page, and you relish the opportunity to use your words.

You don't need a huge vocabulary; just use the one you have with energy, efficiency, and honesty. Let your voice come through. You do need drive, determination, and a sense of humour about your work. Find folly in yourself. Expose yourself to readers. Let them in.

Most of all, you need to stay open to ideas, insights, form, technique, rhythm – new ways of looking at writing. One way to stay open is to bring a character onto your stage and experiment. You sketch her first. You give her a past and some dreams and a place to live and a wardrobe that fits her lifestyle. As she comes onstage, you take notes. She lights a cigarette. What brand is it? Light falls across the glass-topped table to illuminate a film of dust. Is she the housekeeper? Where does the light come from? When she stands up, leaving her chair, where is she going? You won't know until you write it. For a writer, writing is the best test. Immerse yourself in the writer's life. The real writer's life; the writing.

Warming up

Some days you'll wake up and get right to work, jotting notes as your coffee trickles into the pot. You might even wake up in the middle of the night, your mind racing with details, scenes, connections. Words shoot from your hand like bolts of lightning.

On those 'hot days', race to your writing spot, notebook in hand. Ignore the morning doldrums, the pitfalls that distract you. Feel the excitement course through your veins. Your language is fluid, roaring; words splash onto the page. The writing pump is flowing, and you don't dare stop it up. When hunger pains bring you out of the writing fugue, you'll discover that you've written three scenes, two character sketches, and two back stories. This is why you write. On hot days, you find yourself cruising along the road that connects conscious thought and unconscious emotions. You don't have to spend time reintroducing yourself to characters, reconnecting with story. Savour these infrequent gifts.

Not all writing days are hot. Most writers spend hours cleaning their desks, reading, looking up obscure quotes – anything to avoid sitting down to write. If you wake up slowly, filling your coffee cup, walking the dogs, reading the paper, the writing pump is rusty and needs lubrication. Writing is a job with a tyrannical boss. The computer is nothing but an Internet portal, an e-mail machine. Characters are pesky cousins, wanting, whining, weeping.

Establish a writing routine to avoid slacking off. Get each writing session going by warming up. Do mind-maps, clusters, lists. Stretch your writing muscles to clear the cobwebs. Open the mind's eye. Getting into a routine makes your weekends productive. Waiting for inspiration will cost you a lifetime of wasted writing time. Start with warm-ups:

- *Make connections*. Start anywhere: a person, a place, a sacred object. Write a word in the middle of a blank page. Now draw a line out from it. A person connects to death, love, money. A place connects to want, wanderlust, peace. An object connects to a person, a theme, a destiny. While these connections stretch your mind, let them build. Write quickly. Don't judge. You're trying to reach your unconscious. Don't censor.
- *Get organised*. Set goals. This book gives you a course of study; expand it. Tailor your writing sessions. List your character's favourite foods. List the scenes you find most difficult. List your favourite names. Use lists to ask and answer questions. Lists are catalogues of supplies; words are your tools.
- *Writing practice*. Writing practice moves you from your dark, distant cave to the road. Set the timer, put pen to paper, let go. Allow yourself to misspell words. Don't mess with punctuation. Just keep the hand moving. Writing practice is what happens before you tell a story. Use this time to search a character's back story, the details of setting, the points on your story arc. Writing practice allows you to experiment, go crazy.
- *Writing with friends*. Writing with other writers brightens the dark passage ahead. Creative energy permeates your soul, surrounds your being. Groups of writers meet everywhere: coffee shops, bookshops, libraries. Get together to bounce ideas around. Join a group to share your heartache. Writing is a lonely pursuit, and sharing your passions can relax the tensions. Some groups write and then read aloud; other groups exchange pages for critique. Groups can offer any structure you like. Communicate your needs, and other writers will stimulate your mind.
- *Reading aloud*. Writers are artists. The medium is language. Hearing brilliant language read aloud, capturing style bliss, releases endorphins in your brain. Take your time, read from your favourite books. Allow the language to flow from you. As

you read, find your writing centre. Hear the words. Enjoy the images.

- *Exercises*. Do the exercises in this book: they emphasise technique and help you pace your writing, weekend by weekend. These exercises aren't one-off endeavours: use them to get you going. If you feel a twinge every time you think of your antagonist, look over the character questions. If you plan to work on scenes one weekend, redo the scene-building exercises. Use the exercises in this book as a springboard for your mind.

Managing your writing

Most writers power through Chapter 1 and then begin editing. They polish and polish until they have a great opening, and that's it. They spend hours and hours rounding a character, showing a scene, poking a metaphor. Unfortunately, Chapter 1 only gets them to page 10 – if they're lucky. Managing your writing means managing your time. There's a time for revision, and it's once the first draft is done. The first draft is the discovery draft. Even if you do every single exercise and complete every single component to the weekend prescription, you've only completed one draft. You draft, you discover, you revise. Then, and only then, are you done. It's not as long and arduous as you may think. Just follow the steps.

Once you've written Chapter 1, write Chapter 2. When Chapter 2 is done, write Chapter 3. If you spend your precious time and energy too soon, you'll burn out. You'll tell yourself, 'I'll get back to it. I just need to get Chapter 1 perfect.' Get the first draft done.

It's no secret: writing is a process. Respect that, and you've already beaten most of the competition.

Prepare, prepare, prepare

When you read a book, you start at the beginning, move through the middle, and finish at the end. It's simple: page 2 follows page 1. When you watch a film, you take the same linear route. The creation of a book, however, is quite different – just as the shooting of a film is quite different. Films are shot out of sequence: before the actual filming, carpenters build, actors rehearse, directors plan. Books follow the same process. How can you begin writing Chapter 1 without knowing who your characters really are? How can you foreshadow a horrible death when you haven't discovered how your beautiful maiden met her killer?

Preparation is important to all steps of the writing process. Get to know your characters before you put them in scenes and set them in motion. Know every detail about the setting of your novel. Let your characters speak for themselves, and listen to what they say. Film directors know every detail of the script. Great writers prepare. Create a blueprint and follow it.

You start preparing with character work – sketches. You create people out of your thoughts and experiences. When you're done, these characters will speak, act, and react like real people. They aren't real, but they are believable. They dress in the clothes appropriate to their place and time. They speak with inflection and language consistent with their status. It's your job to create characters that are full, exciting people.

After character work, you move on to scene development. Because you've already explored your characters' back stories, you know how they react in certain situations. You put them in motion and believe what you're writing – it's accurate. You have to sketch scenes so that details are authentic. If you're in London, pay in pounds, drive on the left-hand side of the road, avoid a lorry (not a truck).

Do your homework, and the writing is easy. You've got the pieces, now just put them in place.

Freeing your unconscious

Your rational mind makes decisions, pays the bills. Your unconscious mind holds secrets. Your conscious mind processes information in the front of your brain, where you think. Your unconscious mind absorbs details that escape your blurry vision. Your conscious mind understands. Your unconscious mind feels. You will need both to create a saleable novel. Editors look for books that evoke emotion. Grab the readers by the scruff of the neck and scare them. Tapping your unconscious mind is the key to a bitchy protagonist, hot sex, broken bones. The road between the conscious and unconscious minds is guarded by all kinds of trolls: commercialism, politics, fast food. To tap your unconscious, you have to free yourself. Give yourself licence to hate, cry, fail. This happens at the tip of the pencil, the point of the pen, the keys of the keyboard. The rich details that will distinguish your work come from your unconscious. That's where you will find your character's deepest, darkest secrets. That's where you will find your connections.

Tapping your unconscious allows you to see the arc of your story. If, in Chapter 3, your pill-popping football mum crashes her 4x4 and runs from the police, can you find the key to unlock her demons? Has she ever been arrested before? Does her husband know she chases her Prozac with vodka? Most importantly, why? That's a question you can't answer rationally. Of course, she came from a broken home and suffered with an abusive stepfather, but why isn't an unlimited bank account and a tall, dark commodities trader enough? Your only choice is to follow the road into your unconscious and see where it takes you.

Escaping the internal editor: write under the clock

The internal editor is the Judge. It casts doubt, lays shame. It's like a parent, pointing you, the writer, in the right direction. It says, 'Be cautious. Don't talk about drugs. Don't swear. And, my God, don't talk about incest. Avoid the taboo. Tell nice stories.'

Get a kitchen timer. Set it for 20 minutes and write. Free yourself from all rules and all judgements. When you're writing under the clock, the hand keeps moving, trying to keep pace with the mind. Write fast. Write slowly. Write in capitals. Write joined-up. Just keep writing. This is the place to bring together all the ideas that are swirling in your head. This is the place to record those thoughts that you don't talk about at parties. Writing under the clock is your chance to release the tension stored in places your mother never talked about.

Writing under the clock is also your chance to ask questions. Was your antagonist molested? Is your protagonist a teetotaller because her father used to get drunk and beat her? What does a hit of heroin really feel like? There's no judging right or wrong here. Writing under the clock is the beginning of the journey – the quest of discovery. Find that theme that keeps coming back to tickle your brain. Silence your number-crunching mind, and allow yourself the freedom to get the story out of your grey matter and onto the page.

To give you an example of writing under the clock – the speed, the joy, the insights – we have included a model novel-in-progress where you can see a fellow writer following the same path that you follow. The working title of this model novel-in-progress is *Trophy Wives*. The protagonist is a character named Veronica, the same character who appeared in the rain-swept car park earlier in this introduction: 'the rain beats down, her hair is a mess, etc.' As the writing progresses through the weekends, we watch Veronica grow from a nameless girl drenched by rain into a protagonist with enough motivation to drive the novel to a satisfying climax. The model novel helps you trust your own creativity.

Writing to produce word pictures

Good fiction conjures pictures in the reader's mind: the stage on which the characters interact and the action takes place. Every writing teacher uses the phrase 'show, don't tell'. In other words, create word pictures for your reader. This is no small task. Most editors I know reject manuscripts after the first page because of too much summary and too few images.

The key to creating word pictures is detail. In *The Amazing Adventures of Kavalier and Clay*, Michael Chabon uses details to paint pre-WWII through the eyes of comic-book writers. In a brilliant scene with Salvador Dalí, Chabon shows Joe Kavalier racing across a room, dodging and leaping over an underwater breathing apparatus that just happens to be Dalí's attire for the dinner party. The reader sees Dalí's face turn from flushed pink to bright red to terrifying blue. All the while, whirring and clicking fill the background. Chabon uses details on every page to give life to a time and place of his own creation. He uses details to paint images.

It's easy to write something that is weak. It's much harder to find concrete nouns and active verbs that capture the essence of the moment. Great writers manage to separate image from action. Great writers use details like Coke-bottle glasses, hooker nylons, giantess hands. Verbs are just as difficult, but the right strong verb soars above weak, stagnant ones.

Images force writers to make the abstract concrete. To write a novel with potential for success in bookshops and on the screen, write with concrete nouns and active verbs.

Your first word picture is a sketch of your novel's architecture.

part 2 Weekends 1–6:

Plotting your Novel

Writing a novel in the 21st century is made complicated by a world of screens.

It wasn't always like that.

Charles Dickens and Charlotte Brontë and Herman Melville wrote using a bottle of ink and a quill pen. The tip of the pen was called a nib. When the nib got dull, making the writing blotchy, the writer stopped writing to trim the nib with a sharp knife. If the writer was wealthy – every novelist's archetypal dream – then there sat, on the desk, a handy earthen jar packed with extra quills, all with razor-sharp tips, so that, when he or she wrote, the words would be etched into the thick paper.

Not so today.

If you are writing today, there's a good chance you compose on a laptop. You write sitting in an Internet café with a wireless connection, so that, when you are seized in the iron grip of writer's block, you can hit the cyber key and trip out into cyberspace.

If you choose to write at the local neighbourhood pub, you can lift your eyes from the screen of your laptop to the screen on the wall-mounted television and see the gods of our age – sports heroes, film stars, chat-show hosts – and go back to the writing after a while, your head filled with images from the screen.

If you are an early riser, as were Anthony Trollope and William Faulkner, you roll out of bed, grab a cup of coffee, and sit down at your home computer to hit those keys. But first, of course, you take time to check your inbox for e-mail.

At weekends, most writers watch films. If you are young and frisky, you brave the smells and noises of the local cinemas to catch the latest films. If you are old and settled, you rent a couple of videos (if you are like most writers, you approach the world of DVDs with an air of suspicion: how do they cram all those images onto one little disc when it takes me 300 pieces of paper to tell a story in novel form?).

No more corner bookshop

Screens have changed the writing world – and when the writing world changes, the writer must change too.

Remember the corner bookshop – the place where you could browse, where you knew the owner, a withered little old man or sharp-eyed little old lady who could direct you to a really good book? Now we have megastores: big whopper bookstores like Barnes & Noble and Borders.

Now we have Half Price Books and Amazon.com and Powell's Books online. Amazon readers have morphed themselves into reviewers. These reviewers – literature graduates, well-wishers, amateur critics – have replaced the proprietors of the corner bookshop. Amazon.com tracks book sales. And when your book is published, you can check the numbers on Amazon.com to see how you rank in sales compared to other titles sold by Amazon. For the writer in our time, sales on Amazon.com can account for a hefty percentage of books sold.

The writing world has changed, but plotting stays the same

Memorise this definition: *plot is what happens in your story*. Plot is what happens first and what happens next and what happens after that and after that and after that, and how the story ends. That handy definition of plot contains a structure for your story. The structure has three parts: a Beginning, a Middle, and an End.

Beginning is what happens first. Middle is what happens next. End is what happens last.

Because you are writing a novel, and because the novel is a long dramatic structure – like feature films, one-hour TV dramas, operas, epic poems, and theatrical plays – you can think of the three parts as three acts:

- Act One is your Beginning.
- Act Two is your Middle.
- Act Three is your End.

Because plot is the journey of your main character through time and space, smart writers plot with notes and furtive jottings and sequences of cause and effect and synopses and even line-drawings to sketch out progress and direction.

A smart writer works like any creative artist. First, the sketch, to rough out the idea; then the idea fleshed out. The musician starts with a note or a chord that grows into a melody. The painter starts with a series of sketches before moving on to the full-scale construction.

In between the sketches, do some writing. When you write about plot, the writing is a word-sketch. You can start with a line like, 'This is a story about...' and go on for ten minutes, 20 minutes, or half an hour. You might need to write 'This is a story about...' more than once. You can follow 'This is a story about...' with 'This is the story about a character who...', which gives you a tight focus on your protagonist.

On Weekends 1–2, you'll sketch a linear plot. The linear plot, which fits most film scripts, charts rising action through three acts to the climax.

On Weekends 3–4, you'll sketch a cyclic plot. There are two cycles. One is the Heroic Cycle: Departure, Initiation, and Return. The other is the Mythic Journey: Cage, Escape, Quest, Dragon, and Home.

On Weekends 5–6, you'll experience the power of writing down the page – a speed technique that sets fire to your pages.

Weekends 1–2:
Plotting along a straight line

If you were building a bridge, you would start with sketches - an idea here, an idea there. The sketches would blossom into a blueprint. The blueprint would chart out the structure of the bridge.

If you are coming to the novel from the world of the short story, you can use a plot sketch to expand your thinking process, to stretch your mind out across the span of 250–300 pages. You need to keep a toehold in the Beginning - that opening image, that first character entering the story - while you reach out across the unknown, searching for the End.

Doing this search is easier if you know the kind of story you are writing. Veronica, the intrepid, trapped protagonist of our model novel, *Trophy Wives*, starts in poverty, rises to wealth when she marries Paul, and then, at the end, winds up enmeshed in a crime story. This movement from poverty to wealth gives Veronica's path an upward trajectory. Poverty to wealth is an economic measure. In metaphoric terms, Veronica rises from Rags to Riches. The Rags represent poverty; the Riches represent wealth. In spatial terms, Veronica's rise is from low to high, from Lower World to Upper World.

The writing of *Trophy Wives* comes from the Cinderella fairy-tale, where an orphan girl escapes the dirt of virtual slavery to marry a handsome prince. The Cinderella fairy-tale is a good model to illustrate the efficiency of the linear plot. Let's keep our three novel parts (Beginning, Middle, and End) in mind as we develop our first practice sketch.

- *Beginning*: What happens as the story opens? What is the situation? How do we feel about the protagonist? What symbols does the writer use? What is the problem the protagonist must solve? Which characters are introduced? How do they connect to the protagonist?
- *Middle*: What happens at the middle of the story? What actions does the character take? What are the symbols?
- *End*: How does the story end? Is the ending happy? Is the ending

sad? Which characters have survived all the way to the end of the story? What symbols have lasted? How do the symbols work at the climax? (Climax, from the Greek, means the peak of action, where conflicts are resolved.)

Before we answer in words – sentences, paragraphs, fragments, notes – let's sketch a diagram of Cinderella on her rise from Rags to Riches (see Figure 1). Figure 1 shows our protagonist in rags at the beginning. Through a series of actions – dressing for the ball, dancing with the prince, losing the glass slipper on the steps, trying on the glass slipper at the climax – she moves up the economic ladder to riches. The beginning opens with the protagonist in a cage of poverty. The end climaxes with her transformation, from scullery maid buried in ashes into a princess with her hands on the gold of the kingdom. As you develop your novel, take the time to sketch your plot.

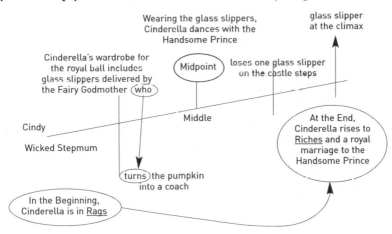

FIGURE 1: THE ASCENT FROM RAGS TO RICHES IN THE CINDERELLA FAIRY-TALE

Guidelines for plotting with a straight-line structure

The rising line represents the path of the Cinderella protagonist. Cinderella starts low and ends high. This line represents the Cinderella protagonist in feature films like *Working Girl* (Melanie Griffith) and *Pretty Woman* (Julia Roberts). In *Working Girl*, the protagonist leaves her briefcase behind in the apartment of the Handsome Prince, played by Harrison Ford. The briefcase, a handbag-substitute which represents an office executive, is the glass slipper of this updated version of the Cinderella story. In *Pretty Woman*, the protagonist gets wardrobe help – and wardrobe advice – from the hotel manager, played by Hector Elizondo, who is the Fairy Godmother figure in this update.

So, once you start your sketch, and the ideas start pouring in, jot those ideas down in sketch form. Here's an example: one of our model novels, *The Amazing Adventures of Kavalier and Clay*, has two protagonists. One of the two protagonists, Josef Kavalier of Prague, is a Rags-to-Riches figure. Josef leaves home by escaping in a coffin from Prague to Lithuania. The year is 1935, the Nazis are coming to his hometown, and his parents send him away to America, the promised land. Josef arrives in New York without money. Like Cinderella, he is a denizen of Lower World. Also like Cinderella, Josef will rise into Upper World. To climb the economic ladder, Josef needs a Fairy Godmother, so along comes his cousin, Sammy Clay, who sees Josef's talent with a paintbrush – the kid is a brilliant artist – and develops a career in creating superheroes for comic books.

Kavalier and Clay is a long novel: it has six sections split among 75 chapters, and the book runs over 600 pages. That's a novel of more than 200,000 words; a manuscript of 800–900 pages. Now imagine, if you will, the strength and experience it took to handle the rough draft, the edited drafts, the typing, keeping track of the manuscript pages. And ask yourself: how did the writer do that?

The answer is: the linear structure. Let's take a look at the finished book and sketch the structure (see Figure 2). Note the similarity between this structure, for a book of more than 600 pages, and the structure of Cinderella:

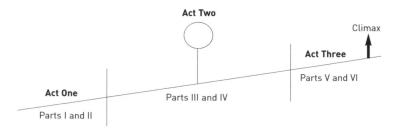

FIGURE 2: STRUCTURE IN *THE AMAZING ADVENTURES OF KAVALIER AND CLAY*

- *Act One* (the Beginning) of *Kavalier and Clay* contains Parts I and II. Each of Chabon's sections has a name. Part I is called 'The Escape Artist'; Part II, which heralds the partnership of Josef and Sammy, is called 'A Couple of Boy Geniuses'.

- *Act Two* (the Middle) contains Parts III and IV. Part III is called 'The Funny Book War', a pointed reference to the life-and-death struggles between the artist (represented by Sammy and Josef) and the corporation (represented by the moguls who run the comic-book business). While the real war – World War II – escalates in Europe, the two boys battle with greed and corruption in America. Part IV, called 'The Golden Age', shows that the boys have won the war at home, while the war away from home is just getting started. Part IV ends with the Japanese bombing of the US naval base at Pearl Harbour. The month is December. The year is 1941.

- *Act Three* (the End) contains Parts V and VI. Part V, called 'Radioman', uses a compressed narrative style to follow the adventures of Josef (now Joe) Kavalier as he serves his new country as a naval radio operator in an isolated ice-base at the end of the world in Antarctica. Part V builds a step to the climax when Josef/Joe shoots an innocent German geologist. Joe's motive is revenge. He wants payback for his dead family, back in Prague. So he kills the only German he can find.

    Part VI, 'The League of the Golden Key', is the final section of Chabon's novel. It begins in 1954, a decade after Joe kills the German in Part V. The technique here is called jump-cutting. It came to us from the the way in which film directors and screenwriters move from one scene to another – or from one time period to another – with a quick camera cut. For a good example of jump-cutting, study this long novel by Michael Chabon.

Now it is time to develop the next sketch, where we practise adding information to the diagram (see Figure 3).

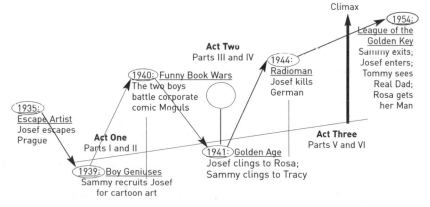

FIGURE 3: TIME AND STRUCTURE IN *THE AMAZING ADVENTURES OF KAVALIER AND CLAY*

When you draw a line on the page, you are thinking on paper. When you divide the horizontal line using vertical lines to mark the acts (think of a curtain falling on a stage play or the timing of commercial breaks on television), you are working with structure. Structure, whether you are building a bridge or building a novel, is an arrangement of parts.

When you draw a sketch for your novel, follow our work on model novels like *Kavalier and Clay*. First, draw a rising line. Next, divide the line into parts: Beginning, Middle, and End. Next, think of the parts as acts; thinking like this takes you into storytelling. Then, add information from your own work.

The type of information you include will vary depending on where you are in the writing process. In the case of *Kavalier and Clay*, we have added dates, and connected the dates to sections of the book. If you follow the dates from 1935 to 1954, you can see a story that stretches out for two decades. You can add character names (Sammy, Josef, Rosa, Tommy, Tracy Bacon), and then you can add those large actions that compress the parts of your story:

1935: Josef escapes Prague
1939: Sammy recruits Josef
1940: Boys battle comic corporate moguls
1941: Josef clings to Rosa; Sammy clings to Tracy
1944: Josef kills German
1954: Sammy exits; Josef enters; Tommy sees real dad; Rosa gets her
      man

By drawing a simple sketch, you have compressed your novel down to a single linear sketch on a single sheet of paper. (If you have a good drawing programme for your computer, like CorelDRAW or Quark Xpress, you can do a simple sketch in your notebook and transfer it to the computer.)

Before we leave the *Kavalier and Clay* sketch, let's take a quick look at the year 1941. What has happened here? If you check the opening line on the opening page of the opening paragraph of Part IV, Chapter 1, you can see the date, 1941, and a number with a dollar sign – $58,832.27. This simple linkage of numbers suggests great wealth. With their comic-book heroes, these two poor boys have increased their wealth. They have made the move from rags to riches. They have flirted with the corridors and boardrooms of Upper World. Joe has found a mate, Rosa. Sammy has found a lover, Tracy.

Now recheck your diagram. Here is the clue. Part IV is located in the second half of Act Two. For any dramatic structure, whether it is a novel or a film script or a script for the stage, Act Two is the testing ground. The toughest test for the writer is the second half of Act Two, where the writer approaches Act Three and the climax.

Exercises

1. Architecture of the novel
Using the rising line that represents action rising to a climax, sketch the architecture of your plot. Use simple terms like Beginning, Middle, and End to divide the rising line into three parts. Add labels for three acts – 1, 2, 3 – and indicate the climax with an arrow.

2. Doodling
With your skeleton sketch on the page, add character names, objects of value like money or jewellery, wardrobe items, vehicles, and weapons. Add landscape items that might offer scene-settings like lake, forest, mountain, cliff, cave, city, street, school, church, skyscraper, graveyard, or wedding chapel. Add a handful of action verbs like run, feel, charge, fight, throw, toss, slice, hit, sew, stitch, drop, fall, climb, soar, fly, lift, elevate, and tremble. Remember that being messy is the heart of the creative process. Neatniks take note.

3. Beginning
Use this startline: 'My novel opens in a (forest, city, bathroom, schoolroom, prison cell, chapel confession booth, phone booth, speeding car, spaceship headed for)…'

4. Middle
Use this startline: 'In the middle of my story, my protagonist (name your protagonist here) makes a turn in the road and comes face to face with…'

5. End
Use this startline: 'The object at the climax of my novel looks like…'

The novel-in-progress: *Trophy Wives*

The linear sketch overleaf shows the writer of our model novel searching for the bones of a novel. From watching films and TV, the writer knows that stories have story segments. Anyone who sits through an hour-long TV drama has noticed that the intensity ratchets up just prior to each commercial break. These breaks on your screen are one clue to laying out the bones of your novel. In the sketch below, the writer develops a story about a Cinderella-heroine named Veronica. At this point, the writer knows that Veronica is in her mid-20s, intelligent, attractive, and broke. On the diagram someone dies. There are names for other characters – Paul, Ashleigh, Anderson, Gwyn – but when you plot you must keep plotting. Save the character work for later. Veronica follows the same ritual climb as Cinderella: up the economic ladder from Rags to Riches. The story starts here, with this diagram (see Figure 4).

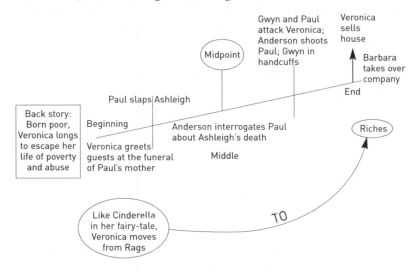

FIGURE 4: *TROPHY WIVES* IS A TWISTED TALE OF RAGS TO RICHES

The protagonist, Veronica, has the plot. Like Cinderella in the fairy-tale, the protagonist is born poor. She grows up poor. On the sketch, the writer depicts Veronica's fate with a rising line that moves from Rags to Riches. As the story opens, she has made the leap from poverty into wealth through marriage, and she stands at the entry of the big house to greet guests at the funeral of her husband's mother. As the writing progresses, and the writer makes discoveries about the characters, the opening scene could change. For the moment, the scene at the front door is a place-holder. There is work to do, like forging connections between Veronica and the other characters. With five characters plus a protagonist, the writer of *Trophy Wives* could have five subplots to manage.

Weekends 3–4:
Plotting along the curve

During Weekends 1–2, you explored the straight-line plot rising to a climax near the end. The straight line is helpful if you are writing a novel with a protagonist on an upward climb that culminates with action to resolve the problems driving the story. One reason why audiences like Cinderella stories is because the resolution is clear and decisive. At the climax, when the glass slipper slides onto her foot, Cinderella ascends to Princesshood, leaving behind the ugly filth of the prison-like house of the Wicked Stepmother. Action at the climax – the trying-on of the slipper – resolves Cinderella's poverty problems. As she transforms into a Princess, she will no longer need a Fairy Godmother to transport pretty party dresses from 'Otherworld'.

The straight-line plot also works for novels as diverse as *The Great Gatsby*, *Lolita*, *Moby-Dick*, *The Maltese Falcon*, *The Accidental Tourist*, *White Teeth*, and *The Amazing Adventures of Kavalier and Clay*, which runs over 600 pages.

The straight-line plot of *The Great Gatsby* climaxes when Jay Gatsby get killed in his pool at West Egg. His death is followed by a funeral in the rain. If you draw a straight line from Gatsby's grave, you end up at the opening of the novel when Nick the Narrator sees Daisy in her white dress floating on a bed that seems to be lifted by the magical, moneyed breeze blowing through East Egg. The season is summer; the scene takes place in Tom's palatial East Egg mansion. Nick lives across the Bay in a rented house next door to Gatsby, whose name comes up in conversation. When Tom gets called to the phone, Daisy becomes agitated, losing her cool. Nick learns from Daisy's friend, Jordan Baker, that Tom has a girl in New York – a reference to Tom's affair with Myrtle Wilson. Daisy does not know Myrtle; she does not know that Gatsby drives a yellow car. Gatsby does not know Tom; he does not know about Tom's affair with Myrtle; he does not know George Wilson, Myrtle's husband, the man who fires the gun that kills Gatsby. *Writing tip*: The straight-line plot is a good technique for isolating your protagonist, while secrets do their work in the subplots. The straight-line plot of Vladimir Nabokov's *Lolita* climaxes when the narrator, an educated European named Humbert Humbert, fires a pistol, killing a nasty man named Clare Quilty, who has stolen Lolita away from Humbert. Narrator Humbert is in a race against time because Lolita is a nymphet – nymphets have a short life, a few brief years between the ages of ten and 16 – and Clare Quilty must die for stealing away the love of Humbert's life, taking away her last moments as a nymphet.

The straight-line plot appears in *Moby-Dick* in a parade of nine ships: the Albatross, the Town-Ho, the Jeroboam, the Virgin, the Rose-Bud, the Samuel Enderby, the Bachelor, the Rachel, and the Delight – each one a floating waystation marking Ahab's progress as he draws nearer to his nemesis, the whale who bit off his leg. When Ahab passes a ship, he asks the same question: 'Have you seen the White Whale?' When the captain of the Albatross tries to answer the question, his trumpet falls into the sea. Ship number nine, the Delight, has just been trounced by Moby-Dick, whale-boats smashed, the ship's rigging in tatters. Ahab asks: 'Have you killed my whale?' The captain of the Delight answers: 'There is no earthly harpoon that will kill Moby-Dick.' But Ahab has a special harpoon, so he keeps going – on a straight line aimed right at Moby-Dick.

During the first two weekends, you had a chance to hone your plotting skills with the straight line rising to climax. During Weekends 3–4, you'll plot your novel using a curved line that curls around to meet itself, following the plot that starts and ends in the same place. While the straight-line plot works for Cinderella and Gatsby and Hamlet, the cyclical plot works for stories like the Odyssey, where the hero leaves home, has adventures galore, and then returns home for the finale. The cyclical plot works for Grail Questers – intrepid knights-errant who sally forth from the castle in search of the symbolic silver salver, dish, or enchanted cup, entering the wilderness, fighting dragons, and rescuing maidens in distress before returning home with the precious thing tucked away in their saddlebags. If your protagonist starts in New York City, drives overland to California to have adventures, and returns to New York City, you would plot using a cycle. In his landmark book, *The Hero with a Thousand Faces*, myth-guru Joseph Campbell canonised this cyclic journey by calling it the Monomyth, or Heroic Cycle, which has three phases: Departure, Initiation, and Return. The three phases of this cyclical journey correspond to the three acts of the straight-line plot. When you work with a three-part structure, you are following the guidance of Aristotle's story-structure laid down in his Poetics: each story must have a Beginning, a Middle, and an End.

Guidelines for plotting the quest for your protagonist

If the straight-line structure does not fit your story, you can work with the cyclical plot structure. If we look at the Big Picture, we see three movements:

1. The protagonist leaves home.
2. The protagonist crosses a threshold into Another World.
3. The protagonist re-enters from Another World, and returns home.

To make use of these adventures in your novel, you need a structure. The structure in Figure 5 follows the counter-clockwise path noted by Campbell in *The Hero with a Thousand Faces*. Phase 1, leaving home, is called Departure. Phase 2, crossing a threshold, is called Initiation. Phase 3, returning home, is called Return.

Figure 5 shows how the Heroic Cycle can help you see the structure of many contemporary novels. This example is *The Namesake*, written by Pulitzer Prize-winner Jhumpa Lahiri.

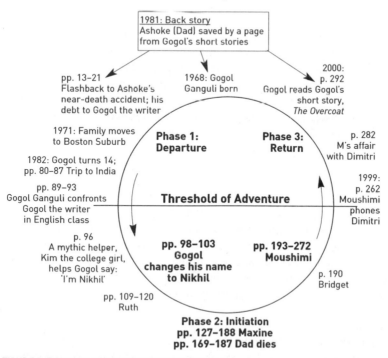

FIGURE 5: TIME AND STRUCTURE IN *THE NAMESAKE*

Gogol Ganguli, the sensitive and retiring hero of *The Namesake*, takes the Heroic Cycle. Born in the late 1960s, Gogol has no choice about his name, which is taken from that of his father's favourite writer, a Russian named Nikolai Gogol (1809–1852). The diagram shows Gogol moving through the three phases of the Heroic Cycle: Departure, Initiation, and Return. Let's take them one at a time.

Departure

Born with a name that makes him strange in America, Gogol straddles two worlds. One is the United States, the world of his birth; the other world is India, and especially Bengal, where his parents come from. His parents named him Gogol because his father, Ashoke, clutched a copy of Gogol's short stories as a train crash in India buried him under a pile of rubble. A searcher's flashlight beam found a page of the book held by Ashoke. When his son is born in America, Ashoke needs to give him a name for the novel's first Departure – a sudden trip back to the old country – so Gogol Ganguli becomes the namesake of Nikolai Gogol. As the boy grows up, his idea of departure is leaving his name behind.

Initiation

To leave his name behind, to depart from the customs of India, Gogol needs help. His mythic helper is Kim, the college girl, with whom he has a chance meeting at a party. She tells him her name; he replies, not with Gogol, but with Nikhil. Kim is the first in a sequence of five females who help Gogol with his initiation. After he changes his name to Nikhil in court, Gogol meets Ruth. When Ruth deserts him for England, Gogol mopes around New York until he meets Maxine, an American goddess, who brings this sad lad into the bosom of her family. Gogol breaks off with Maxine when his father dies. We're at the bottom of the cycle now, the low place that Joseph Campbell calls the 'nadir'. After Maxine, Gogol has an affair with Bridget, a married lady. And after Bridget, he meets Moushimi, female number five, whom he first encountered in childhood. After a year of marriage to Gogol, Moushimi phones Dimitri Dejardins, a man from her teenaged past and, when he reappears in her life, a Frenchman who can really cook. Moushimi's phone call launches an affair with Dimitri that separates her from Gogol.

Return

Separated from Moushimi, Gogol – who still calls himself Nikhil – returns home. The final scene shows Gogol upstairs in his mother's house, reading the short stories of Nikolai Gogol, and understanding, for the first time, his father's reason for giving him the name Gogol.

Taking your protagonist on the Mythic Journey

If the Heroic Cycle does not feel right for your story, you can move your plot over to the Mythic Journey, which is more flexible because it allows the writer to work inside the narrator's mind. The Mythic Journey has five stations: Cage, Escape, Quest, Dragon Confrontation, and Home. Having this more complex structure makes it easier for some writers to reach the end of the story. Each station has a specific function. Your story opens with your protagonist locked in a cage; the cage leads to escape; escape leads to the quest; the quest leads to the dragon; getting by the dragon, your protagonist heads for home.

1. *Cage* is an enclosure that restricts: prison, monk's cell, marriage, poverty (economic prison), school, rule, society, church, the mind, the trough of depression.
2. *Escape* is action motivated by restriction: Cinderella escapes the House of the Wicked Stepmother; Ann Lord, the protagonist of Susan Minot's novel *Evening*, escapes the City for a weekend on the Island and falls in love; Roy Hobbs escapes death in Act One of Bernard Malamud's *The Natural*, but the silver bullet, an unwanted sacred object, still lurks in his chest (an escape with a twist).
3. *Quest* operates on two levels: the exterior level is a physical journey with physical landmarks such as street signs, road markers, buildings, familiar stuff; the interior level is a journey of the human spirit, where the road signs turn archetypal, pointing the way to salvation or damnation. Models for your quest include Dante trekking through Hell; Jane Eyre climbing the staircase at Thornfield; Ahab meeting the nine ships on his hunt for Moby-Dick; Almasy in Michael Ondaatje's *The English Patient* hunting for the Cave of Swimmers; the knight-errant who seeks the Holy Grail; the sleuth who seeks the killer. As the quest gets tougher, it becomes a Road of Trials – more tests for the protagonist.
4. *Dragon Confrontation* is a collision of forces: Good vs. Evil; Light vs. Dark. The dragon is the fairy-tale representation of your antagonist. If you're writing a mystery, the dragon is the killer, the selfish monster who takes human life without payment. If you're writing an epic, the dragon is a monster like Grendel or Moby-Dick or the Wicked Wolf or Cinderella's Wicked Stepmother. The

29

dragon in Shakespeare's *Hamlet* is Uncle Claudius, the deadly king who lurks offstage. To reach the dragon of Elsinore, Hamlet plots; he schemes; he traverses a complex labyrinth of castle rooms, dead bodies, graves, madness, and his mother's treachery. (In *Hamlet*, the mother is a Death Crone.) Archetypes boost your brain towards insight. At the climax, Hamlet kills the uncle (and King Replacer) with a dagger.

5. *Home* is a sigh of relief, a reward brought by closure. Home for Cinderella is the castle on the hill; home for Mr Norman Bates, protagonist of Hitchcock's *Psycho*, is incarceration; home for Jane Eyre is a house where she can care for Mr Rochester (she has money; he does not); home for Roy Hobbs in the movie version of *The Natural* is back on the farm (in the novel, Roy hits the city streets).

Getting help from other writers

Figure 6 (opposite) shows you the Mythic Journey at work in another contemporary novel, Paulo Coelho's *The Alchemist*. The plot of Coelho's book follows the protagonist from Spain to Africa and back to Spain. The protagonist is a shepherd boy who likes books. His name is Santiago, which is Spanish for James. But the word 'Santiago' is close to 'santo', the Spanish word for 'saint', and as the protagonist goes deeper into the desert, readers sense a deep spiritual connection with events in the desert from biblical times. Coelho's book has sold in the millions. It has been translated into a dozen languages. Let's look at Figure 6.

A cage for Santiago

Santiago, the intrepid shepherd-boy protagonist in Paulo Coelho's *The Alchemist*, is trapped in a cage that combines his profession with the culture of rural Spain. His parents send Santiago to study for the priesthood. He wants to travel. The only people who travel, his father says, are the shepherds. So Santiago becomes a shepherd. He is a good boy, very industrious, so he is trapped by his sheep. A voice in a dream tells him to seek treasure in Egypt, somewhere near the Pyramids.

Escape for Santiago

He escapes the cage in two ways: first, by handing over six sheep – one-tenth of his flock of 60 sheep – to an old man who gives him some magic stones; and second, by selling the sheep that remain. In

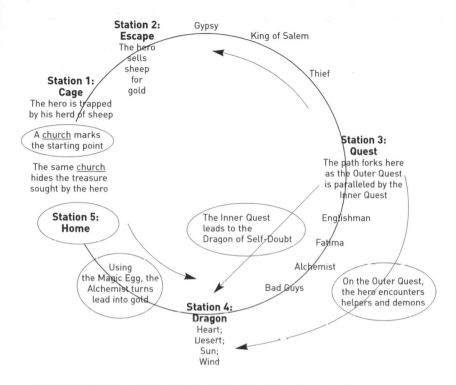

Station 2: Gypsy
Escape King of Salem
The hero
sells
sheep
for
gold

Station 1: Thief
Cage
The hero is trapped
by his herd of sheep

A <u>church</u> marks
the starting point

Station 3:
Quest
The same <u>church</u>
hides the treasure
sought by the hero
The path forks here
as the Outer Quest
is paralleled by the
Inner Quest

Station 5:
Home
The Inner Quest
leads to the
Dragon of Self-Doubt
Englishman

Fatima

Using
the Magic Egg, the
Alchemist turns
lead into gold
Alchemist

Bad Guys
On the Outer Quest,
the hero encounters
helpers and demons

Station 4:
Dragon
Heart;
Desert;
Sun;
Wind

FIGURE 6: THE FIVE STATIONS OF THE MYTHIC JOURNEY IN *THE ALCHEMIST*

Africa, a thief steals Santiago's gold, clouding the intensity of his escape. Various guides point him towards Egypt. For Santiago, the shepherd boy, the quest starts at this point.

Santiago takes the quest

Santiago joins a caravan heading into the desert. On the caravan is an Englishman with many books. While Santiago discards his single book because it is a burden, the Englishman carries several camel-loads of books. The Englishman is a guide, a mythic helper. He points Santiago towards alchemy and the Alchemist of the book's title. Santiago reads the books and gets excited about big-name alchemists – Helvetius, Elias, Fulcanelli – who could turn metals like lead into gold. From the Englishman, Santiago learns of the Philosopher's Stone, the source of wealth and everlasting life. The boy learns that alchemists follow their Personal Legend. They discover the Soul of the World. They find the Philosopher's Stone and the Elixir of Life. The book is an instrument of knowledge.

At an oasis, the Englishman hunts for the Alchemist and Santiago meets Fatima, the girl of his dreams. Looking into the eyes of Fatima, he feels the Soul of the World surging inside him and he knows at once that the language of the world is love. The boy sees a hawk descending to attack another hawk and warns the chieftain about desert bandits. This reading of the flight of the hawks is a special knowledge; this special knowledge brings Santiago to the attention of the Alchemist.

Because of Santiago, the warriors of the oasis win the battle against the desert bandits. Santiago says goodbye to Fatima and follows the Alchemist into the desert, where he gathers the wisdom to confront the dragon of self-doubt.

Santiago confronts the dragon

Stopped by armed bandits, the Alchemist produces a yellow egg made of glass (the Philosopher's Stone) and a small vial of clear liquid (the Elixir of Life). The Alchemist uses Santiago's gold to buy them three days. If Santiago can become the wind, he will save both their lives. Santiago talks to the desert and the desert talks back. He talks to the sun and the wind and they talk back. The wind talks back with a sandstorm that buries the bad guys. The wind has many names – scirocco, levanter, simum – but when the boy reaches into the wind with the hand that has written all things, he reaches through the names, all the way to the Soul of the World, and that is ultimate knowledge: a force with all names and no name. The sandstorm stops, the dust settles, and the two questers – Santiago and the Alchemist – continue their journey.

Looking back, Santiago sees that he has just confronted the dragon of self-doubt. It is the end of his journey, time to head home.

Home for Santiago

Before they part, the Alchemist slices a sliver of the yellow egg into a pan of hot lead, and the lead turns to gold. The gold is payback for the money given to the bad guys in the desert. As he digs for his treasure, Santiago is captured by more bandits. The bandit leader, seeing the gold, tells of a dream he had: that he should go to Spain, find a ruined church where shepherds slept with their sheep, find the sycamore that grew from the ruins of a church, and dig in the roots for treasure.

Back home in Spain, Santiago digs in the roots of the sycamore and finds gold Spanish coins, enough money to get him back to the desert, back to Fatima.

To Santiago, Fatima is also home.

Exercises

1. Plotting with the Mythic Journey
You have six startlines to work through, beginning with, 'This is a story about a character who...', which functions as a warm-up.

Startline: 'This is a story about a character who...'
Startline: 'The cage for my protagonist tastes like...'
Startline: 'My protagonist escapes the cage when...'
Startline: 'On her Road of Trials, the protagonist encounters...'
Startline: 'To defeat the dragon, my protagonist must...'
Startline: 'My protagonist reaches home when...'

Writing times are ten minutes for each startline.

2. Plotting with the Heroic Cycle
There are three parts to the Heroic Cycle – Departure, Initiation, and Return – which feels a lot like three acts bent into a smooth curve. You can develop your own startlines, but the main thing is to get your protagonist across two thresholds, and then back into society.

Startline: 'This is a story about a heroic character who...'
Startline: 'The hero leaves home when he/she hears the call of adventure and then...'
Startline: 'Crossing the First Threshold, the hero enters a land (world, universe, society) called...'
Startline: 'Crossing the Second Threshold, the hero re-enters the world he/she left behind with a feeling of...'

Writing times are ten minutes for each startline.

The novel-in-progress: *Trophy Wives*

Although we plotted our model novel, *Trophy Wives*, along the rising line, we can also plot those same events along the curve. The story opens with the protagonist, Veronica, trapped in a cage.

Helped by a helper, Veronica escapes the cage. She goes on a quest to find tools (evidence) and the wisdom to use the tools (strategy) to confront the dragon.

The dragon hides behind the mask. Because of what she learned on the quest, Veronica has the power to strip off the mask. Stripping off the mask, she sees the true face of the dragon.

Because she confronts the dragon, the protagonist is now free to head home. After reading the lesson on plotting along the curve, the writer of *Trophy Wives* does a quick sketch of the architecture of the novel (see Figure 7).

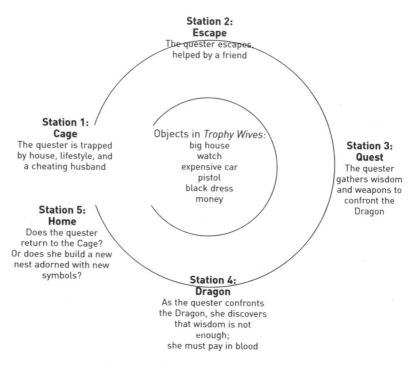

Station 2:
Escape
The quester escapes, helped by a friend

Station 1:
Cage
The quester is trapped by house, lifestyle, and a cheating husband

Objects in *Trophy Wives:*
big house
watch
expensive car
pistol
black dress
money

Station 3:
Quest
The quester gathers wisdom and weapons to confront the Dragon

Station 5:
Home
Does the quester return to the Cage? Or does she build a new nest adorned with new symbols?

Station 4:
Dragon
As the quester confronts the Dragon, she discovers that wisdom is not enough; she must pay in blood

FIGURE 7: USING THE MYTHIC JOURNEY TO PLOT *TROPHY WIVES*

The purpose of the architectural sketch is to bring your protagonist to the end of your story. For writers who get stuck at the beginning – the observable behaviour pattern here is writing Chapter 1 over and over again – the Mythic Journey gets the protagonist moving. At the end, there is a sense of closure. Down the road, as the story develops, the writer can return to this sketch and fill in the details. For *Trophy Wives*, we have the following story parts to work with:

- A protagonist in a cage
- A helper who could wear a mask (false helper)
- A short-tempered husband
- A pistol
- A corpse

- Big money
- Sibling rivalry
- A detective

To forge these ingredients into a story, we need another technique. It has to be something that frees up the writing; a writing tool that pulls the writer away from the restriction – or even the cage – of the paragraph. That technique, borrowed from poetry and screen-writing, is called 'spinning', and we'll explore it in the next chapter.

Spinning your novel down the page

Writing down the page speeds up your prose. When your prose speeds up, your brain catches fire. When your brain catches fire, ideas spark. If you're writing down the page – writing short lines, leaving lots of white space – your brain has room to work. Writing down the page instead of writing in paragraphs sets you free from the laws of syntax – subject, verb, object, full stop here, comma there, capital letter there – and when you evade punctuation, leaving behind the markers for standard English prose, then you have the freedom to fly.

Punctuation is a useful tool.

But not when you create.

Punctuation forces you to stop and think.

Thinking about what you write when you are writing 'hot' activates the left-brain editor, the narrow-eyed judge, the carping interior critic.

You move from writing hot to writing cold.

Not good.

After the sketches, here comes fireball prose

Spinning down the page takes its form – stopping the sentence before the string of words reaches the right-hand margin, carriage return, zip, and you're back to the left to start all over again – from poetry, and also from a compression device developed by Robert J Ray and Jack Remick in their writing workshops. The compression device is called Image and Action.

Image and Action grew out of a three-week crash course called 'Bootcamp for Screenwriters', taught to kick-start the screenwriting programme at the Distance Learning School at the University of Washington in Seattle. Image and Action developed because the film script is a lean form (lots of white space) that draws the eye down the page instead of across it.

The toughest enemy in screenwriting is exposition.

Exposition means stopping to explain.

The story goes along and suddenly the Author steps onstage, the house lights go up, the Author grabs the spotlight or the microphone or the megaphone and says: 'Here, Dear Reader, we must halt this story for a passage or two of explanation, yes, explanation without which there is no earthly way you could understand my complex tale, so fraught with ambiguity, so rife with irony about the state of the world in our time, that...'

For screenwriting, exposition is The Monster That Eats Time.

Making films is expensive.

Exposition kills story.

Exposition is a disease that hides in narration. If you chop it out of narration, exposition slides over into dialogue and monologue. It's easy to spot in a screenplay: any dialogue that runs over three lines is exposition trying to hide behind dialogue.

Exposition is harder to spot in the novel, which is built with big fat paragraphs made with black ink. With Image and Action, though, the novelist with a trained eye can eliminate the need for exposition – stopping the story to explain the story – by compressing the story into actions that are visual (the boy smacks the ball) and images that are mostly visual (the boy wears a green T-shirt), but that can also be auditory (the smack of the bat on the ball) or kinetic (hot sweat under his arms as the boy drops the bat and runs for first base).

Novel-writers sometimes balk at writing down the page.

That's the left brain talking.

The left brain is a problem.

The solution to the problem is heat.

When you get hot, you leave the left brain in the dust.

In the rearview mirror.

Cursing. Threatening revenge. Scowling at your speed.

Choices for the writer

You can work the following down-the-page exercise in two ways. First, you can alternate Image and Action, making sure to write the word 'Image' or the word 'Action', followed by a colon (:) or dash (–), depending on how dependent you are on punctuation. Second, you can write down the page.

Image and Action
Here's an example of Image and Action. See how quickly you can guess the book or film adaptation.

In the example below, K stands for Katharine. Almasy has the point of view. Clifton is the husband of K. Clifton's first name is Geoffrey. Candaules is the King of Lydia. He is married to the Queen. Gyges is a spear-carrier – warrior – in the army of Lydia.

Action: K climbs from plane.
Image: Khaki shorts, bony knees.
Action: K staring at a tarpaulin.
Image: K reading.
Action: K watches Almasy while husband talks.
Image: Her knees, ankles, arms.
Action: K wants to borrow Herodotus.
Action: K offers Almasy a cup of water.
Image: Clifton's cognac bottle.
Action: K reads from Herodotus.
Action: Candaules describing wife's beauty to Gyges.
Action: K signals husband. (Are you listening, Geoffrey?)
Action: K sinks into quicksand.
Image: K reading, eyes down, never looking up.
Action: Gyges views the Queen naked.
Action: The Queen spots Gyges leaving the bedchamber.
Image: Gyges kneeling before the Queen.
Action: Two choices – kill the King or die.
Action: Gyges kills Candaules.
Image: Poems about Gyges, written in trimeter.
Image: Gyges as a cog in a love story.
Action: K stops reading, looks up, exits quicksand.
Action: Almasy falls in love.
Image: K and husband dancing in Cairo.
Image: Nervous grip of an arm on a cliff.
Action: Almasy writing his book.
Image: K invades the page he's writing.
Image: K's body parts – mouth, knee, stomach.
Action: Almasy undresses K with writing.
Image: K's body like a long bow rising from bed.
Image: Hassanein Bey's lawn.
Action: K asks to be ravished.
Image: K hands knife to Almasy.

If you have not guessed already, this example of Image and Action covers several scenes and lots of typed pages from Michael Ondaatje's novel *The English Patient*. One way to measure success is by prizes. Ondaatje won the Booker Prize, England's highest literary honour. And the film, by British director-screenwriter Anthony Minghella, received a bushel basket filled with Oscars.

The syntax of this Image and Action exercise contains complete sentences ('K asks to be ravished.' 'Gyges views the Queen naked.') and also fragments ('Almasy writing his book.' 'K's body like a long bow rising from bed.'). When you do Image and Action, you use the key words followed by punctuation to provide your left brain with recognisable markers. While the left brain is busy with colons and dashes and full stops, the right brain – that wild creative creature – is free to tell the story.

Plan B: ripping down the page

You might start writing down the page with Image and Action. Then, when you feel the heat, and you are ready to leave the left-brain editor behind, you stop writing Image and Action and colon and dash and you rip down the page.

In the page-rip below, there are two protagonists – one named Sammy, one named Josef (later Joe). S&J means Sammy and Joe.

Here is another example of writing down the page to discover your plot.

Sammy meets Joe/mystery of cousin blood
Joe fails to escape from Prague/needs help
Joe fails to escape from chains/needs help from Tommy
Joe gets laid/escapes in coffin with help
Sammy and Joe join forces to create funny books
S&J make deal with Anapol
S&J invade Rathole/intruder inside
Mighty Molecule deserts Sammy and Mom
Joe flies/escape-artist born
Joe gets $3 for drawing of Rosa Saks
S&J brainstorm future of Escape Artist Hero
Adventures of Max Mayflower (Tommy, J's brother)
Joe orders his thoughts into comic panels
S&J recruit Rathole Gang/boy bonding/teamwork
S&J create their first book
S&J barter with Anapol over wages
Mum's letters pull Joe's brain back to Prague
Joe's dad is dead/German consulate closing
Max Schmeling knocks Joe out

Tommy is Josef's brother. Sammy lives in New York City, but the brothers (Josef and Tommy) live in Prague, Czechoslovakia. The time is the mid-1930s. Rosa Saks is the female character who connects Sammy and Joe. Rosa lives in New York City. Anapol is a big business figure, a denizen of New York, who uses the talents of Sammy (a writer and ideas guy) and Joe (a magician and artist guy) to build a corporate empire in mid-20th-century America. Max Schmeling is a famous boxer of German descent. The appearance of Max Schmeling, a real historic figure, in a book of fiction, gives you some idea of the complexity of this tale. The novel is *The Amazing Adventures of Kavalier and Clay* by Michael Chabon. Like the other novels chosen for this book, *Kavalier and Clay* won a prize – not the Booker, but the Pulitzer. When a novel is chosen for a prize, budding novelists, if they are smart, will pay attention to the novelist's technique.

Exercises

1. Deep breathing
Sit back, relax, take some deep breaths. Count to ten. Count from ten back to one. Let your mind rove across the structure of your novel. If you're listening to music, let the music take your mind. Fly on a wave of sound.

2. Writing down the page
Open your eyes. Grab your laptop or your notebook. Start writing. Don't worry about sentences or words. Don't stop to fix grammar or spelling. When your first line reaches the middle of the page, hit the Enter key and write another line. Here's an example:

This is a story about
Cinderella girl named
Veronica a girl who grows up poor
A girl who marries a rich man
A girl who sells her body to get comfy
A girl who...

Write for a while – 20–30 minutes. When the timer beeps, stop writing. If you wrote on the laptop, plug into the printer and print out your words. If you wrote in the notebook, type it into the laptop and don't change a word. Changing words lets the editor in.

3. Rest

Take a break. Have a coffee. Meditate. Go for a walk. Don't talk to anyone. Don't make all those phone calls. Forget your e-mail. Stay in your writing brain.

4. Read what you wrote down the page

Look for pattern created by repetition. What names repeat? What verbs repeat? What objects repeat? What dialogue lines repeat? What locations repeat? Use circles and lines to focus your brain. As you track your repetition, identify locations or actions that might turn into scenes; locations like: forest, road, crossroad, kitchen, bathroom, bedroom, shopping centre, coffee shop, dugout, trench, cave, warrior cave, gate, portal, dock, etc. Mark these locations on your printed page. Then number the locations.

5. Time span

If you write down the page three or four times, your brain will cough up most of the story. However, the events in the story might not be in the perfect order. To put them in order, enlist help from your left-brain editor. Your editor loves to count, loves to re-order, loves to micro-manage the smallest detail. Your editor, who lives in real time, wants your novel to be in real time. Time moves in a line from one minute to the next. The time span of *Kavalier and Clay* is 20 years. The time span of Ian McEwan's novel *Amsterdam*, on the other hand, is a couple of months – February to early spring. Reading over your down-the-page writings, define a time span for your novel, be it hours, days, weeks, years, or decades. Then date each scene, add time of day and place, and use this information to create a chronology.

6. The chronology

For a sample chronology, see overleaf, where we have added dates to events from Act One of Michael Chabon's *Kavalier and Clay*. If you like, you can use that same model – chapter, date, point of view, object, action – to build a chronology for your novel. As you build your chronology, take the time to look back over your shoulder and remember the two hours of down-the-page writing that gave you all this information.

Chapter	Date	POV	Object	Action
1	1939	Sammy	Ink	Sammy & Joe join forces to create funny books
2	1939	Sammy	Radios	S&J make deal with Anapol/barter
3	1939	Sammy	Cigarettes	S&J invade Rathole/intruder inside
4	FB	Sammy	Steam Room	Mighty Molecule deserts Sammy & Mom
5	1939	Sammy	Ladder	Joe flies/escape artist born
6	1939	Joe	Rosa Drawing	Joe gets $3 for drawing of Rosa Saks
7	1939	Joe	Golden Key	S&J brainstorm future of Escape Artist Hero
8	1939	S&J	Golden Key	Adventures of Max Mayflower (Tommy, J's brother)
9	1939	Joe	Cigarettes/ Gum	Joe orders his thoughts into comic panels
10	1939	Joe	Ink Blob	S&J recruit Rathole Gang/boy bonding/teamwork
11	1939	Sammy	The Book	S&J create their first book
12	1939	Sammy	Money	S&J barter with Anapol over wages
13	1940	Joe	Envelopes	Mom's letters pull Joe's brain back to Prague
14	1940	Joe	Letter	Joe's dad is dead/German consulate closing
15	1940	Joe	Booze	Max Schmeling knocks Joe out

TABLE 1: A SAMPLE CHRONOLOGY FOR *KAVALIER AND CLAY*

The novel-in-progress: *Trophy Wives*

After creating two structural sketches, the writer of *Trophy Wives* runs up against a wall. The diagrams, while displaying the larger movements of the novel, have failed to deliver up a sequence of scenes. This is not abnormal. The creative process is hit and miss, touch and go. One day you're hot, the next day you're cold. When one tool does not deliver, you try another tool.

From the structural diagram, the writer moves into writing down the page (short lines, speed, lots of white space). Now that the back story is secure, the opening of the novel shifts forwards. Our protagonist is married. She lives with her husband in an upscale dwelling in a large metropolitan city in America. The downpage writing opens with the protagonist greeting guests. She wears black. The guests wear black. No one is smiling. The protagonist's husband's mother has just died.

The first scene is set in the entrance to a large home.

By writing down the page, the writer generates more scenes.

Foyer. A big house on Nob Hill in San Francisco.
Veronica in black,
stands in the foyer, receiving guests.
Thank you for coming.
Veronica goes to the kitchen to direct the staff.
Den. Paul sits at his father's desk in the den.
Pistol on the desk.
Ashleigh Bennett walks into the den.
She locks the door behind her.
Paul puts his father's gun in his pocket.
Are you okay?
My parents are gone.
I'm here for you.
She moves behind him.
She rubs his shoulders.
He stands, turns kisses her.
Veronica moves through the drawing room.
She stops in front of Barbara, Paul's sister.
How are you holding up?
Where is Paul?
In the den.
Moving. Barbara walks away.
She cuts through the kitchen and across the great room.
She stops and straightens a picture on the wall.
She reaches the den's French doors.
As she reaches to knock, Ashleigh Bennett exits.
They collide.
Ms Bennett.
Den. Barbara walks into the den.

Smirks at her brother.

Paul walks to the window, stares out.

Do you trust her, Paul?

Like I trust you, sis.

Bedroom. Veronica sits at her dressing table in the bedroom.

Paul enters, holds out his arms.

Veronica stands and walks to Paul.

He smells like perfume.

He reaches for her.

She steps back.

Paul walks out.

Veronica wakes up early.

She dresses quietly in tennis clothes.

Tennis Club. Veronica walks into the pro shop.

Are you ready for me?

The tennis pro is handsome, lean, younger than Paul.

Hey, my star pupil.

I need a workout, Veronica says.

You want it, Mrs Watson, you've got it.

Line space.

By leaving the paragraph behind and writing down the page, the writer produces a scene-sequence that might be used to start the novel. The writing took ten minutes and generated half a dozen scenes. Some of the scenes are labelled with places – Foyer, Den, Bedroom, Tennis Club – and others by character names: Veronica and Barbara. The first step is writing it down the page. The second step is a quick analysis using your TWN checklist: time, place, character, object, and ritual. Please remember that you don't have to run the checklist in any precise order. You might begin with character or ritual, and wind up with object. Right now, we will begin with place.

Place: the scenes come from changes of setting, from foyer to den, from den to drawing room, from drawing room to kitchen, and so on. The technique used here – the jump-cut – is borrowed from the craft of film-making.

Time: the time is mid-afternoon or mid-morning.

Character: the protagonist is Veronica. She is female, in her late 20s, attractive, married to Paul. No sign of education or career. No mention of children so far.

There are two antagonists. Antag1 is Paul. He is male, late 20s or early 30s, handsome, rich, hard-hitting, married to Veronica. At this point, we assume that Paul has money, perhaps inherited. He could have a corporate career. So far, there has been no mention of children for Paul and Veronica. Antag2, at this point, seems to be Barbara, Paul's smirky sister.

The tennis pro is a possible helper. But Veronica would probably trust a female more.

Ritual: greeting guests, kissing, changing clothes, playing tennis.

Objects: pistol, black dress, tennis clothes. If the writer shows Veronica playing tennis, she'll be using a tennis racquet. It's important to create lots of objects early in the writing. An object planted early has time to grow with the writing.

Secrets: something's going on between Paul and Ashleigh.

After you run the checklist, you can use a grid to compress the information. This grid was created in Microsoft Word.

Scene	Place	Character	Object	Ritual
1: Foyer	Big House	Veronica	Later	Handshake/ mourning
2: Den	Big House	Paul/Ashleigh	Pistol	Foreplay
3: Drawing Room	Big House	Veronica/Barbara	Later	Stand-off
4: Kitchen	Big House	Barbara/Ashleigh	Picture	Hunting
5: Den	Big House	Barbara/Paul	Insert Photo	Sibling Rivalry
6: Bedroom	Big House	Veronica/Paul	Perfume	Rejection
7: Pro Shop	Club	Veronica/Pro	White Dress	Tennis = what?
8: Field Test	Test Site	Paul/Suits	Spy Plane	Commerce

TABLE 2: RUNNING THE TWN CHECKLIST – *TROPHY WIVES*

Using the grid to play what-if

Six scenes in the house show the characters making edgy contact. Let's use the character connections to play what-if: Paul and Barbara are siblings. Veronica is Paul's wife. Veronica clashes with Barbara. What if their clash is sibling jealousy brought on by buried incest?

What if Barbara resents all of Paul's women? What if Ashleigh Bennett is an accountant and what if she cooks the books for Paul? That would give her a hold over him. And a motive for using his father's gun. At this point, we see Veronica moving from room to room, watching, being unhappy and withdrawn. Is she afraid of Paul? Is she wary of Barbara? How much does Veronica know about Ashleigh? In the bedroom scene, Veronica smells Ashleigh's perfume in the bedroom. Has she smelled it before? What if Ashleigh has a friend at the Securities and Exchange Commission?

The grid shows one visible resource-base – the big house – and a house this size has to be supported with money, so what if the death of Paul's mother has instant consequences: the family business started by the father of Paul and Barbara now passes to them. Now we have a plot; a situation straight from today's headlines, where corporate executives steal from their stockholders, where accountants cook the books. How much does Barbara know about Ashleigh?

With these scenes, these characters, and these what-ifs, we shift now to several weekends of character work. Where did Veronica meet Paul? Who's in league with Barbara? Does the tennis pro help Veronica? Or is there a masked helper waiting in the wings?

part 3 Weekends 7–14:

Sculpting Your Characters

When you start your book, you might begin with a concept, jotting down an idea for a fictional situation. 'This is a story', you might write, 'about economic success (money, a fancy home, material possessions) after being trapped in a life of poverty.' Or you might begin with a close-up that pulls the reader in tightly on the detail: 'The rag, filthy with dirt and accumulated cinders, left tell-tale streaks on the grey stones of the hearth.' Or you might begin with the familiar voice of the storyteller: 'Once upon a time, in a kingdom to the west, there lived a cinder-maid who detested ashes. Her name was...'

This movement – from idea to image to opening line – is a handy three-step process; one that you can use to start your own work. You clarify the movement – it could be coming of age, hunting down a killer, or rising up from rags to riches – with a statement of your central idea. You explore the situation with an image linked to the idea. And when you write your opening lines to introduce the character, you echo the voice of the storyteller, perhaps heard in childhood, because you know you can change it later, when you rewrite.

Cinderella is a great character to use as an example for your own work. She has tenacity, drive, and incredible staying power. The theme of her story, rags to riches, provides clear direction for her movement in the story: up from the cinders. The moral (hard work and honesty will get you through) has wide audience appeal.

The Cinderella myth appears in many different incarnations. In *My Fair Lady*, she's Eliza, a cocky Cockney lass with an accent that inspires Professor Henry Higgins to play Fairy Godmother before she transforms him into her Handsome Prince. In *Pretty Woman*, Julia Roberts made her name as a Cinderella character. Cinderella crosses cultural boundaries: in Germany she is little Aschenbrodel; in France she is La Petite Cendrillon.

When you create your female characters, there's a good chance you'll borrow, either consciously or unconsciously, from the character of Cinderella. Here's why:

- First, her beauty, concealed by metaphorical cinders, enables her to be reborn when she gets cleaned up.
- Second, under all the layers of costume, Cinderella is afraid. She's afraid of being alone. Her father's dead, gone away. She's afraid she will never love again. She's afraid of the power her stepmother has over her. Without voicing it, Cinderella lets us know by her actions that she wants out. Her father's house, now in the

hands of the Wicked Stepmother, is her trap. To solve the problem – to escape the trap – her only course is to land herself a Prince.

- Third, landing the Prince will give Cinderella her safe harbour.

Determining what your characters want

You can give your character life by answering key questions early in the writing. What does my character want? What's stopping her from getting it? How far will she go to get what she wants? Whom will she betray? Is she hungry enough to kill for what she wants? Your deep character work will pay off fast and big. If you don't like the verb 'wants', you can use 'desires' or 'yearns for'.

Start with 'want lists' for your characters. Take ten minutes and list every possible want that each of your characters might have. Start simple: money, food, shelter. Go deeper: love, sex, acceptance. Go deeper still: motherly approval, life without guilt, freedom from addiction. You can find simple examples everywhere: a woman wants her mother's approval for how she raises her children. A man wants his father's approval for his chosen career. These wants lead to dramatic consequences for your characters. If they go unfulfilled, what will your characters use to fill the void? Who stands in the way of fulfilling them? This drama sparks emotion that drives the story, making your reader laugh, cry, scream. This is what keeps your reader interested. This is what your reader pays good money for.

Drama in your novel starts with character. What does she want? How badly does she want it? What's in her way? What will she give up to get it? What are her obsessions? How will she do when she fails? What will she do when she succeeds?

Understanding character and motive

Once you've decided what your character wants, you have another crucial question to answer: why? Motive – from the Latin *movere*, to move – is what forces your character through the pages of your novel.

A motive is an emotion or a desire that incites a person to act. The husband who murders his mistress is driven by fear. In Chapter 1, his mistress is angry: the husband won't leave his wife and kids. In Chapter 2, on a weekend trip to Vegas, the mistress drinks too much, threatening to go to the wife and reveal their indiscretions. In Chapter 3, Vegas police find her body in a dumpster, stripped naked and strangled. The husband goes home alone. The husband wanted freedom from his mistress; the mistress wanted the husband to leave his wife. The husband acted on his want: his motive.

The two characters' competing wants give the story spice, conflict. They are people with different pasts, convening presents. The mistress was motivated by dreams of her own family, the husband she couldn't have. When these two characters cross paths, and both can't fulfil their wants, your novel starts to pick up pace. The reader starts to live the conflict with the characters.

Clashes like these create excellent drama in your novel.

Developing characters and character roles

Characters operate in roles that set expectations for the reader. This is the most subtle form of structure in your novel. Your lead character is the protagonist. Most traditional lead characters are good guys or good girls: Indiana Jones, Harry Potter, Bridget Jones, Cinderella. They are heroes, heroines. Their hearts are pure. They fight the good fight, and they win in the end. The dragon – the character who stands in the way, blocking the protagonist's journey (need, want, desire) – is the antagonist. *Anti-* means against, and the drama in your story comes from pitting the protagonist, representing good, against the antagonist, representing evil.

Harry Potter, the protagonist in a series of books written for children and young adults, wants to be a normal boy, attending Hogwarts School of Witchcraft and Wizardry, in the magical world of witches and wizards in present-day England. Harry's desire, simple enough on the surface, is opposed by Lord Voldemort, an archetypal antagonist whose presence in the fantasy world created by J K Rowling creates wonderful drama.

To make your conflict more interesting, to give it body and depth, you will bring on a cast of supporting characters. These lesser characters assist the protagonist and antagonist, carrying some of the load. When a gang of antagonists outnumbers your protagonist, you recruit helper characters to even the odds. Harry Potter, outnumbered and outmatched by Voldemort and his followers, the Death Eaters, finds help in his schoolmates and the teachers at Hogwarts. Since it's economical and necessary to exploit what you bring onstage, you explore these minor characters, adding significant details that decorate your scenes and enrich your story. Ron Weasley, Harry's best friend, is tall, gangly, full of wild ideas that often turn out to be true. Supporting characters are a place for you to introduce eccentric details that spice up your story. To exploit a particular character trait, give supporting characters what your protagonist wants. Harry Potter just wants to be a normal boy with a family who loves him. Ron Weasley has exactly that. Ron's family is poor, but he has five brothers, a sister, and parents that dote on all the children. By injecting Harry into scenes with the Weasley family, Rowling amplifies Harry's wants.

As a writer, examine character traits like Harry's craving for a normal life, and begin to ask yourself these questions: How can I use this trait in my story? Do my character's wants and needs create drama? What if, for example, your character is a zookeeper who doesn't like animals? A teacher who doesn't like children? A salesman who can't sell? A mother who regrets having children? A B-movie queen?

This last example, a B-movie queen, gave author Elmore Leonard a perfect helper character for his cult classic, *Get Shorty*. Her name is Karen Flores. She's pulled onstage when Chili Palmer, the protagonist, tracks down Harry Zimm at Karen's house. Karen is a voluptuous redhead who has made her name doing bad horror flicks. She sees through Chili's tough-guy act, but she also sees he's a clever guy, sharp enough to make a great movie.

By bringing Karen Flores on, Leonard gives the reader a movie expert, a connector, a voice of reason. Karen knows how the movie business works, and she's not a dreamer like Harry Zimm. Flores does not talk fancy. Instead, she gives Chili straight talk, talk he understands. Flores was married to Martin Weir, the A-list star who will ensure the success of Chili's movie. She gives Chili access to the tools that will help him fulfil his want. Along the way, Flores gives Chili insight into getting this movie done. In fictional terms, she is the helper who guides him into the machinery of Hollywood filmmaking.

Helper characters support your protagonist from plot point to plot point. They do the heavy lifting, the 'schmoozing' – whatever is necessary to let your main characters fulfil their wants.

Finding motivation for your character

The verb 'wants' – he wants, she wants, the enemy wants – is your key for unlocking motive. Motive gives your characters a reason to act. Their actions – what they do – put them in conflict with themselves, with each other, and, sometimes, with the universe. This conflict drives your novel.

If you take the time to dig down into character, you'll come up with a core motive for the conflict. To dig into your character, first give her a name: let's say Veronica. Then ask questions: What does Veronica want? Does she want children? A family? Money? Romance? A house with a white picket fence? An apartment on the beach? To marry a politician who becomes President so she can be First Lady? Then, answer every question, unearth motivation: What if Veronica was born poor? What if her deep drive is for economic security? What if her first target is a handsome man with money? What if her second target is any man with money?

A few ifs and what-ifs lead you to discoveries about character which point directly to a fictional situation. For example, you find that Veronica, who has certain Cinderella-like traits, wants to escape from her poor-girl past.

Building character through discovery

To energise your discovery process – to give yourself permission to discover – work with what comes up on the page as you do your writing. If you bring a character onstage semi-rehearsed and only half-dressed, without knowing what she's doing there, don't be suprised when she fluffs a line of dialogue. Now that your character is onstage, give her some attention. What is she doing with her hands? If she's adjusting the strings on her tennis racquet, she could be on a tennis court. If she's carrying shopping in the rain, the tennis court vanishes and is replaced by a car park. The season is winter and the weather is wet and cold; the rain is falling, the wind blowing her hair, and she cries when she drops the shopping because it is winter-time inside the character. If it's winter, what is she wearing? If she's wearing designer clothes, she could have money. If, however, she's wearing faded Levi cut-offs, she could be poor. To find out, let her react to the situation. How does it feel to be wearing jeans and a leaky raincoat when the man in the Porsche wears a Burberry and Mephisto shoes? Does it make her feel depressed? Or does her predicament fuel her desires to climb out of the muck?

As you track these characters through the opening pages of your manuscript, trying to discover what they're doing, keep asking questions: Who are these people? Where are they going? What do they want? What's stopping them? How smart are they? Where are they coming from? How well do they know each other? Whose story is this? Discovery writings should flow wild and free, like white birds loosed from the cage.

Deep characters help you to nail dialogue. Put your sexy protagonist onstage. What does she do with her hands? What kind of shoes
does she wear? When she goes to the office party, does she wear the
Armani suit or the slinky Bebe dress? Is she jealous of the doctor's
wife? Is she comfortable in her own skin?

In discovery, you explore your characters' wants, motives, and
motivations.

Weekends 7–8:

Creating a character sketch

A character sketch is a snapshot of a person who will eventually appear in your novel. The particulars of the sketch come from your personal experience – a woman in the queue at the supermarket, the plumber with a limp who fixes your toilet, the man at the bus stop who talks to himself. You measure each person, writing down in your notebook what you see. You note each detail: height, weight, race, build, hair. Notice the gestures she makes, the clothes she wears. Work fast. Use keywords, buzzwords. A character sketch isn't a place to perfect sentence structure – it's a place to build a foundation for characters in your novel.

Character work develops your writer's eye, moving you from real detail (concrete observations of the living) to fictional detail (assumptions you make based on your observations). This is the process of creative guesswork. In creative guesswork, you invade the privacy of a stranger to make writerly assumptions about lifestyle.

Character assumptions combine the details and traits you witness in the real world. You bring all your notes together to begin to form a character for the pages of your novel. You start with concrete observations about a stranger: she wears a Casio watch, torn jeans, Nike trainers. She walks quickly to her old Honda Civic. She carries two plastic shopping bags, one in each hand. The rain pelts her, but she doesn't stop or slow down. At the car, she fumbles with her keys. She drops a bag, and a jar of mayonnaise breaks. She leans down and picks up the bag and the wet shopping. She sets them aside and picks up the broken glass. She cleans up her mess. She is a good person. She is poor. Her apartment is down the road from the shops. She commutes into the city for college. When her car won't start, her life begins to crumble. She doesn't have money to get it fixed. She needs the car to better her life. She has a motive.

You watch her, working the sketch over in your mind. With your small notebook (the one you always keep with you) you jot down notes: Honda Civic, Casio, torn jeans, sad. Caring, cleans up her mess. She's unhappy. She's pretty. She doesn't care about her appearance.

She wants to better her life and life throws her challenges. You start to envision her home. It's small, cramped. The apartment building is a long way from her life in college. It's cheap, and she can afford it. She wants to get out.

The character sketch is a quick exercise, but one of the most important you will do. Writing down details, you start to make connections. Your characters are the heart of your novel. Their lives produce drama, and drama makes a book sing. As you begin to collect details, the doorway from your conscious to your unconscious opens. You start to feel your character's wants. They are believable. They are real.

Fifteen minutes and you're ready for the writing. You have the foundation for a character. She might be the protagonist, or she might be a helper. You don't know yet. You need to get to know her better.

Learning by example: the stranger in the room

The sketch below is a study of Veronica, the protagonist of *Trophy Wives*, whom we first met in the supermarket car park. For the character sketch, we relocate her to a coffee shop, where she is reading a book, taking notes on a yellow legal pad.

Sketch: stranger in the room

Height:	5' 5"
Weight:	120lbs
Sex:	female
Age:	24
Date of birth:	1 July 1980
Place of birth:	Browning, Montana, Blackfoot Indian Reservation
Hair:	black, silky
Clothes:	simple, classic, worn
Shoes:	Nike trainers, Payless Shoe Source, seconds
Jewellery:	her only jewellery is her mother's beaded necklace
Financial status:	born poor, will marry very rich, will pay the price
Health:	hassled, stressed, weary
Fatal flaw:	she loves too deeply
Mind:	sharp, pragmatic, precise, sensitive, hesitant about romance

Face:	chiselled, high cheekbones, wide mouth
Eyes:	blue, sharp, look right at you, show little trust
Pose:	stands straight, shoulders square, hiding her need to hunker down
Build:	slight, trim, fit, too thin, right on the edge of unhealthy
Arms:	strong, lean, sculpted
Legs:	dark, runner's legs, slender, sexy
Imperfections:	scar on chin
Home:	small apartment in Oakland, bad neighbourhood; she lives in the small apartment alone, moving in when her mother committed suicide
Favourite room:	her bedroom, set up for an office, with computer, books, pens
View from the window:	alley
Habits:	twists hair, rubs hands
Vehicle:	beaten-up 1986 Honda Civic hatchback
Name:	Veronica
Primary motivation:	wants to escape her life of poverty

Guidelines for creating your sketch

A character sketch frames the character using specific details – female, fit, black hair, Nike trainers, torn jeans – which generates creative guesswork, where you call on your imagination to do more character work, adding more details: a shabby apartment in Oakland, a window overlooking the alley, a mother who committed suicide.

Possessions are clues about lifestyle. Veronica is poor. She has an old car that won't start and a small apartment in a bad neighbourhood. She commutes into the city for college because she can't afford to live near the University. Why is she alone? Where will she go? As you sketch in these details, you build a profile of a person from the outside. Keep the sketch focused on the exterior. It doesn't take a lot of time – ten minutes, maybe 15 – to jot down the details. But there's a lot you don't know yet. You don't know, for example, about friends, parents, siblings. You don't know which room she sleeps in. You don't know who else might sleep in the house.

This is important. Not knowing gives you a reason to find out. Not knowing triggers your mind to ask questions that get behind details: Did she always live alone? Why does she clean up the car park? Does she have a man in her life? Why is she sad?

Do several sketches, training your writer's eye to focus on physical details. You will get better with practice, and you'll do sketches for as long as you're a writer. It's a fluid movement: your eye sees, your hand records. The sketch teaches you again and again to notice the world, to use the details around you in your writing. And with each sketch, you're hoping to create a character, a stranger in the room, who will bring drama to your novel and drive a successful plot.

Exercises

Use the following exercises to take the baby steps to creating characters. Use these steps to explore the people who will grace your pages. Most successful novels are character-driven, and you are in the crucial stage of creating those people. Spend time creating solid characters; it will pay off as you create the story around them.

1. Stranger in the room

Take your writer's notebook to a public place - a coffee shop, a restaurant, a bar, a library, a waiting room, a park. Do three character sketches as you look at strangers. For each character, fill in these categories:

Height:
Weight:
Sex:
Age:
Date of birth:
Place of birth:
Hair:
Clothes:
Shoes:
Jewellery:
Financial status:
Health:
Fatal flaw:
Mind:
Face:
Pose:
Build:
Arms:

Legs:
Imperfections:
Home:
Favourite room:
View from the window:
Habits:
Vehicle:
Name:
Primary motivation:

2. What if?

What-if questions set your characters in motion. You can ask ridiculous questions, create out-of-the-blue scenarios that give your characters problems to solve: What if a car hit her? What if she went to a party and met someone? What if she was caught shoplifting? What if she wakes up in jail? In a strange bed?

Or you can ask questions in sequence: What if she is born poor? What if she gets pregnant by a rich boy? What if her husband has an affair? What if her husband's mistress disappears? What if her sister-in-law tries to take back the family fortune? What if the husband goes to jail? What if the kids go to live with the grandparents? What if the police detective who arrests the husband wants favours? What if the favours are sexual? What if the detective and the sister-in-law both want the same thing: money?

Ask the question, then let the answers spin out. What-if questions are great for story development and character continuity. Ask what-if questions for all three of the characters you did sketches for.

3. Casting director

Now that you've done three sketches and answered your what-if questions, cast your characters. One character looks good for a protagonist; one looks like an excellent helper/catalyst – but the antagonist looks iffy, so you need to ask more what-if questions. If that doesn't sharpen your character, try another sketch. You will have to live with your characters for the next 51 weeks, so cast accordingly.

Getting help from other writers

The protagonist of *Fortune's Rocks*, by Anita Shreve, is a girl named Olympia Biddeford. At the age of 15, in the month of June, in the year 1899, Olympia – who has fallen deeply in love for the one and only time in her life – gets pregnant. The father of her baby is twice her age, plus another decade. He is married. He has three children. The year of Olympia's child's birth is 1900. Olympia is 16 and unmarried. The child is taken from her. When she is strong enough, Olympia goes on a hunt for her lost child.

This is a good book to study for the straight-line plot because Olympia is too young to have much back story. Therefore, the plot is linear. A character sketch of Olympia reveals secrets you can use in developing your protagonist.

Name:	Olympia Biddeford
Sex:	female
Age:	15 on page 1; 27 at the end
Height:	5' 8"
Weight:	120lbs
Imperfections:	emotion mottles her face and throat, making her look sick

Body parts:

Mouth:	her mouth deserves a portrait in itself
Feet:	page 1 has her barefoot; likes sand between her toes
Hair:	rich, thick, heavy, demands many hairpins; colour of oak, then brightened by sun at Fortune's Rocks
Arms:	an inch longer than last year; growing girl
Chin:	touched by Haskell during a family photo session
Throat:	touched by Haskell, chin to throat, Act One

Wardrobe:

Page 1, on the beach. Olympia walks barefoot to the water. Her linen hat is off. Her boots are left behind at the sea wall. She stands out because it's 'Man Time' on the beach. Bare feet, skirt hem of her peach dress soaked by salt water. Under the dress, she wears stockings.

Bedroom, dressing for dinner. She discards this costume: a sailor-girl dress, white and navy blue; sailor piping around the bodice, a sailor's collar. Her hair is loose, tied with a ribbon. She's 15 and wants to look older.

Bedroom, re-dressing for dinner. She dons a 'white handkerchief' linen blouse, a long black woollen skirt with a high, fitted waist. She discards the ribbon, too girlish. She piles her hair in a high knot.

Bedroom, dressing for bed in a thin nightdress of white linen. Putting on the dress, she discovers that her arms are an inch longer than the sleeves. Protagonist grows up.

Bedroom, dressing for the birthday party. A silk dress that clings to her body. The most revealing thing she has ever worn. She is 15, on the cusp of 16. She is pregnant. Her hair sparkles with gold highlights from the sun. Hair done up in a double bun, secured with combs of pearl. (*Wardrobe and structure*: this costume starts the scene-sequence that makes up Shreve's midpoint.)

Favourite rooms:

First, there is the sunroom, under construction in the house that her lover Dr Haskell is building on the beach at Fortune's Rocks. While Haskell's wife is away, Olympia and the doctor make love in that room.

Second, there is her bedroom, a private sanctuary where she dresses.

Third, there is the deconsecrated chapel in her father's house at Fortune's Rocks. Olympia uses this chapel as a retreat. On the night of her 16th birthday, she meets Haskell in a final clasp of love.

What the character wants: Olympia wants a life with Dr Haskell. She is the intruder into his family circle; he welcomes her into his arms, but not his life. She is driven by the laws of sociobiology: she wants genetic success. She has good genes. Dr Haskell has good genes that show up in his children, who are healthy and smart.

Obstacle: Olympia's obstacle is society. She is too young. She is unmarried. She breaks rules. Society, in the form of parents and other adults, makes her pay.

Antagonists:

1. Antag 1 is a smart-aleck poet named Cote. At the novel's midpoint, he leads Mrs Haskell to a telescope that is trained on the chapel where Olympia clasps Dr Haskell for the last time.

2. Antag 2 is Mrs Haskell, the wife and mother who stands in Olympia's way.

3. Antag 3 is Olympia's father, a stalwart upholder of society's laws. He controls the resource-base of money and property.

4. Antag 4 is Olympia's mother, a beautiful woman who spends much of her life in bed.

5. Antag 5 is a farmer in western Massachusetts who wants to donate his sperm to Olympia's womb.

6. Antag 6 is the adoptive parent of Olympia's lost child.

7. Antag 7 is the lawyer who opposes Olympia's attempt to retrieve her lost child.

Line space.

A good character sketch generates details that you can use when you write your novel. The dressing rituals guide Olympia to the novel's midpoint, where her affair with the doctor is revealed. The seven antagonists mark Olympia's journey from Act One to the courtroom climax in Act Three. Gather your details about wardrobe and ritual. Tuck them away in your notebook, on your hard drive. They will come in handy.

Weekends 9–10:
Back story

The stranger in the room has a past, a history. The technical term for talking about the past in fiction is back story. Back story is what happened before the character entered the story. You won't need to create an entire personal history for your characters, but you will need to find motive, big events. Before she showed up, dressed impeccably, to pose for your character sketch, your stranger (Veronica) was somewhere else. She bathed and dressed and checked her hair in the mirror. Then she grabbed her yellow legal pad, left the room, locked the door behind her, and headed to the coffee shop. You use creative guesswork to establish where she came from, not only in space, but also in time. What happened in her past that left her scarred, stamping her with a character trait that you can use?

Secrets lurk in the past. The stranger looks composed; she's taking notes; she's sipping her tea – but what secrets is she hiding? What juicy stuff can you dig up to provide motivation for this character? To find out, play what-if. What if she had a lousy childhood? What if she was born unwanted? What if her mother worked as a waitress or a maid? What if her mother brought strange men home to the shabby apartment where the stranger was trying to study? What if she went to college to become an actress? What if she slept with a teacher who promised to leave his wife and marry her? What if the teacher's wife found them together?

To heighten the drama, you deepen the pain. What if she had an abortion that almost killed her? Or try a logical extension from your character sketch – her blue-collar background. What if she ran out of money and the only way she could make it through school was to work as an escort? What if she sold her body? What if she takes money from men to exact her own special revenge on the entire male gender? Why is she getting revenge?

The what-ifs boils down to motive. Writing back story is a process of constructing character motivations. You unearth motives for your characters in the same way that a therapist looks for the causes of depression in his patients. You ask questions. You dig into the past and find trauma. Trauma in childhood leaves us helpless and afraid. Fear makes us cold. We can't move. We cry a lot. We withdraw inside ourselves. In Chabon's *The Amazing Adventures of Kavalier and Clay*, Joe Kavalier's motive is guilt about his brother. Joe escaped Nazi Germany, leaving his parents and brother behind. Throughout the novel, Chabon uses Joe's guilt as the motivation for all his actions.

Follow Chabon's lead: use back story. For example, the following scene explores a moment from Veronica's past.

Learning by example: Veronica's back story

Veronica exits the supermarket. The rain beats down. She stares at the rain, feeling the drops on her face. She takes in a deep breath. Her shopping bags are paper; her hair is a mess. As she runs for her car, the rain stings her cheeks. Her foot finds a puddle and she feels cold through her toes and she cannot find the car. Then a voice calls out, 'Miss, are you all right?' but she does not stop. She feels her fingers losing their grip on the shopping. She is at the car, fumbling for keys, when one shopping bag drops. She hears the crunch of glass breaking. Stooping to pick up the dropped bag, she sees a black car. A vintage Porsche. A man coming at her, through the rain.

She unlocks the door. Gets behind the wheel, hands shaking. She turns the key and there is an edgy, whining sound. The car does not start. She looks through the window. The man is there. A tall man in a trench coat. A Burberry, like a model in a magazine. He does not knock on the window. He just waits in the rain.

She rolls down the window.

'Can I help?' he asks.

'It won't start.'

'I'm not a mechanic,' he says. 'But I can call for help.'

'I don't know,' she says.

'You're wet,' he says. 'Are you okay?'

'I don't know.'

'Don't go away,' he says. 'I have a phone in the car.'

Veronica nods, but says nothing. She waits. He comes back. He offers to buy her a cup of coffee. 'Tea?', she asks. Her life is over. She is cold. The damned raincoat leaks. Her hair is plastered across the front of her face. She's wearing a baggy sweater and jeans with a hole in one knee. Her feet are freezing. In the coffee shop, she's still shivering. 'What do you like? They have terrific espresso.' 'Tea,' she says. 'I stopped drinking coffee.' 'Tea it is,' he says. He tells her his name is Paul. Shaking her head, she decides to call him The Man. She sits in a booth against the wall, watching the rain through the window. It feels safe here, safe and warm. She is tired, battered by the rain. The waitress at the coffee shop makes eyes at the man. He looks very tall. He is an older man. Mid-30s or early 40s. He wears Mephisto shoes. As he returns to the table, Veronica shrugs out of her raincoat and a book drops on the floor. Her paperback copy of *Jane Eyre*. Before she can lean over to pick it up, the man has it back on the table.

She opens the book. The pages are wet on the margin. Her careful notes, made in blue ink, are smeared. Veronica cries, the tears hot and wet. The man hands her a tissue. She nods, blows her nose. Poor Jane Eyre. The tea is hot. Veronica holds the cup close to her face with both hands. She hates her life. The man indicates her copy of *Jane Eyre*.

'Good book. Sad story.'

'It's the story of my life,' she says.

'Hemingway is my writer.'

'I read it first when I was ten, Jane's age when the book opens. Her story is my story.'

'What are all those marginal notes?'

'For my thesis.'

'You're a student?'

'Yeah, I'm almost done.'

'That's good. School is important,' he says. 'How is your tea?'

'I feel better, thank you.'

'Are you on scholarship?'

'Yes. And I work at the library.'

'Doing what?'

'Information clerk, at the reference desk.'

They talk. His father has just died. He's busy running the company started by his father. They have a second cup of tea. He opens the book, reads a line. He has a nice voice. His eyes are sad. He seems to be opening up to her. She feels the waitress watching. She is pretty, a blonde with a good figure. Veronica feels small and dark, wiped out by the bright-eyed blonde. She finishes half her tea and stands up.

'Can I give you a lift?', he asks.

'I'd appreciate that,' she says.

The man follows her out to the Porsche.

In the car, the man hands her his business card. He needs a dedicated researcher, he says. Someone with a brain to analyse some reports, synthesise information. It's not great money, but it's steady work.

Veronica says nothing. She needs money. The man looks well-off. What would it be like working for him? She has nothing to wear to a real job. She guides him to the corner near her apartment. She's avoiding her life. The Porsche stops. She needs money today. Her head spins. He opens the car door for her, offers to walk her to her door. She says, 'No thank you, you have done enough.'

At the entrance door, she looks back to see the man watching her. Veronica shivers, a ripple of excitement. He is still watching as she enters the building.

Guidelines for writing back story

When you write back story, make some notes, block out a scene or two, and then track the objects. Look at the objects that surface in this writing. Veronica's back story starts in the rain. She's wet, the shopping is heavy and her car won't start. When she drops a shopping bag, she breaks glass. The broken glass is an object that turns into a symbol. The breakage of the glass represents the crack in Veronica's life. She is Cinderella in a beaten-up car. Soaked by rain, Veronica battles the elements.

The broken glass and the unstartable car attract the attention of the handsome prince. His vehicle is a vintage Porsche. He wears a Burberry raincoat. He uses a magical object – a hot cup of tea – to bring her back from the edge of doom into his circle of wealth and power. Like Cinderella from the fairy-tale, Veronica's beauty shines through the mask of poverty and despair. When she removes her raincoat, out falls a copy of *Jane Eyre*. The prince who has rescued her has seen the film, but he has not read the book. This simple object – the paperback copy of *Jane Eyre* – is not only a conversation piece, but it is also a container for the dreams of Veronica. *Jane Eyre*, she tells him, is the story of her life. This dialogue line is made possible by the novel (object) that falls (action) from her raincoat (object), which got wet in the rain (weather), which she removes because she is cold (touch, kinaesthesia). With that brief summary, we can deploy the TWN checklist:

Time:	afternoon.
Place:	the city is San Francisco; the characters meet in a car park. The car park is wet.
Character:	the characters are Veronica (our protagonist) and a man named Paul. Writing about Paul, the writer is care-

Objects: ful to refer to him as 'the man'. By not using Paul's name, the writer controls the point of view, and keeps the man at an appropriate distance.

Objects: the objects are shopping, plastic bags, raincoat, 'clunker' car, sleek car, books, teacups, tables, chairs, a serving bar.

Dialogue: the subject of the dialogue is Veronica's quest for education. The subject is triggered by the annotated copy of *Jane Eyre*, the object which falls out of her pocket. The dialogue reveals her dream: finishing school. She's smart enough to work at the reference desk. She probably knows computers. The man in the raincoat runs a company and he can use her skills. The dialogue triggers the barter ritual.

Ritual: the barter ritual comes from needs and wants. Veronica needs money. The man wants her for himself. What if they make a deal?

Notes: at this point, we do not know whether or not this man is telling the truth. He understands buying and selling. Perhaps he thinks Veronica is an easy conquest. To know more, we must keep writing. Before you write, you might build a chronology.

Chronology for the protagonist

To find motivation for your character, you probe the past. You need an entry point, a place to begin exploring, a doorway. Take a few moments during the week to build a list of dates for your character. Start with the date of birth. Our heroine, Veronica, is in her mid-20s, so her birthday would be in the early 1980s.

1980: born Browning, Montana, Blackfoot Indian Reservation
1983: father runs off
1985: moves to LA, mother gets job as housemaid for a television producer
1996: her mother loses her job, works as an escort
1997: first sexual experience, boyfriend of aunt; Veronica is 15
1998: first love, a rich boy, ends up hurt
1998: scholarship to Santa Clara University
2003: works at the library information desk, from Santa Clara
2004: meets Paul Watson, her future husband, in the rainswept car park

2004: marries her older man; moves into a big house on Nob Hill
2004: husband's mother dies

A list of dates will open doorways into your character's past, expos-
ing motivation. When you write your back story, you'll have several
possible starting points to choose from. Your character's life is a con-
tinuum, a timeline, like your own life. Each date is a point on a con-
tinuum, and your story is a piece of the larger timeline.

Back story is for the author, not for the reader. Whether they
come out in dialogue or flashback or exposition, it's important to
pay attention to significant details. Back story helps the writer find
motive. And motive, while essential to a character's movements and
actions, is not essential to a reader's enjoyment of the story.

In the following exercises, you will develop your own back story.

Exercises

1. Chronology: dates as doorways
Build a chronology of dates for each character. Key dates give you
doorways into the past, and you should get your characters'
chronologies in shape before you dive into the past. A list of dates is
like a ladder, with easy steps connecting the past of each of your
characters to the time at which they enter your story. To get the
birthdays of your characters, subtract their ages from the year in
which your story takes place. With the birthdays as an anchor, jot
down a list of dates and events from your character's life: first day of
school, first kiss, first crush, parents' divorce, death of a grandparent,
death of a friend, military wedding night. Allow the images to roll
as you probe the past.

For cultural and historical continuity – the references you will
make to details – you can research the year of your story in *The
Timetables of History*, or similar classic reference books.

2. Writing the back story
Working from one key date in the chronology, write back stories for
each of your main characters. Begin with an overview, and move
deeper in the scene that becomes a turning point in your character's past. Write under the clock – write on each character in your
notebook for 15 minutes. Lock down your writing by including one
or more of the five senses: taste, touch, hearing, smell, sight.

Take a short break. Close your eyes. Breathe deeply. Read your
material. Don't judge, but add quirky details. What are you forget-

ting? What happy moments still bring the character joy? What makes the character sad?

3. Wants list

Start a wants list. What does Character A want? What does Character B want? How do your characters clash? Where in the story do their wants clash? Keep adding to your wants list as new thoughts pop into your brain.

4. Stay organised

Complete back-story work for all the characters you sketched during Weekend 1. Place the work in individual folders to keep it organised. Keep everything about each character together. Have fun. Make their lives interesting and dynamic.

Getting help from other writers

As you move through the back-story exercises, creating your characters, look at your favourite authors. Where were your favourite characters before the stories began? What motivates them to act?

Tim O'Brien's *The Things They Carried*, a Vietnam war story based on O'Brien's experiences, illustrates the power of back story. As the characters patrol the jungle, the reader learns what each man carries and why. The war provides a timeline: these boys were pulled away from their lives in America, and O'Brien contrasts their civilian lives with their military lives to show motivation.

First-Lieutenant Jimmy Cross carries a picture of the love he left behind, Martha. He also carries a pebble sent to him by his lost love. Love becomes a distraction, and his men die because he has lost focus. The reader never sees Cross at home in New Jersey, but because he carries the picture and the pebble, the reader knows that Cross feels a strong commitment to this woman.

Kiowa, another of O'Brien's characters, carries an illustrated *New Testament*, his grandmother's distrust of the white man, and his grandfather's feathered hunting hatchet. These details about Kiowa show his state of mind, and his reliance on heritage. These details show the reader Kiowa's motivations. Kiowa's story, before *The Things They Carried* begins, is one of Native American life in the 1960s – a very troubled, complex existence.

Later in *The Things They Carried*, we learn that Lieutenant Cross burns Martha's picture and tosses out the pebble she sent him. Remembering his life before Vietnam (his back story) causes him too much anguish and distracts him from the dangers of war. His wants, his motivations, create drama and make him an excellent character.

In your own life, you know people who wear their thoughts and feelings out in the open. Unless you've experienced the close-knit bond of a unit in combat, you don't know the same kinds of details O'Brien does, but you will know the kinds of details that signal back story in your social group. The wife of a friend spends lavishly on Christmas. Growing up, her family barely had enough money for one present for the children. Your boss shows his nervousness at office parties. His parents dragged him to family gatherings, a show-piece of the success of their marriage.

Think about this motive for one of your characters: holding on to the past keeps him or her from living in the present.

Weekends 11–12:
Writing a dream

Writing a dream opens a door into your character's unconscious, a nice balance for the realistic detail of your character sketch. The sketch gives you exterior surfaces: clothes, possessions, settings. The dream explores the secret interior: desires, longings, neuroses and traumas.

You write dreams for your character for at least three reasons:

- First, dreams are a shortcut – a window to the soul that helps you learn more about your characters. Dreams bring you close to the players in your novel. If Chuck Palahniuk hadn't written a dream for Tyler Durden in *Fight Club*, he might never have discovered the sleepy world that bred underworld fighting and anarchy.
- Second, dream writing allows you to experiment with images and symbols, where you connect with the power of writing. If this is your first encounter with symbolism, get ready to be rewired. We live in a world filled with symbols, most of which pass away with no recognition. When you write dreams, use the startline, 'In a dream, I…' Write in your journal for ten minutes without ending a sentence. Let the energy pour out of you: you will be surprised at the vibrant, expressive words that form coherent, brilliant images. Writing dreams gives you an opportunity to explore the symbols that will take readers into other worlds. Once you've written a few dreams in your notebook, transfer the dreams into your word processor, adding details. Practise creating a scene.
- Third, writing dreams helps you let go, freeing yourself from inhibition and soaring for a few moments on the wings of language. When you begin with the startline, 'In a dream, I…', silence your internal editor. Send him or her far away.

Learning by example: Veronica's dream

Veronica is alone. Her breath leaks from her lips, making clouds. No heat because no money. No money because no work. The room is long. The furniture is old. Veronica looks into the mirror, its edges rimmed with ice. She looks young, then older, then old. Her black hair turns grey, then white. Her face turns into a skull. She puts her hands to her face. Her cheeks are cold. She looks down. Her bedroom slippers are falling off her feet. Her toes are white. The white of her toes spreads to her feet, whitening the ankles, the shin bones, the knees. Her dark skin turns white and then the door opens and her mother enters with a man.

Her mother wears a leather dress made of doeskin chewed by the women of the tribe sitting in a circle around a blazing fire humming as they sink their white teeth into the hide of the dead deer and Veronica tastes the blood of the deer as she stands up to embrace her mother who smiles down at her with light in her eyes saying, 'Hello honey, this is Charley, be nice to him while Mama changes her uniform,' and Veronica cries, 'Look at me, Mama, I'm older than you, look in the mirror,' and this man Charley is a big fat man with a cigar between his teeth, the smoke curling up from the cigar and he holds the cigar like a wand pointing the hot tip at Veronica while he blows smoke into her face and she looks into the mirror to see that her face has turned to smoke, and she grabs a pot from the top of the electric stove, swinging it like a baseball bat holding on with both hands pivoting like she does at school when she slaps that ball over the stiff arms over the outstretched gloves of the boys who taunt her in the halls and the silver pot slams against the head of Charley and blood spurts out and her mother stands in the doorway wearing a ballet costume a tight bodice with little pink flowers along the neckline and a pink tutu that fluffs up around her dark thighs and her mother says, 'Get his money before he wakes up honey and let's split this place,' and Veronica digs in the back pockets but finds nothing and then digs in his jacket pocket inside feeling his heart beating under the blue striped shirt and her fingers find the wallet so fat with money and she grabs Mama's hand and they race together out the door, leaving the man behind them on the floor and on the street they hear sirens wailing and behind her Veronica sees the flashing red lights on the roofs of the cars a hundred police cars arranged in a V shape and V stands for Veronica and Mama falls behind and Veronica keeps running hearing the squeal of tires and the explosion of bullets just like on the television and Mama crying, 'She did it that bitch of a daughter did it' and Veronica runs along a corridor of ice her feet burning feeling fire in her lungs and she runs up a twisting road to a high hill with a house in the clouds and a golden gate opening to let her through and the front door opens and a woman in black holds out both hands saying, 'Thank you so much for coming, my husband is in the study if you would like to leave your condolences,' and the woman in black looks like old photos of Veronica's mother, those same high Blackfoot cheekbones passed down from Grandmother to Mother to the Daughter who runs through the big house wearing a doeskin dress running down a long corridor with closed doors on each side and on each door the name of a woman...

Notes on Veronica's dream

This dream takes us inside the unconscious mind of Veronica, the protagonist of *Trophy Wives* – our model novel-in-progress. The dream opens with a series of short sentences, establishing character (Veronica and her mother), place (a long room), an object (the ice mirror), and Charley, a man brought into the house by Veronica's mother.

The dream starts with a movie-like time-collapse as the protagonist sees herself getting old and turning to ice in the mirror. The ice represents her frozen self, the withdrawn character who meets Paul Watson in the car park in the rain. The ice inside the protagonist sets up a problem in search of a solution that adds forward thrust to the plot – how will Veronica escape from the ice? – and sets up the possibilities for dramatic conflict. Which characters will help Veronica thaw out? And which characters will keep her locked in the deep freeze?

In the second paragraph, the short sentences vanish, to be replaced by one long sentence that runs over 500 words in a fun, semi-chaotic stream-of-consciousness syntax that you should try when you write dreams for your characters. This long sentence opens with a cluster of images – leather dress, women in a circle, white teeth, hide of the deer, blood of the deer – that evoke Veronica's Blackfoot heritage. If she can return to this image-cluster in the novel, she might gain strength from these women.

The circle of women gives way to dialogue as her mother orders Veronica to be nice to Charley, and as Veronica tries to assume control by switching roles with her mother: the face in the mirror looks ancient. This role-reversal recurs again when her mother appears wearing the ballet costume of a little girl. Left alone with Charley and his suggestive cigar, Veronica is horrified to see her face turned to smoke. To escape the smoke, she bangs Charley's head with a pot. Blood oozes from Charley's head. Her mother in her ballet costume turns the conversation to money – the reason she brought Charley home in the first place. And Veronica is trapped in a world of chaos ruled by greedy adults.

Emboldened by Charley's fat wallet, Veronica escapes her mother, who blames her daughter for Charley's blood, and runs up the hill to the house in the clouds, where she meets herself in the foyer – an echo from the scene-sequence earlier, where Veronica stands at the door greeting mourners who have come to pay their respects to Paul and his sister Barbara. The two costumes that appear at the end of the dream – one black dress and one Indian dress made of doeskin – represent the protagonist's divided self. The writer has used the dream to dramatise the two halves of Veronica Watson. She is poor. She is rich. She is young. She is old. She is white. She is Native American.

As you write a dream for your character, keep one eye on Veronica. She can teach us a lot.

Guidelines for Writing a Dream

Your goal is to write a dream that explores the mind of your character. In the character sketch, you started building your character with bits of information like age, sex, birthplace, birthday, occupation, income, likes and dislikes, needs. With this information, you explored a scene from your character's back story; an event in the past that affected the character in the narrative present that starts on page 1 and runs to the end of the novel. If you work hard, the sketch and the back story will connect. The sketch on Veronica, for example, noted that she was a poor girl, and the back story connected her to a man with money. Her problem is poverty, scratching out a living while she finishes college. In the dream, the writer of *Trophy Wives* dramatises the problem (poverty) and the solution (taking money from men) which is not really a solution (pot, blood, police cars), and the dreamer ends up a split personality in the big house where the story opens. Veronica's dream showcases three writing strategies for you to borrow for your own work: repetition, altering logical sequence, and letting go.

Repetition
When you repeat words in a passage, the repetition builds an echo effect. You let the words drift down through the writing like the recurring notes that make chords in a piece of music. If the repeated words are strung out, the echoes trailing like threads through a piece of cloth, repetition weaves a support fabric for the events in

your story. When repetition bunches up to form word-clusters, it hauls your images into the foreground where they attract the attention of the reader. When you repeat a word, you're tagging it as important; when you fail to repeat a word, you take the risk of losing it in the jungle of other words. If you use too much repetition, don't worry; you can trim the excess away when you rewrite. The trick here is to repeat a word until you get control through repetition.

The echo words in Veronica's dream – mirror, smoke, face, deer, Mama, V, Veronica, pot, blood, turns, look, digs – are everyday words angled in a kind of 'dream warp' that spins out of control when Veronica's face turns to smoke in the mirror, when she hits Charley with the pot, and when Mama steps out of her mothering role into a pink tutu. By repeating a simple verb like turns, you intensify the idea of transformation. By repeating a word like mirror, you can create the terrible image of a character growing old before our eyes. The fascinating thing about repetition is that you cannot feel the power without doing the work, without repeating the same word over and over and over until until until… Until you feel the power.

Altering logical sequence
The rhythms of cause and effect stabilise the world as we know it. You turn the key; the lock opens. You feel cold air on your neck; the cold air makes you hunch down, pulling the collar of your coat tight.

When you dabble with cause and effect, you increase the chances of writing something new. For example, in her dream, Veronica whacks Charley because her face turns to smoke because he is smoking a cigar. She registers no emotion. No fear, no rage, just a dreamer whacking an intruder, preparing the dream-world for Mama, who enters, wearing a pink tutu. Before Mama left for her costume change – a transformation of an adult female into a toy dancer – Veronica pointed out her own face in the mirror, calling attention to time out of sequence and a dream-world where a young girl had turned into a crone. In Veronica's dream, playing with the routine of cause and effect coughs up terrible truths about Mama and men and money: Charley is here, in this tawdry room, to get fleeced, to give up his money. And we also realise that Mama wants help from Veronica, and that the role of women is to take money from men. Is this what drives Veronica, a poor girl in a car park, to take the measure of Paul Watson in his Burberry raincoat?

When you write your dream, you can run wild with reversals of everyday logic, and you can keep the balance with a mixture of action and reaction that seems logical and right. When Veronica hits Charley, the blow makes his head bleed. She looks up to see Mama in the doorway. Mama orders Veronica to get Charley's money. Cause and effect brings the cops, and Mama's accusation ('She did it...') sends Veronica on the run. The dream is peopled by monsters. Charley is the monster with a cigar. Mama is the monster in a silly pink tutu. In this world, it is logical to run, to escape, to flee from the Lower World of greed and poverty to the Upper World of wealth: the house in the clouds.

Dream logic, built on a chain of images woven together by repetition, leads Veronica to her place of refuge.

Letting go

The first paragraph sets the stage: Veronica alone in a room. The sentences are short, the cadences like everyday prose. The first paragraph is a warm-up for the second paragraph (beginning with 'Her mother wears a leather dress made of doeskin...'), which stretches out for more than 500 words. Try writing your own long, stretched-out sentence today. Take a deep breath, let go, and when you come to a place where your internal editor whispers, 'Put a full stop here,' you use a simple connector like 'and' or 'then' or 'and then' or 'when' or 'so' or 'but'... and that way you can keep the words going, across the page, down the page, while you repeat those echo words to create that sense of transformation we understand as dreamlike.

As the Veronica sentence expands, it gains momentum, building to the final image: a young woman in a black dress greeting people in the foyer of a large house on the hill – the same house that opens the story called *Trophy Wives*. Now that the writer has written a dream, we have a better understanding of the person in the plain black dress. She grew up poor and now she is married to money. Money is the big symbol in the dream, and also in Veronica's waking life as she settles into her marriage with Paul. With her need for money and what it buys – safety, warmth, comfort, stability, a place in the world – would she have married Paul if he had been poor?

When you let go with your writing, you raise issues that will shape your story. The message in this dream is clear: Mama exchanges sex for money. The intent is also clear: Mama brings Charley home because she wants help from Veronica. When you let go with your writing, you not only create a thicker texture, but you also create more work for yourself as the novelist. Did Veronica help her mother to take money from men? Did her mother force Veronica to grant sexual favours to strange men? Did Veronica end her mother's tyrannical control with a pot in a sick-smelling room somewhere in her past? Or did she let fly at Charley only in her dreams? Veronica's dream raises the question: when will she break free?

The writer can find out by writing. By letting go.

Exercises

1. Writing a dream

Close your eyes, take a few deep breaths, and let your mind roam free as it plays with images and symbols. Concentrate on your breathing, the rise and fall of your chest, that point on your nose where the air goes out. Examine the process of your breathing (this takes your mind off the real world). When you feel relaxed, open your eyes and make a list of symbols and images. For easy reference, keep a separate file of these. When you can't think of any more, start a new dream. Take a couple of minutes to do the list. Use one of these three startlines to write a dream for one of your characters:

'In the dream, I...'
'In the dream, he...'
'In the dream, she...'

Write for 10–15 minutes, timing yourself to distract the internal editor. If you get stuck, repeat the startline, looping back, a kind of whipstitch with language. After you get rolling, allow your sentence to lengthen, expanding as it builds momentum.

When the timer rings, take a short break. Walk around. Breathe deeply. Don't talk to anyone. Don't read. Don't watch TV.

2. Getting close to words

When you return from your break, circle the key words in your dream, using a coloured pencil. Circling key words (the words that repeat) pulls you close to your language. When you have circled your key words, jot them down on a page in your notebook. At the top of the page, print 'Symbols and Images'. When a symbol or an image appears in your writing, add it to your list. This list prepares you to write dreams for your other characters.

3. Writing more dreams

Write a dream for each of your main characters. Practise your deep breathing. If your first dreamer was female, your next dreamer might be male. If you're writing about a homicidal maniac, the dream is essential to exploring his madness. If you're writing about a teenaged virgin, struggling to find her place as her friends take ecstasy and have sex parties, dreams will reflect choice, confidence, independence. The beginning of the dream is your anchor – come back to it if you want, or sever the rope and drift in the deep seas of the mind. Use the same startline ('In the dream, he...') and write for 15 minutes. If you didn't try a long sentence in your first dream, now is the time to do that. Repeat key words. Feel the pulse of your dreamer.

Getting help from other writers

In Dan Brown's *The Da Vinci Code*, Robert Langdon, the protagonist, is a symbologist who uses his immense knowledge to find the Holy Grail. Brown uses symbols as plot devices to keep the action moving; he also uses symbols as points of connection for his characters. His explanations and analysis of Leonardo da Vinci's paintings reach to the heart of symbols in religious works. Brown shows how logical connections can keep a plot moving.

The Da Vinci Code also serves as a good example for the use of dreams in fiction. Louvre curator Jacques Saunière is murdered in the opening chapter, and his granddaughter Sophie Neveu joins forces with Robert Langdon to solve the murder and find the Grail. As the two move through the novel, Sophie makes connections to her past while battling thoughts and emotions evoked by her grandfather's pagan practices.

Brown uses flashbacks from Neveu's childhood to introduce ideas and information that help the reader better understand what the characters in the story are confronting. In addition, Brown uses distant memories, or dreams, to illustrate conflict within the characters. The effect is greater drama and a more interesting read.

The novel-in-progress: *Trophy Wives*

Following our advice – to write a dream for each of your main characters – the writer of *Trophy Wives*, our novel-in-progress, writes a dream for Paul Watson. At this point, early in the writing, the writer has given equal weight to Paul and Veronica. This is a good technique because it allows you to study the characters, to get to know them as they become more solid. Paul's dream starts in the air, as he floats over a graveyard. The theme of the dream is death, maybe murder, and the writer keeps repeating key objects attached to Paul, like the Breitling watch and the Heckler and Koch pistol. Both these objects belonged to Paul's father. As you read this dream, circle the words that are repeated.

In the dream, Paul floats across the sky, green down below, as he soars over a crowd of people wearing black, a circle of mourners around a hole in the grass. The hole is rectangular, coffin-shaped. Paul angles his arms for a landing. His feet touch the grass and he is standing beside Ashleigh Bennett. She wears a red dress and red stockings and a little red hat. Her white hand holds the arm of Paul's father. 'What time is it?' Ashleigh asks. Paul and his father lift their wrists to their eyes. '11:30,' they say in unison. 'My watch,' his father says. 'I love that watch. Yours now, along with everything else.' Dad passes the watch to Paul. 'It's a Breitling, you know, with a winder-upper.' 'What time is it?' Ashleigh asks again. Paul and his father lift their wrists to their faces. Together, they call out: 'The time now is 12:30, Eastern Daylight.' His father unfastens the sharkskin strap and slides the watch off his white wrist. Standing in the coffin, he hands Paul the Breitling watch. 'Take good care of it. See the way the moon-light hits the crystal, sapphire. Unbreakable.' The iridium numbers glow on the face, illuminating the stainless steel bezel. Paul takes the Breitling, pulls back his French cuffs, slides it onto his wrist, fastens the strap, and shoots his cuffs. Just right. 'And this, you might need this.' His father pulls the Heckler and Koch pistol from inside his jacket. 'Willie McGuiness,' he says. 'Who?' 'I won that from Willie McGuiness in a card game. Nice guy.' Dad hands Paul a handkerchief. 'Wipe your face.' 'Why?' 'There is blood on your face.' 'Why?' 'You're bleeding because she scratched you.' 'Who?' There is blood on his father's face, on the hand that passes the pistol. Paul takes the pistol, the bloody grip staining his skin. The blood runs down Paul's legs. Lucky he wore grey today. Grey is a fadeaway colour. Behind the father and son, a judge, a senator, the mayor, union members, wives, widows with tears in their eyes. 'Come on in, Paul.' Paul climbs into the coffin, lies down next to his father. Ashleigh Bennett leans over the coffin, her face framed by blonde hair. 'Time to go, boys.' Paul raises the pistol, but Ashleigh is fast. She lowers the lid, it closes with a soft muffled sound. Paul pulls the trigger. The explosion fills the coffin. His eyes spark from the muzzle flash and he rides the bullet out of the chamber, smelling gunpowder, feeling the heat. Paul is the slug that rockets out of the casing, feels it connect with tissue, tearing through bone, fracturing the skull. Paul rips a track into the grey matter. What happened here? Why did this brain inside this skull sell him out? Ashleigh's hand on the coffin, her face looking down, her mouth saying: 'I phoned my friend at the SEC and they're giving me witness protection. Bye now.' The lid closes. She locks it with a hex key made of gold. 'You are dead,' Paul says. 'The girl is vicious,' Dad says. 'I knew one just like her, before I met your mother.' Ashleigh Bennett closing the coffin now. She takes the hex key and locks the lid down. She rubs the coffin with her left hand. She pats it twice. A pastor reads from *Psalms* as the coffin drops away, into the hole. Ashleigh Bennett tosses roses into the hole. 'What time is it?' '1:30,' Paul says. The crystal on the Breitling glinting. The Heckler and Koch in his right hand. The muzzle flash. The slugs leaps from the cartridge, striking Ashleigh Bennett in the throat, in that dimple between the collar bones, and he remembers putting his lips on that place, that little depression at the base of the throat. Ashleigh gasps. Blood oozes from her mouth. Ashleigh crumples, then drops into the hole.

Notes on Paul's dream

Because he has money, Paul Watson is the solution to Veronica's poverty. Buried in the solution, however, is another problem – a husband who has a flaw. Let's follow that idea of the flaw. The dream forges a connection between Paul and Ashleigh Bennett. He loves her; she betrays him; he kills her. As we search for a motive, we can play what-if. What if Veronica's husband is drawn to innocence? What if he uses women, then tosses them away? What if he is breaking off a relationship with Ashleigh when he meets Veronica? What if he plays the replacement ritual with Ashleigh, and what if that turns her against him, and what if she is a key employee of his company, and what if she possesses a secret that can hurt him?

Remember that you can play the what-if game at any time – it's all part of the rush you feel when writing a novel. You never know when a whimsical what-if might become the key that unlocks a character.

Weekends 13–14:

Dressing your character

Dressing your character brings him back from the recesses of dream and back story. You have a sense of who he is, where he goes, what he wants. Now it's time to dress him, style him – for his personal history and his personal taste to be developed. While your character dresses, preparing for the stage – the setting you create – he performs a ritual. This ritual helps define his personality, his age, his lifestyle. Define this ritual by asking questions: How long does he take in the shower? What runs through his mind while shaving, staring into his own eyes? How does he react when the grey hairs outnumber the brown ones?

Does he dress quickly, with practised efficiency? Or does he fuss over ties, shoes, belts? Does he dress smart casual? Does he dress in the uniform of a blue-collar worker? Are his suits laid out, waiting for his approval? Does he sift through piles of identical pinstriped shirts, smelling each one, hoping for a 'clean' one? What kind of watch does he wear? Is it a Swiss, precision-movement Omega? Is it a scratched Casio? Does he run downstairs, half-dressed, cursing his wife for the backlog of laundry?

If he dresses with efficiency, is he a cool customer? If he begins his day under control, will he lose his grip later? When he runs downstairs, does he trip on toys strewn across the floor? Is his wife already out of the house, on the train to a more prestigious job? Is he jealous of her designer clothes? Is his wife a homemaker? Is she competition for the head of the pack?

Exteriors are dangerous. As a writer, you spend time crafting the appearance of your characters, like a make-up artist preparing an actor for a scene. Take time to consider the impact of appearance on readers. Make their exteriors consistent and believable. As we found in dream writing, details build meaning, whether you're working with symbols from the interior or costume jewellery from the vast universe of the exterior. One way to create meaning is through repetition: work boots, work boots, work boots. He left his work boots at the back door to avoid tracking mud into the house. He laced the work boots tight, preparing for a long day under the hot sun. His work boots left an imprint for the police to use as evidence.

You are the writer. It's your story, and you create the characters who drive it. You choose what to repeat, and the repetition signals to the reader what's important.

You've built characters for your novel; you've done sketches, and you've written dreams and back stories. Now it's time to array your characters with uniforms that match their lives. Give them make-up. Style them, and get them ready for the stage. The outfits they select offer clues, not only about where they are going – the office, the club, on holiday, to prison, to school – but also about what they expect when they arrive on the scene. Below, we have used Veronica's husband, Paul, as an example. He's out of the house and living in the company apartment. He's in his early 40s and feeling the effects of stress and age.

Learning by example: Paul, dressing

Paul's dressing room is L-shaped. The carpet is charcoal, the walls are white, and the skylight opening is controlled by a button on the wall beside the chest of drawers. The drawers are built-in; they slide in and out with a soft, expensive whisper. Across from the drawers is a long wall of suits, casual trousers, jackets. Paul owns three tuxedoes and four dinner jackets – two white, one red, one dove-grey. Above the racks are shelves for Paul's shoe collection, stored in labelled boxes: Office, Walking, Tennis, Jogging, Formal, Climbing, Golf, Knockabout, Beach, Europe, Deck, Dad. From his father, Paul learned how to polish his own shoes, to get his fingers black with shoe polish. Not long before the old man died, they would polish shoes together, facing each other in the garage, and Paul remembers the smell of shoe polish and saddle soap. He has not polished a shoe since the funeral.

Paul enters the dressing room through wide French doors, white frames, polished brass handles, and glass panes gleaming. He is barefoot, he wears his thick grey terrycloth robe. He feels tired as he moves along the racks of clothes. What do you wear to the court room? What threads do you drape across your body to impress the rat-faced judge? Do you wear a jacket and slacks and no tie? Do you wear tennis clothes to put him down? Do you wear brown for bad taste? Grey for fade-out? Black for a funeral? Or do you wear blue to show him that you understand power? If Paul had a black judge's robe, he would wear that. He exhales. His breath stinks. He grabs a

81

grey suit. Five years old, a gift from Dad. He grabs a white shirt from Dad's laundryman. Charley Lee, Shirt Washer. Exchanges the white shirt for a grey shirt, new, from Brooks Brothers, grabs a grey tie, hunts through the shoeboxes until he finds a pair of black Ecco City Walkers. Dad wore Ecco shoes long before they were popular. They shine up better, he would say. Built to last. Grey socks to complete the ensemble. Grey is halfway to funereal black. His dad died, leaving a mess behind and a warning as he lay on his hospital bed. 'Good-looking woman, Paul. She's smart and she knows how to dress and she's good with numbers, but be careful you don't get on her bad side. That one, she's got knives for fingernails.'

Paul hangs the suit next to the mirror. It is full-length, with a dark mahogany frame, and it travelled with Paul's parents from the two-room apartment in Fresno to the small house in Oakland where Paul was born and then across the San Francisco Bay to the apartment on the edge of the Haight and finally to Dad's house on Nob Hill where Paul cannot take a step without seeing his father's face, his father's bedroom slippers, his father's body getting old and bent and creaky with age.

Paul's father wore Jockey shorts and so does Paul. He likes boxers, not briefs. His chest measures 45 inches, so he buys his T-shirts in extra-large, knowing they will shrink after two washings. He likes cotton because polyester makes his skin feel itchy. He checks himself in the mirror. Six feet tall, tired face, a pot belly that arrived overnight, a surprise. He steps away from the mirror, onto the scales. They are chrome and steel, with two slider bars, and they came from the changing room of the Men's Club, purchased by Paul's father for ten dollars when the club went upscale modern. He sets the bottom slider at 150, then he inches the top slider to the right, 35, 40, 44, inching it along, pound by pound, click by click. When the slider reaches 50, the little metal arrow has not moved. Paul grunts, shoves the bottom slider to 200, then moves the top slider back, 20, 19, 15, 13. The arrow levels out. Mr Paul Watson, of Nob Hill, San Francisco, California, weighs in at 213 pounds. Six weeks ago, he weighed 180 and felt good.

The grey trousers are tight around his belly. He discards the belt and locates his grey braces, stockbroker gear, just the right uniform to inspire confidence in new clients. His hands fumble with the buttons. He steps out of the grey trousers, sits on the bench. He feels sweaty, and then chilled. What this money manager needs is a drink. Show up in court with booze on your tongue. Good morning, your Honour, let me blow in your little rat face.

Okay. One more look in the mirror. Shirt looks good. Braces buttoned on. He remembers his father called them galluses. Trousers have a good crease. The grey tie matches the grey of his face this morning. He sits on the bench again. The shoes feel tight. Maybe the booze from the last six weeks ran down his leg to pool in his feet. He shakes his head at himself. If his mother were here, she could help him with his shoes. 'When you get old like me, Paulie, you'll need someone to help with that.' Paul leans over, aware of his growing pot belly. His head swirls and he grips the edge of the dressing bench. He pushes himself up, takes another deep breath, stares at his face in the mirror. He straps on the Breitling, another behest from Dad. It feels right on his wrist. It's the only thing in the day that does feel right. He removes the grey suit coat from the hanger. He starts to shrug into it, then stops when he hears a car door slamming outside. He walks to the big window and looks down. On the curved driveway below is a green Cadillac, the vehicle of his lawyer, his taxi service to court. Paul shivers. The sun is hidden behind a bank of clouds and Paul Watson feels silver fog in his bones.

Guidelines for dressing your character

Dressing your characters gives you the chance to experiment. You experiment with colour, fabrics, textures, brand names. You experiment with details. You give your character flash, flare, life. As your character dresses, costuming himself for the scene that's about to begin, you work with reflections: memories triggered by objects, lines of dialogue recalled from another time. If he's dressing in a cheap motel, you make use of the ubiquitous green light over the bathroom sink.

In Paul's dressing scene, he's headed for the courtroom while his head pounds with a hangover. He's alone in the house on Nob Hill and he keeps remembering his dad, the same power-figure who showed up in Paul's dream at the end of the dream section. He is frustrated and nervous and he shows his anxiety by coughing.

To write your dressing scene, bring in the list you made last week in your notebook – the notations about layout, shelves, clothes. Focus on the dressing room as the container, a metaphor for your character's lifestyle. Is it crammed with clothes? Is there dust in the corners? Are the shoes kept in their original boxes? How big is the dressing room? If it's a walk-in one, is it like a narrow corridor? Or a garage large enough for two Cadillac 4 x 4s? What's on the floor of the dressing room? Polished wood makes a noise when the characters walk. A soft carpet feels cushy. Keep remembering Cinderella from the famous fairy-tale. She put on a party dress so she could attend a ball. The right wardrobe was her ticket, her entry pass. Without the party dress, the girl cannot go to the party. Paul Watson feels the same pressure as he dresses for his court appearance. At this point in the story, the writer of *Trophy Wives* is writing for discovery, working each sentence, not knowing the full story, not knowing the events that lead to this dressing scene. If you can keep the hand moving, keep the fingers on those keys, and pay attention to details, then your story will grow. The dressing scene gets Paul ready for the courtroom scene. You can write that scene next, making a connection between these two scenes, and you will have new characters to create. In the case of *Trophy Wives*, we have the rat-faced judge and the lawyer in the green Cadillac. Who are these characters? What do they want? What are they wearing?

You dress your characters not only to get in touch with costuming – the art of masking – but also to get them ready for the next scene. Dressing is a ritual, mounting the horse, donning armour for the battlefield, zipping up the pretty dress for the party, climbing into tennis clothes for the Club, dressing in a hurry for school. Take your time and go for concrete detail. You're giving your character a face to present to the world.

Paul lives in a house worth millions. He's 40 years old and his body is showing signs of age. Details from the setting merge with details about Paul's physical appearance to make him human. When you write, you work with sense perception because the five senses help to nail down point of view: 'One more look in the mirror. Shirt looks good. Braces buttoned on. He remembers his father called them galluses. Trousers have a good crease. The grey tie matches the grey of his face this morning. He sits on the bench again. The shoes feel tight.' Then you deepen the sensation: 'Paul leans over, aware of his pot belly. His head swirls and he grips the edge of the dressing bench.' Paul is in transition. His life is disintegrating around him. He's headed for court. What will happen next?

As you dress your character, keep these questions in mind: What does your character want? Will he get it? Who will your character meet when he walks out the door? Who waits for your character in the next scene?

Getting help from other writers

Zadie Smith's characters in *White Teeth* are dressed for their state and their stature. Archie wears corduroy and button-down, short-sleeve shirts. Samad wears a tuxedo made from the same fabric as the tablecloths in his cousin's restaurant. Clara wears no bra, she's 'independent, even of gravity'.

Smith crafts her characters with details that provide rich insights to her readers. Archie is a blue-collar stiff who finds his station comfortable. Samad detests his lot in life. Moving to London afforded him a better lifestyle than he had in India, but he wants more. His tuxedo chokes him. Clara is an independent woman who will raise an independent daughter. Clara breaks away from her mother's apocalyptic religious convictions and lives free. She raises her daughter in the same way.

By looking at the costumes Smith dresses her characters in, readers learn about their lives, their feelings, their motivations. Smith is a good example of a writer who shows her characters instead of just telling readers about them.

Exercises

Well done! You've made it through 14 weekends. You've survived. You've worked hard. You've written, and you've learned tricks of the novelist's trade. You've learned about language, repetition, rhythm. Over the past eight weekends you've invented characters, and now they are ready to step onto the stage and begin their stories.

Even if you don't have a full cast of characters, cast the ones who are ready. If holes appear as you begin, go back to character work and fill in the missing material, the missing details. Good characters are the foundation of your novel. Don't hesitate to go back and shore up the foundation.

Cast one protagonist and one main antagonist. Cast one helper/guide/catalyst. Write their parts out in your notebook: their names, ages, sexes, ethnicities. Give them their roles. Give them time, and give yourself time to accept their roles. True characters grow; the roles you assign now might not stick, but taking the time to cast them gets you started. Casting your characters gives them an assignment for your first scene.

1. Describe a dressing room

Sit on the floor of your dressing room. Take a deep breath: what do you smell? Reach out and touch the wall, the floor, a shoe, a piece of clothing. What do the different surfaces feel like? Can you hear any-thing? Open your eyes and list the first five things that you see. The list is a warm-up device. Now, using a simple startline like, 'Sitting on the floor of my dressing room, I see…', write for ten minutes.

2. Dressing your main character

Dress your character to prepare her to move onstage into your story. For details, you can start with your own clothes, the reality of textures and colours and smells that you know so well. Or you can invent a fantasy wardrobe, using garments (and labels and prices) from fashion magazines (*Vogue, Elle, Cosmopolitan*) and also from direct-mail catalogues (Spiegel, Sears, Neiman-Marcus, Land's End, Victoria's Secret, J Crew). Use the wardrobe to define your charac-ter, to present her to the reader.

Assemble a wardrobe: garments from drawers, garments hanging in a closet. Take ten minutes during the week to list the contents of your dressing room. Here's a list from Veronica's, in her home on Nob Hill – the poor girl now has money:

mahogany cabinets, drawers
French doors
La Perla underwear, stockings
Ugg bedroom slippers
silk-covered bench
emerald from Colombia (wall safe downstairs)
middle drawers: tennis, jogging, swimming, gym workout, etc.
Manolo Blahnik shoes
Nike trainers
skirts, Dolce & Gabbana
Vera Wang dresses
Burberry raincoat

3. Dress your other characters

In timed writings of five minutes each, dress your other characters. These wardrobes don't have to be complete; they just need to pro-vide enough information to define the character. With practice, you'll complete these wardrobe activities a lot faster. Add your com-pleted work to each character's folder.

4. Start a ritual activity list for each character

Ritual activity – small, connected actions that are performed again and again – defines your characters while at the same time informing the reader about process. Dressing is important because it's part of the image we present to the world; what T S Eliot called 'to prepare a face to meet the faces that we meet'. Start a list of other rituals (washing, shaving, slicing an onion, loading a gun, sharpening a harpoon, building a box) that help to define your characters. Add to this list as ritual activities appear in your writing. Put your lists into the appropriate character folders.

5. Try a scene-change

Take a few minutes and try a scene-change. Move your character from the dressing room/bedroom – the safety of the private world – to another setting, the public world full of danger and adventure. For stability, keep her in the same costume. For practice, write about your character from the point of view of another character.

Character work is watching your characters handle weapons, money, jewellery, furniture, cooking utensils, vehicles, and wardrobe items. Sometimes your characters back away from centre stage, easing out of the spotlight to take refuge in the shadows. That happened to F Scott Fitzgerald and his character Jay Gatsby, the Man from the West who wants to capture Daisy Fay Buchanan, the Girl from the East.

The Great Gatsby was finished. Fitzgerald sent it to his editor, the legendary Maxwell Perkins at Scribner's. Perkins liked the book, but he found the character of Gatsby vague, dim, shadowy. Gatsby felt older than he was, Perkins said. There was no satisfactory explanation for his vast wealth. The face-off between Tom Buchanan (Daisy's husband) and Gatsby at the Plaza Hotel in New York City – the scene that precedes Daisy's killing of Myrtle Wilson with Gatsby's yellow car – sagged because Tom was forced to spar with an opponent in the shadows.

We read classics to find the secrets of the immortals. *The Great Gatsby* was published in 1925, over three-quarters of a century ago. It sold well – an estimated 55,000 copies – and then faded away, to become lost in the parties of the Roaring Twenties, and then in the Great Depression. Today, *The Great Gatsby* is still selling (some estimates put annual sales at 300,000 copies) and it has generated at least four film-versions, the latest one starring Paul Rudd as Nick and Mira Sorvino as Daisy. If you are an aspiring novelist, you know the power of film in our time. One film from a book is nice; two is nicer; four films is the stuff of legend. We know that *The Great Gatsby* is still around. So, how did Fitzgerald bring

Gatsby back onto centre stage? How did he get the man of shadows into the spotlight?

Fitzgerald's solution is a lesson for aspiring novelists. He kept writing. He wrote dialogue until Gatsby could say a word like 'money' and it would be Gatsby's voice talking. And he attached objects to his main character. He gave Gatsby a mansion. He gave him a yellow car. And he gave him a wardrobe of suits and ties and shoes and rainbow shirts. If you remember, the rainbow shirts appear in a scene in Gatsby's bedroom near the middle of the novel. There are three characters present – Gatsby, Daisy, and Nick (the narrator). The time is afternoon, the rain has stopped falling, and Gatsby and Daisy have just rekindled their love after being separated for several years. Gatsby is happy. He's got his lady again. Daisy was lost and now she's back with Gatsby – not only in his house, but in his bedroom. Gatsby wants to show off, to shoot fireworks, so he grabs his coloured shirts and tosses them into the air. The scene explodes on the page. Shirts fly into the air like balloons. Daisy is delighted. She loves spectacle. But Nick is nervous. All these shirts will have to be laundered all over again.

The spewing of the shirts into the late-afternoon light brings Daisy even closer. As Nick leaves them alone, there is no mention of love-making, but the implication is there, in the bedroom, as the day slips toward twilight, and the lovers reunite in a physical way.

When you run into trouble with a character, stop, take some deep breaths, and then attach an object to the character. Start with wardrobe items, and remember Gatsby's coloured shirts.

part 4 Weekends 15–20:

Plotting Your Novel – Plan B

As you discovered during Weekends 1–4, plotting your novel starts with an idea, a notion, a character with a problem, a scene – the materials of a story sketched into a diagram. You draw a line. The line represents the path of your protagonist. The line can be ruler-straight, rising from left to right to the climax, the high point of the action. Or the line can be a circle that represents a journey or a quest. The circle is handy if you are writing a book like *The Alchemist*, where the protagonist returns, at the end of the book, to the place at which he started.

On this line, whether it is curved or straight, you can hang the names of the main characters; the five or six people who carry the most weight in your story, who take most of the ink on the page. Add objects to the diagram. In fiction, objects are visible things with weight, shape and substance – things like money, jewellery, weapons, vehicles, furniture and wardrobe items. If you lower your nose to a handful of cash money, you can smell the paper, the ink, and the sweat left by other hands. If you run your hand over the sharp-edged blade of a sword or a kitchen knife, you verify its dangerous sharpness by touch. Objects help the writer get a grip on the world of sensory perception, and this is one simple way to bring reality into your fiction.

When you're writing a piece of fiction, you might divide objects into two groups: those you can move, carry, hide, or store away for the winter; and those that are fixed, stable and hard to move. Movable objects would include that list above – money, weapons, jewellery, vehicles, etc. – and fixed objects would include houses, skyscrapers, castles, caves, gardens, swimming pools, trees, mountains, very large rocks, and other landmarks that don't move around. In *The Great Gatsby*, for example, a traveller on the road through the Valley of Ashes looks up and sees a billboard advertising the services of an optometrist, Dr T J Eckleberg, who looks down on the wasteland like God. Dr Eckleberg wears glasses; he has eyes like eggs. And the symbolism of his egg-like eyes is an echo of the two opposing landmarks that dominate the book: East Egg, which represents old money; and West Egg, where Gatsby lives in the garish mansion which he has rented to impress Daisy Fay Buchanan, his lost Louisville love, and where, almost every night, he throws parties with dancing and music and bathtub booze, hoping that Daisy will look across the Bay and feel the magnetic pull of his love. Objects, whether they are small or large, are important to the writer because, through repetition and careful handling, they can blossom into powerful symbols.

If you have read *Jane Eyre*, for example, you have felt the awesome power of Thornfield Hall, an English country house owned by Mr Rochester, and the symbol, for lonely Jane, of warmth and comfort and safety from the elements. These two houses – Thornfield Hall and Gatsby's mansion – accrue meaning through repetition. They keep coming back, taking up space on the page. Therefore, because of the power of repetition, they grow in the reader's mind. If you do not repeat your set of objects, three things will happen: first, you will not create the symbols that you need; second, without symbols, your book will have a thin texture, which readers will perceive as weakness; and third, your book will not feel cohesive.

When you plotted your novel during those first six weekends, you used line-drawings to explore the architecture of your novel. You added weight to the line-drawings by spinning some sentences down the page. Scenes developed and objects rose to the surface. Characters entered your story. They had dreams, they got dressed, and you poked around in the past to discover motives for their actions in the present.

The next six weekends give you another chance to work out your plot. First, you will practise letting your objects tell the story. Second, you will make a tough decision about your protagonist. Will you have one protagonist, like in *Jane Eyre*? Will you have two protagonists, like in *Amsterdam* and *The Amazing Adventures of Kavalier and Clay*? Will you have three protagonists, like Zadie Smith in *White Teeth*? Will you have four protagonists, like in *The English Patient*?

Our advice is to stick with one protagonist – that's enough heavy lifting – but so many writers on our writing courses are drawn to multiple protagonists that we feel obliged to include a lesson on how some novelists handle more than one.

After your work on objects and protagonists, you will have enough material (and enough questions and loose ends) to write a working synopsis. The working synopsis is a tracking device. You should write a new synopsis whenever you get stuck. Writing the synopsis gives you an overview of your work, a feeling for the whole novel before you finish it. A working synopsis allows you to pull back, away from the words on the page, and see the Big Picture. Model synopses can help: if you want to read some excellent synopses, get yourself a book of plots for grand opera (*The Wordsworth Book of Opera* is good), or study the tightly written mini-plots in *The Oxford Companion to American [or English] Literature*.

Weekends 15–16:
Plotting with sacred objects

Choosing the perfect object for your novel

The harpoon is a perfect object in *Moby-Dick*. Take away the harpoon, and you reduce the power of Ahab's crazy hunt for the white whale that bit off his leg in the back story. Take away the harpoon, and you kill the power of the climax, where Ahab flings the harpoon at his nemesis, crying: 'Thus, I give up the spear!'

The glass slipper is a perfect object for Cinderella. Take away the glass slipper, and you lose large chunks of story: first, the dressing scene, where Cinderella puts her dainty foot into the slipper; second, the dancing scene, where Cinderella waltzes with the Handsome Prince; third, the escape scene as the clock strikes midnight and Cinderella loses one slipper on the steps of the castle; and fourth, the trying-on scene at the climax, where, in the Walt Disney version, the Wicked Stepmother breaks one glass slipper, and where Cinderella – the shrewd heroine driven by poverty and the grey grit of ashes – produces the second slipper, which vaults her from Lower World to Upper World.

According to *The Cinderella Casebook*, there are more than 4,000 versions of the Cinderella story. Most of these versions depict a girl of low status ascending to a position of high status through the shoe test, a suspenseful trying-on of a magic slipper. In some versions, the slipper is made of fur; in others, the slipper is made of glass. Whether it is made of fur or glass, the slipper is a good example of a special object. It has the power to make a Princess. It has exactitude. If the slipper gets lost or broken, there is a twin waiting in the wings. The slipper as object appears not only at the climax in Act Three, but also earlier, in Acts One and Two. Among writers, this is called 'planting the object'.

When you work with objects, you should plant them early in the writing. You should plant more objects than you think you need, before you know for certain which objects will help you tell the story, because you won't know that until you reach the end of your novel and look back across the landscape. At that point, you can loop back to your opening, pencil in hand, and make your object-list. You write objects now, filling your pages, because you are writing fast and you have nothing to lose. Don't edit when you create. Just write those word-pictures.

When you create a new character, make it a habit to attach an object or two. It looks simple, but when we perform the Friendly Object Check in a fiction class – when we go around the room asking each writer about his or her objects – we are often met with confusion. Some writers look away; others look down. There are nervous rustlings in the room, murmurs in the group. Then a hand goes up, a writer with a question: 'Could you please define an object?' Silly question, but we hear it over and over.

Objects, we say, are the things in this list based on *Moby-Dick*: Harpoon. Whaleboat. Lance. Sail. Sextant. Tiller made from a whale's jaw. Ivory leg made from whalebone. Ecuadorian Doubloon. Coffin.

Change the objects and you tell a different story. Objects in Cinderella are a party dress and glass slippers and a pumpkin turned into a carriage and a clock that strikes midnight and, in the Grimm Brothers' version, a sacred tree that grows from the grave of Cinderella's mother. Objects in *The English Patient* include Almasy's book, *The Histories of Herodotus*, where he parks his heart; a flower pressed between the book's pages; a desert campfire surrounded by men and one lone female; a champagne bottle that points to the female, prompting her to tell a story about a sexual triad in the past (Gyges, Candaules, and Queen Omphale) that mirrors another sexual triad in the desert in the 1930s (Almasy, Katharine, and her husband Geoffrey); a yellow aeroplane that becomes a deadly weapon; oil under the sand; photos of the desert taken to locate the oil; the Cave of Swimmers; wall-paintings of swimmers; a map of the desert; a woman's body superimposed on the map.

Our everyday lives are filled with objects – wardrobe items, jewellery, weapons, writing materials, silverware, glassware, furniture, vehicles, books, papers, computers, mice, cursors, screens, speakers, DVDs, spoons, forks, knives, teacups, camcorders, iPods – but when we write, we sometimes avoid writing about objects. Without objects, the writing gets abstract. To stay connected, you must turn your mind into a container for objects. Fill up the container, packing it full. When it feels full, dump the contents of your mind onto the page, onto a simple structural diagram, like the one overleaf. Let the objects fall where they fall. On the line, off the line, hanging in space. Just get them down on the page. Take a look at them, and then play with the objects, moving them around, until they tell the story. The objects below are from Cinderella. See how they fall.

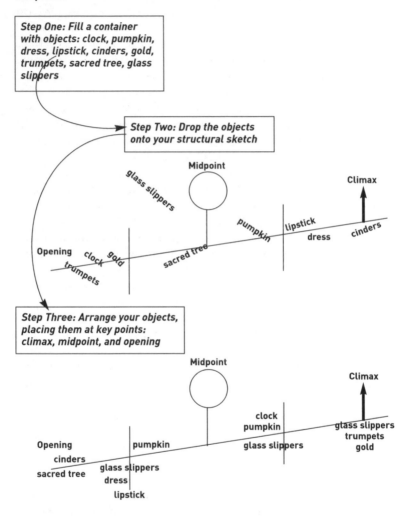

FIGURE 8: ARRANGING THE OBJECTS IN THE CINDERELLA FAIRY-TALE

If we arrange the objects to tell a story, the glass slippers enter the story near the end of Act One as part of the wardrobe brought by the Fairy Godmother. In some versions of the Cinderella story, the slippers are a product of the sacred tree which grew from the grave of Cinderella's dead mother. In the Grimm Brothers' Cinderella, Cinderella grows proactive, planting a branch from a tree that knocks off her father's hat while he is riding home, then watering the tree with her tears.

The glass slippers are breakable. They dominate the story of Cinderella. In a Cinderella film called *Working Girl*, the lost slipper (an object left behind) is replaced by the briefcase of Tess McGill, played to perfection by Melanie Griffith, which gives the Handsome Prince, played by Harrison Ford, the opportunity to see her again when he delivers the briefcase. The right object in the right hands creates story.

Objects tell the story in *The Great Gatsby*

If you have read *The Great Gatsby*, you probably remember the yellow car. The car is a convertible. It enters the story in Chapter 4, when Gatsby arrives in Nick's driveway. The month is July. Gatsby's parties have failed to attract Daisy, and Gatsby wants help from Nick, who is Daisy's cousin. The yellow car is gorgeous, monstrous, lush. It seems to catch sunlight in the windshield, which Fitzgerald describes as a 'labyrinth of a thousand suns'. The upholstery is green leather. Gatsby's yellow car is garish, but Gatsby, a poor boy from Out West, sees the car as a symbol of having arrived. And he has no idea that the yellow car will turn into a deadly weapon.

There are two climaxes in *The Great Gatsby*. Climax One takes place in the Valley of Ashes, outside Wilson's Garage, when Daisy uses the yellow car to run down Myrtle Wilson – the blue-collar mistress of Daisy's husband, Tom. Climax Two takes place in Gatsby's swimming pool at the rented house in West Egg, where Jay Gatsby takes a swim. The season hangs on the cusp of late summer/early autumn. There are dead leaves in the pool, where Gatsby is alone, floating on a blow-up mattress. There are servants in the big house. There is a big yellow car hidden away in a garage. One servant remembers hearing shots. One bullet for Gatsby. One for his killer's suicide. The killer is George Wilson, a garage mechanic and the owner of Wilson's Garage in the Valley of Ashes and the husband of Myrtle, Daisy's victim. George kills Gatsby because Gatsby owns the yellow car. George does not know that Daisy was driving when the car struck down his wife. Daisy knows. Her husband Tom knows. Nick the narrator knows. Gatsby dies because of his connection to an object.

As you work out the plot for your novel, keep those objects coming. Attach the objects to characters. Let the objects make connections between scenes. In *The Great Gatsby*, the yellow car connects to Wilson's gun – both are deadly weapons – and it connects, because of its function and body size and look, to other wheeled vehicles. By tracking these three objects (generic car, gun, yellow car) through the novel, we can begin to feel the connective power of repeated objects:

- In Chapter 2, Nick overhears George Wilson asking to buy Tom's car. This Valley of Ashes scene at Wilson's Garage sets up the moment of mistaken revelation later, when Myrtle sees Tom driving the yellow car which sends her to her death at the climax.
- In Chapter 3, a party guest named Owl Eyes smashes a car in front of Gatsby's mansion. No one is hurt in this minor smash-up. Things change when Daisy kills Myrtle with the yellow car.
- In Chapter 4, the yellow car enters the story in a blaze of horns and elaborate description as Gatsby arrives to take Nick to lunch with Meyer Wolfsheim – Gatsby's business partner in the bootlegging business, and the man who fixed the World Series. Here, Fitzgerald uses the car to connect Gatsby with corruption.
- In Chapter 4, on the way into town in the yellow car, Gatsby and Nick pass a hearse. The hearse represents death. The yellow car speeds on past. This time.
- Later in Chapter 4, Jordan Baker remembers Daisy's white roadster in a flashback. She remembers Daisy herself in a white dress in the back story. White is the disguise worn by Daisy, the Death Crone who will murder her husband's mistress. Jordan Baker remembers Tom's car accident in California that broke the arm of a hotel maid, one of Tom's girls.
- In Chapter 7, Tom Buchanan, Daisy's husband, swaps cars with Gatsby for the drive into town. Behind the wheel of the yellow car, Tom stops for gas in the Valley of Ashes, where Myrtle Wilson (Tom's mistress) – looking down from a second-story window – mistakes Jordan Baker in the back seat for Daisy. When Tom offers to sell the yellow car to Wilson, he leaves the impression that he is the owner.
- In Chapter 7, Gatsby and Daisy leave the city for East Egg with Gatsby back at the wheel. Daisy is on edge because she had to witness a verbal struggle between Gatsby and Tom. Before the yellow car reaches the Valley of Ashes, Gatsby lets Daisy drive, hoping to calm her nerves. With this driver-swap, Daisy now sits where her husband sat on the journey into the city. Myrtle,

thinking that the husband is still driving, tries to stop the car and gets slammed by the wife.

- In Chapter 8, Nick advises Gatsby to hide the yellow car and leave town. Gatsby, a romantic hero up to his eyeballs in twisted love, refuses.
- In Chapter 8, back at Wilson's Garage, widowed husband George Wilson analyses the crime scene. Seeking revenge on the driver of the yellow car, he goes to Tom's house. Tom sends Wilson to Gatsby's mansion in West Egg.
- Later in Chapter 8, George Wilson, Myrtle's grieving husband, kills Gatsby in his swimming pool at West Egg. He finds Gatsby by tracking the yellow car according to Tom's tip. Lots of irony here: instead of killing the man who stole his wife, he kills the man who stole Tom's wife. Gatsby is the scapegoat. He pays for crashing the gates at East Egg.
- In Chapter 9, as he recalls the afternoon of Gatsby's death, Tom defends his action of telling Wilson where to find the yellow car. Wilson was crazy, Tom says. Tom was afraid for his own life. So he told Tom the truth. Gatsby owned the yellow car.

If you use objects in your writing, they will do good work. They will not only help you make connections between scenes, but if you attach an object to each character, you can keep a better grip on your growing cast of characters. Gatsby's yellow car is like Cinderella's slipper: when the object changes hands, the characters go into action. Tom takes possession of Gatsby's car, creating the same ripple of dramatic tension that Cinderella's Wicked Stepmother does when she grabs the glass slipper, smashing it on the floor, in the hope of smashing Cinderella's future as Princess. A great object has 'legs'. The yellow car has been at the climax of the four film versions of *The Great Gatsby*. And what would Cinderella be without the fragile, magical glass slippers?

Does this repetition technique work for any old object? To answer that question, let's look at an object from Zadie Smith's *White Teeth*.

Getting help from other writers

Zadie Smith, the author of *White Teeth*, opens her triple-protagonist novel with a man in a car. Smith's character's ritual is attempted suicide, a form of self-execution. There are two objects in the opening: a car and a bullet. The car, with its noxious exhaust fumes, is the deadly weapon of choice. The bullet, left over from World War II, is buried in the man's thigh. The character who opens the novel with his failed suicide attempt is Archie Jones, one of Smith's three protagonists. The setting in this opening scene is a London street, but flashbacks throughout the book whisk the reader back in time to Italy and India and Jamaica. Like any good novelist, Smith uses a repeated object (the bullet) to tighten up the time-shifts in her complex book.

A buried bullet opens the novel. There is another story here, which will drop the reader into a flashback at the end of Part I. Another bullet closes the novel at the end of Part IV, the climax of *White Teeth*, where a crazed killer tries to murder Archie, the character whose attempted suicide opened the book. The murder weapon at the climax is a pistol. The setting is a community gathering in a London suburb. Two bullets, strategically placed – one at the end, the other at the beginning – tells us that the object is important.

Because the author has chosen to deploy three major narrators (Samad, Archie, and Irie) and, near the end of the book, as the novel moves towards its climax, to divide the telling of the story amongst a small army of minor narrators, the bullet from the pistol sends a message to the reader: since he receives a bullet, this narrator is more important than the reader once thought. Having been shot, Archie Jones rises up above Samad and Irie. In this hubbub of voices and accents, this world of immigration and displacement, the bullet is a shock. A surprise. A stab of violence into a noisy clot of people gathered together on the edge of London to discuss taking action.

The bullet is action.

The bullet ends discussion.

The bullet rips the mask off the face of society.

This is the lesson you need to learn from novels like *White Teeth*: if you repeat an object across a short span – half a dozen paragraphs, for example – you can feel the writing getting tighter. Repetition of the object is like a thick thread weaving itself through the fabric of your work. The same thing happens when you repeat an object across a longer span, like the chapters of *White Teeth*.

In the book, which won the Whitbread Prize, the bullet at the book's climax connects that event to the events which close Parts I and II. Let's track the bullet through the novel.

Object One: a bullet from 1945

The first bullet in *White Teeth* surfaces during World War II, when a rifle misfires, wounding Samad Iqbal, one of the three narrators. The bullet appears in the first section of the book, which is entitled 'Archie, 1974, 1945'. The year 1945 is important, because, at the end of Archie's section, there is a long flashback to Italy near the end of the war. The bullet surfaces in a flashback within a flashback, as Samad Iqbal tells Archie the story of how he was wounded when a rifle misfired.

Samad is a Muslim from Bengal. The bullet, which paralysed his hand, came from the rifle of a Sikh soldier in the Indian Army. The flashback allows Archie Jones, the narrator of the Archie section, to tell the story about his intention to execute a prisoner of war called Dr Sick. After a lengthy prelude – a suspense device packed with more stories, lots of irony about the war, and carefully wrought puns – Archie marches Dr Sick out of sight, offstage, away from the reader's eyes. There is a touch of Greek theatre here. When the Greeks chopped off a head or put out an eye, they moved the violence offstage. The writer hides the shooting from us by shifting to Samad's point of view. For a long suspenseful moment, the reader waits with Samad. There is dialogue between Dr Sick and Archie. Is Archie going to kill him? Looks that way, says Archie. Is Dr Sick allowed to beg? Go right ahead, says Archie.

Time passes. Samad waits, perched on the Jeep. A shot rings out. Hearing the shot, Samad jumps, transferring his response to the reader. After five minutes have passed, Samad observes Archie walking back onto the stage of the story.

Archie is bleeding. He is limping. It is night-time. Archie winds in and out of the light cast by the Jeep's headlights.

As the Archie narrative section ends, there is no verbal confirmation of the execution of Dr Sick. The bullet left the gun. It travelled, as far as we know, into Dr Sick, moving at high velocity. Will the reader ever find out why Archie is bleeding?

Object Two: a bullet from 1857

The second bullet surfaces in another flashback, this one from the point of view of Samad, the narrator of the second section of *White Teeth* entitled 'Samad, 1984, 1857'.

There is a pattern here. With her use of numbers – 1974, 1945 and 1984, 1857 – Smith opens the gateway to the past. She employs flashbacks to create a climax for her first two sections. The linking object is the bullet.

The bullet from the rifle of the Sikh soldier destroys Samad's hand.

The bullet from Archie's gun boomerangs back to Archie. The bullet from 1857 comes from the gun of an Indian hero named

Mangal Pande, a soldier in the British Army during the days made famous in the western world by the poetry and fiction of writers like Rudyard Kipling.

The bullet from 1857 takes centre stage because, to conquer the subcontinent, and then to keep order, the British built an army of Sikhs, Muslims and Hindus. Soldiers in this army were called sepoys. Mangal Pande was a sepoy when a rumour ran through the ranks about a new type of British bullet.

Because this was 1857, bullets came wrapped in casings. Before a sepoy could load a bullet into his weapon, he had to bite through the casing. The rumour that swept through the ranks was that the casings, and the bullets they held, were packed in grease. The grease that cradled these bullets - imagine enough bullets to equip a British colonial army - came from pigs and cows.

Pigs are pork. Muslims do not eat pork.

Cows are sacred to Hindus.

The bullets shifted turf. No longer a piece of gear, a cog that fit into the machine that made the British Empire rich and stable, the bullets were seen by the sepoys as a British plot to destroy the very fabric of India. Biting into the grease would destroy a man's honour.

Enraged and insulted by these bullets packed in grease, Mangal Pande gets drunk and tries to shoot his lieutenant, a British officer. The bullet misses, so Pande wounds the officer with his sword. As sepoys rush to restrain their comrade, Pande aims his rifle at his own head and tries to pull the trigger with his big toe. The suicide attempt fails. The British Army tribunal sentences Mangal Pande to hang. His hanging starts the Sepoy Rebellion - fought over a bullet packed in animal fat - and threatens the power of the British Empire.

The diagram opposite (see Figure 9) shows the trajectory of the bullet, a sacred object in *White Teeth*, from Section One, narrated by Archie, to Section Two, narrated by Samad, and then to the climax, where the point of view jumps from Millat (one of Samad's sons) to Archie and then to Samad and then back to Archie for a flashback to 1945, where we discover that:

Archie Jones did not shoot Dr Sick in 1945.
But Dr Sick did shoot Archie.

That's why the writer shifted the point of view to Samad.

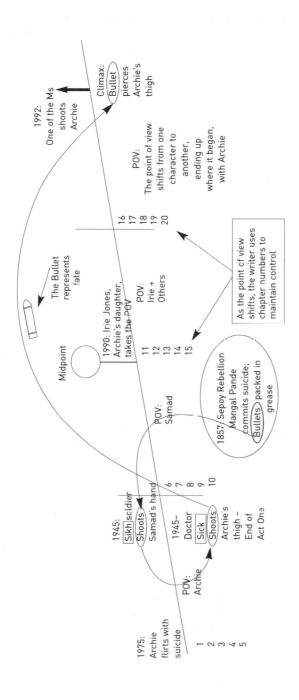

FIGURE 9: TRACKING THE MAGIC BULLET IN *WHITE TEETH*

Object Three: a bullet from 2000 – to create suspense

But now in Part IV, called 'Magid, Millat, and Marcus, 1992–1999', the bullet shot by Millat (one of the three Ms) cuts through the confusion. The bullet exits the muzzle of the gun held by Millat, who is remembering Al Pacino when he (Pacino) shot the police captain in the Italian café in *The Godfather*. (Mark this for your novel: Contemporary writers use film clips the way novelists in the 19th century used classical references to the ancient, ruined worlds of Greece and Rome. Here, the writer selects a violent scene from a violent American film to underscore, by analogy and implication, the violence of our time.)

And while the bullet slows down, travelling in slow motion through the changes in point of view, Smith's technique gives Archie Jones time to think. He's trying to make a decision as the bullet approaches. The decision involves himself and his old Army buddy, Samad Iqbal. The thinking is tinged with racism: Archie is a white guy, and an Englishman; Iqbal is a brown guy, a Muslim from Bengali.

Before you turn to those final pages to find out what Archie was thinking, stop and study the architectural sketch (Figure 9) based on the flight of the bullet from 1857 to 1945 to the beginning of the 21st century.

As you can see from Figure 9, Zadie Smith plotted her novel using a three-act dramatic structure, a variation on the same linear sketch you tested for your novel when you first started reading this book. The diagram also shows four sections – Archie, Samad, Irie (Archie's lovely daughter), and the three Ms (Magid, Millat, Marcus) – which the writer has then divided into five chapters each, giving a pleasant, choreographed balance to each section.

The chapters are indicated by the strings of numbers (1, 2, 3, 4, 5, etc.) running in four columns along the bottom of the diagram. Each chapter has its own title, which is a good way to control your work. *White Teeth* has the same number of chapters (20) as Anne Tyler's *The Accidental Tourist*, which also uses a dramatic, straight-line structure divided into three acts. In *White Teeth*, the four sections provide the perfect balance to a dramatic structure. Act Two is roughly the same length, the same bulk, and the same weight as Acts One and Three. As you plot your own novel, you would be smart to stop writing, stop drawing, and release the left-brain editor. Let the editor nose around, hunting for structure. Keep the editor on a short leash, though; use that choke chain when you have to. And you'll come up with a clean structure, like this:

- Act One, Part I – Chapters 1–5
- Act Two, Parts II and III – Chapters 6–15
- Act Three, Part IV – Chapters 16–20

Guidelines for plotting with sacred objects

1. Make a list of objects for your novel

If you were writing a novel about two lovers in Las Vegas, your list might include slot machines, dice, card tables, roulette wheels, and that croupier's stick used to pull the money away from the players. If one of your characters was a drunk, then you would add bottles of booze, cases of beer, cigarettes, jiggers of whisky. If you were writing a novel about whaling in the 19th century, your list would include harpoons, lances, ropes, whaling boats, a flagon of ale, and cauldrons for boiling off the oil. In *Moby-Dick*, the model for whaling stories, Captain Ahab nails a gold coin to a mainmast as a reward for whoever first sights the white whale. The gold coin, a doubloon from Ecuador, enters the story in Chapter 36, 'The Quarter-Deck'; reappears in Chapter 99, 'The Doubloon', in a film close-up that shows the reader the symbolic designs on the coin; and then appears once again in Chapter 133, 'The Chase – First Day', when Ahab has the first sighting and awards the coin to himself.

2. Attach objects to characters

How simple this is, and yet how many novice writers fail to make the attachments. A single object tags a character. This makes it easy for the reader. If the object has value, then there's a chance that some other character will covet the object, yearn for it, maybe even take it away. Money is a good object for most characters. In *Leaving Las Vegas*, Ben the Drunk has money, and that's how he makes contact with Sera, the Las Vegas prostitute who will become the love of his short life. Ben spots Sera on the Strip. He pulls over to the curb. He asks a question from the car: 'Are you working?' The loaded question marks Sera as a 'working girl', which means a prostitute. Because Ben has money, he can buy an hour of Sera's time. For an hour, thinking only of money to pay off her pimp, she will work for him.

Money is the downfall of Emma Bovary, the female protagonist of Gustave Flaubert's novel *Madame Bovary*. Re-read this classic novel, published in 1857, and mark the references to money, wealth, medical fees, payments, debts, and financial ruin. Emma marries Charles to escape her father's farm. Emma is a die-hard romantic with a body that attracts two local lovers, Leon and Rodolphe.

Because she confuses fantasy with reality, Emma thinks that one of these men will run off with her to a lover's paradise. To keep looking good, she buys more clothes. When the cash runs out, Emma falls into the hands of a merchant who gives her a credit line that allows her to buy more than she can afford. When the merchant presses her for payment, Emma collects medical fees in advance from her husband's patients. Because she collects more money than he can earn, the husband is ruined. Struggling to bridge this cultural chasm between reality and fantasy, Madame Bovary meets a grisly fate: death by arsenic. Poison leads to deathbed; deathbed leads to coffin; coffin leads to grave. A trail of objects marks the downfall of the protagonist.

Emma Bovary's objects are clothes and money. She uses the money to buy clothes to make herself feel better, to lift her mood from the dark depths of depression into a light that is temporary. Emma's downfall comes when she uses the resources of one man, her husband, to finance her escapades with two others.

3. Use your objects to create action

When Jay Gatsby hands over the wheel of the yellow car to Daisy, he has no idea that Daisy will turn the machine into a murder weapon. Does Daisy know what she is doing? Or is the hit-and-run an unlucky accident? Whether Daisy knows or not, she gets her husband back the minute that George Wilson kills Gatsby. Study the actions swirling around the yellow car, starting in Chapter 7. First, Tom Buchanan takes Gatsby's place behind the wheel, an act of temporary possession that lasts long enough to convince Myrtle (the mistress) and George (the cuckold) that the car belongs to him. Second, Myrtle mistakes Jordan Baker, sitting in the back seat, for Daisy – Tom's wife. Third, after he crosses verbal swords with Gatsby in the New York hotel, Tom sends Daisy home with Gatsby in the yellow car. Fourth, on the road back to East Egg, Gatsby swaps spots with Daisy, letting her drive because she is nervous, hoping like a romantic fool that getting her white hands on the wheel will soothe her nerves. Fifth, Daisy whacks Myrtle, using the yellow car as a deadly weapon. Sixth, to protect Daisy and himself, Tom sends Wilson the cuckold to Gatsby's mansion.

The yellow car in *The Great Gatsby* works with the same power as the statue of the black bird in Dashiell Hammett's *The Maltese Falcon*. That novel has 20 chapters; the statue appears in 14 of those chapters. You can track the appearances in a handy list in *The Weekend Novelist Writes a Mystery*. The action created by the black bird is death – a string of bodies that extends from the back story, where greedy people kill to get their hands on the object, and into the narrative present after page 1. There is a really good scene in Chapter 16, entitled 'The Third Murder', which gives a hint of what happens when a character tries to possess the bird. The scene takes place in the office of the sleuth, Sam Spade, where he briefs Effie Perrine, his faithful secretary, on recent events in the case. The briefing is interrupted by a visitor. He is seven feet tall, wearing a black overcoat and carrying a package about the size of a football. As he stands framed in Spade's doorway, the man starts bleeding at the mouth. Blood runs down his throat. He grabs the football package with both hands. Then he falls forward, releasing the package which rolls across the floor. The intruder is dead, killed because he held the black bird. The detective, a shrewd private investigator, is too smart to hold onto the bird. In the next chapter, he checks the bird into left-luggage. Then he posts the receipt to himself, using a false name, to be retrieved just in time for the climax. The lesson from *The Maltese Falcon*: finding the right object can make a writer famous.

Exercises

1. Gather your objects in a list
Objects can be wardrobe items, jewellery, vehicles, weapons, money, furniture, rocks, trees, pebbles on the beach, pearls in the sea. Make more than one list. Which list of objects defines your story?

2. Attach an object to each character
Give one object to your protagonist. One object to your antagonist. One object to your helper. Place character and object in a specific location: a room, a field, a forest, a plane, a desert tank, a bar in Soho, a dining room in Indianapolis, an outdoor café in Paris. Does the same object still cling to the character, or does the change in location suggest another object?

3. Use your architectural diagram
Dump objects from your mind onto your latest structural sketch. Let your hand move freely and don't try to guide the objects; just let them drift down, like snowflakes. When they have all landed, take a break, and when you come back refreshed, move the objects on the diagram and see what story they want to tell. Is it a rags-to-riches story about a protagonist's climb up the economic ladder? Is it a tale

of revenge with a hunter going after the blood of his enemy? Is it a story about two lovers in an underworld city that represents hell? Is it a story about a doomed hero who dies because he forces his way into a sacred circle where he is not wanted, and where he does not belong?

4. Insert objects into your dialogue

If you have two characters talking on the page, insert an object into your dialogue. Have your characters talk about the object. For example:

A: What is that in your hand?
B: Nothing.
A: Show it to me.
B: Nothing, I said. Nothing.

The novel-in-progress: *Trophy Wives*

The grid below shows the writer of *Trophy Wives* locking down on objects.

Character	Role	Object	Wants/Needs	Fate
Veronica	Protagonist	Copy of *Jane Eyre*/House	Independence Wealth Security	Lives
Paul	Antagonist	Father's Breitling Watch Father's Gun	Control California Semiconductor	Dies
Gwyn	Helper	Dirt The Earth	Love Recognition Stability	Dies
Barbara	Antagonist	California Semiconductor Gun	Control of California Semiconductor Approval	Lives
Anderson	Helper	Badge	Solve the Crime	Lives
Ashleigh	Victim	Money	Career Success	Dies

TABLE 3: LOCKING DOWN ON OBJECTS IN *TROPHY WIVES*

Let's examine the objects. Paul Watson has inherited two objects from his dad: a watch and a pistol. While this might not happen in real life, it works very well in a rough draft, because it keeps the object in the forefront of the writer's brain. The watch appears again in Paul's dream with the graveyard setting, when Dad passes the watch to his son. In this dream, the writer links the watch and the pistol. To match the husband's inheritance, the writer of *Trophy Wives* has attached a book to Veronica. The book, *Jane Eyre*, is the story of Veronica's life. On the inside cover, in a flowery hand, are these words from Veronica's dead mother: 'To my baby Ronnie, with love from your Ma.' The book appears in the coffee shop, where Veronica sips a hot cup of tea after being rescued by Paul in the car park.

Veronica's precious book is like the precious book in *The English Patient*. The title is *The Histories*; the author is Herodotus; the book belongs to Count Almasy, the desert-explorer-protagonist, who carried the book with him into the desert. He jotted notes in it. He pasted in his drawings of the caves. The book was his friend and companion. As we discover when he refuses to hand over the book to Katharine Clifton, the beautiful English girl with the jealous husband, the book contains Almasy's heart. In a later scene, when he offers Katherine the book, he also offers her his heart on a silver platter.

Because *Jane Eyre* is attached to the protagonist, the writer of *Trophy Wives* can build the book into a symbol. Barbara does not yet have an object – more work to do. Ashleigh's object is her computer. She is an accountant who works for Paul's company.

Weekends 17–18:
Plotting with more than one protagonist

We pause for a quick review of literary terms. Protagonist is a Greek word meaning 'the one who leads'. Antagonist, another Greek word, means 'the one who opposes'. If you pit one protagonist against one antagonist, their struggle (also called a contest or competition) will create dramatic conflict – the heart of any good story. For example, the protagonist in the Cinderella fairy-tale is Cinderella herself; the antagonist is the Wicked Stepmother. Cinderella gets help from her Fairy Godmother, who, in some versions of the story, is the ghost of Cinderella's dead mother. The Wicked Stepmother, who blocks Cinderella's access to the royal ball, gets support from the Evil Step-sisters, each of whom has their black heart set on becoming the Princess. Any writer who doubts the power of such elegant dramatic simplicity (protagonist vs. antagonist) should take another look at the persistent survival of the Cinderella figure in today's books and films. She is there, for example, in the Julia Roberts call-girl protagonist in *Pretty Woman*. She is there in Helen Hunt's waitress-mum protagonist in *As Good As It Gets*. She is there in the secretary-who-would-be-a-broker protagonist in *Working Girl*.

If you are a weekend novelist just starting out, you should focus your writing powers on a single protagonist. However, from long experience of running writers' workshops, we realise that lots of writers will attempt to split their lead character into two (the double protagonist) or three (the triple protagonist) or four (the quadruple protagonist). From close questioning of dozens of first-time novelists, we have discovered the source of the urge to develop more than one protagonist: it comes from the screen, from popular television sit-coms like *Friends* (six protagonists); from popular weekly television dramas like *ER* (six or more protagonists), which runs multiple story-lines about doctors and nurses and patients in an emergency room in a hospital in Chicago; from soap operas like *Days of Our Lives*; from 'buddy' films like *Lethal Weapon*, which stars two cops, or *Thelma and Louise*, where two attractive women, driven by circumstance, turn to a life of crime.

To satisfy this urge for more than one protagonist, we have analysed the device in two contemporary novels: Ian McEwan's *Amsterdam*, which has two protagonists; and Zadie Smith's *White Teeth*, which – as we noted earlier – has three. Having more than one protagonist splits the attention (and perhaps the loyalty) of the reader. There are structural problems, like when does Protag2 enter the story? And there are problems of space, because your antagonist needs room to work, and protagonists, by their very nature, take up lots of space. We'll start by looking at *Amsterdam*. It's a fascinating book, tightly written, and it offers lots of solutions on managing the double protagonist.

Getting help from other writers

Ian McEwan's *Amsterdam*, which won the Booker Prize, has two protagonists. Protagonist 1 is Clive Linley, a composer who works on a new musical score, slaving away in London and the English Lake District in order to meet a deadline for a performance in, you guessed it, Amsterdam. Protagonist 2 is Vernon Halliday, the editor of a British tabloid newspaper called *The Judge*. In the old days, before he became deskbound, Vernon was a roving correspondent, a word-craftsman of good reputation.

The protagonists are friends. They are both educated; they live in comfortable homes. Clive is a bachelor. Vernon is married to Mandy, who is barely seen by the reader until the final scene, when Vernon has died and she is about to answer the doorbell. Nice dramatic irony here: the reader knows who's ringing the doorbell, but Mandy, Vernon's widow, does not. This final scene from *Amsterdam* gives you a blueprint for deploying the double-protagonist device: use it to create dramatic irony.

Dramatic irony comes to us from the Greek Chorus, that collective body of sonorous voices that used poetic portents to warn the protagonist about danger up ahead.

'Lo,' spake the Chorus, 'yon Sphinx lies ahead. Walk with care, O Man.'

'Don't bother me,' said the protagonist. 'There's this lady I've got to meet.'

The Chorus spoke to the protagonist. The protagonist did not hear, but the audience did, producing dramatic irony. In our time, the Chorus has evolved into the Omniscient Author, who delivers the same portents using exposition. In the hands of a master craftsman like Ian McEwan, this device has further evolved into a zigzag structure of dancing protagonists. When Protagonist 1 has the story, Protagonist 2 is unaware of the action. When Protagonist 2 shares a thought with the reader, they are keeping a secret from Protagonist 1. The reader watches them dance – first Clive, then Vernon, then Clive, then Vernon, with an occasional break when the point of view shifts to another character.

In order to see the full range of possibilities for the double-protagonist device, we need to look at the shifts in point of view in *Amsterdam*. Like *Leaving Las Vegas* and *White Teeth*, *Amsterdam* is divided into sections, and then each section is divided into chapters. Whereas *Leaving Las Vegas* and *White Teeth* have four sections, *Amsterdam* has five. In the table below, you can see the section number, the chapter(s) within that section, and the character who has the point of view.

Part	Chapter	POV	Notes
I	Chapters 1–2	Clive Linley	Composer sweating big symphony
II	Chapters 1–5	Vernon Halliday	Editor sweating falling sales, photos
III	Chapters 1–3	Clive Linley	Lake Country, witnesses rape
IV	Chapter 1	Rose Garmony	Wife of Julian, Foreign Secretary
	Chapters 2–4	Vernon Halliday	
	Chapter 5	George Lane	Husband of Molly, photos
	Chapter 6	Frank Dibben	Replaces Vernon as editor
V	Chapters 1, 2, 4	Clive Linley	Booze, police, Amsterdam
	Chapters 2, 5	Vernon Halliday	Depression, Amsterdam
	Chapter 6	George, Garmony	George has the POV as book ends

TABLE 4: MORE THAN ONE PROTAGONIST: SHIFTING THE POINT OF VIEW IN *AMSTERDAM*

As you can see from the table, the novel opens with a patterned rhythm, as Clive passes the baton to Vernon, Vernon back to Clive. The rhythm changes in Part IV, which opens in the point of view of Rose Garmony, the wife of Julian. As Rose exits, Vernon snatches back the point of view, then loses it to George in Chapter 5, and then loses it again. In Chapter 6, Frank Dibben takes over the point of view and his presence signals that Vernon is out of a job.

In Part V, Vernon and Clive toss the point of view back and forth until the final chapter, where the two Gs – George and Garmony – travel to Amsterdam to fetch the dead bodies of our two protagonists.

Mini-guidelines for working the double protagonist

If you have chosen to deploy the double-protagonist device, make sure that:

1. You know why you are using this technique.
2. You work out the rhythms – the changes in the point of view – before you plunge into the writing.
3. Once you have worked out the larger rhythms (point of view confers power on the holder), you work out the architecture of the book.

The architecture of Ian McEwan's *Amsterdam*

Amsterdam is a story about the power of a strong female in the company of weak males. Molly Lane is dead, but her ghost haunts her ex-lovers, including Clive and Vernon, who encounter Julian Garmony outside the chapel in London where Molly is being cremated.

Amsterdam is the story of two educated men who kill each other.

Amsterdam is the story of a husband who seeks revenge on his dead wife's ex-lovers.

To represent the downward journeys of our two protagonists – Vernon Halliday, editor, and Clive Linley, composer – we use a circle structure (see Figure 10). To represent the object in the subtext – Molly's photos – we use an inner circle. As Clive and Vernon exit the cremation scene, the photos move with Molly's husband George to a house in London, where George offers the photos to Vernon for publication in *The Judge*, to raise the readership. The photos, revealed near the midpoint, show Julian Garmony, the British Foreign Secretary, wearing a dress and some dainty feminine underthings. As the inner circle progresses, we see the photos published in *The Judge*. And at the double climax in *Amsterdam* – when you choose the double-protagonist device, you must have two climaxes – Molly's ghost appears to both her ex-lovers, calling them back.

To represent the point-of-view trade-off between Clive and Vernon, we use a zigzagging line (see the right side of Figure 10, with both Vernon and Clive enclosed in a small bubble). The trade-off, built on past friendships and the body of Molly, starts with a mutual death-pact. Life is so horrible, the two protagonists agree, that they should die together. If you go, take me with you. If I go, you go too. The death-pact strikes through everything – photos, Rose Garmony's TV defence of her husband, Clive's botched symphony, Vernon's loss of his job to the office geek Frank Dibben – and like a curse from Classical Greece, the pact brings the two old friends together in Amsterdam.

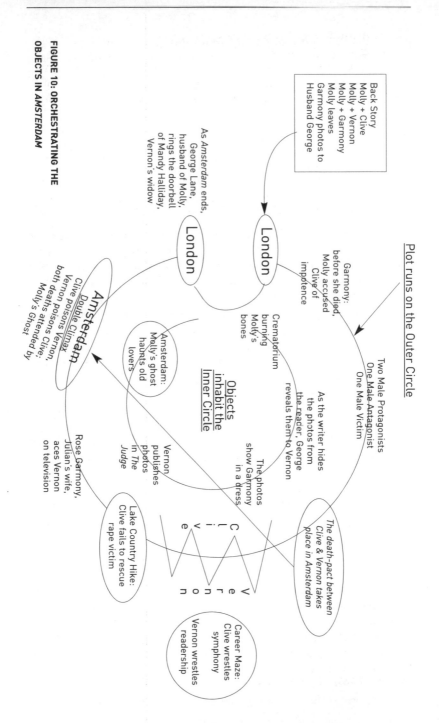

FIGURE 10: ORCHESTRATING THE
OBJECTS IN AMSTERDAM

The method of death is poison.

One good gulp, and you're dead.

The box at the top left of Figure 10 is a compressed summary of action in the back story. Back story, you may recall, is what happens before page 1 – trauma, pain, lost love, pleasure – the events that drive the characters through the story. The back story for *Amsterdam*, for example, contains Molly's love affairs with Clive, Vernon and Garmony, and also her photos of Garmony, which she leaves in the hands of her clever and vengeful husband, George Lane.

With an architectural sketch like Figure 10 to stabilise your structure, you can develop information about each item on your TWN checklist: Time, Place, Character, Object, and Ritual. For example, here are the checkpoints for *Amsterdam*:

Time: *Amsterdam* starts in February, at the funeral of Molly Lane, photographer. The day is cold. The novel ends in early spring, with buds sprouting. Time is less important than Place.

Place: the novel opens in London, takes a detour to the Lake District in the middle (Part III), and climaxes in Amsterdam. The novel ends in London, with George Lane, Molly's widower, calling on Mandy Halliday, Vernon's widow.

Character: *Amsterdam* has six main characters. When you are this far along in the writing, you have enough information to build a power grid. This grid compresses information like: Name, Role, Connections, Wants/Needs, Entry Point, and Fate. When you have read through the sample grid below, create one for your novel-in-progress.

Name	Role	Connection	Wants/Needs	Entry Pt	Fate
Clive	Protag 1	M's old lover	To grow up	Book 1	Dies
Vernon	Protag 2	M's old lover	To get even	Book 1	Dies
George	Antag 1	M's husband	To get even	Book 1	Lives
Garmony	Helper	M's old lover	To change identities	Book 1	Lives
Molly	Antag 2	She is M	To get even with men	Book 1	Dies
Rose	Antag 3	Jealous of M	To protect her children	Book 4	Lives

TABLE 5: A POWER GRID FOR *AMSTERDAM*

Objects/Symbols/Landmarks:
Photos: an object from the back story – a packet of Molly Lane's Garmony-in-drag photos – becomes the sacred object of the book. The object is even more important in a novel that deploys the double-protagonist device: it provides a thick thread that runs through the fabric of the work, appearing, then disappearing beneath the surface of the novel, where it lurks in the subtext until it is time to reappear. Molly's photos of the British Foreign Secretary were taken before her death. On the surface, George wants to punish Garmony, the Foreign Secretary, for having sexual relations with his wife; in his heart, he also wants to punish ex-lovers Vernon and Clive. Photos are part of the symbolism of the modern media.

TV/Cameras/Newspaper: Vernon works for a newspaper. Before he can publish Molly's photos, they show up on TV. Rose Garmony uses a TV interview to defend her husband by attacking Vernon.

Nature: objects and symbolism from the natural world dominate Part III, when Clive escapes London to hike the Lake District. Nature triggers Clive's creativity. As he concludes the composition of his symphonic masterpiece, he hears a woman shouting. Choosing not to break his train of creative thought, Clive hides behind a rock (using an object of nature to conceal himself), while the woman gets raped by the Lakeland Rapist.

Poison: the potion used by Vernon and Clive to kill each other in Amsterdam.

Booze: when Clive gets drunk, he destroys his symphony.

Rituals: the ritual in *Amsterdam* is the passing of a baton – a packet of Molly's photos – that helps both protagonists to cross the Great Threshold, from Life to Death. In classical mythology, this crossing is represented by the River Styx, where Charon, the hooded boatman, ferries the dead across to Hades. In *Amsterdam*, the River Styx is a city called Amsterdam. The other baton, of course, is poison. The death-pact is like a curse from the Egyptian Sphinx. Once cast, the curse cannot be lifted. Therefore, at the climax, which occurs in Amsterdam, Clive poisons Vernon and Vernon poisons Clive.

Lessons from *Amsterdam*

The alternating point of view – Clive to Vernon, Vernon to Clive – establishes a rhythm, a comfort zone for the reader. If you can imagine the point of view as a camera eye, first we see the story from Clive's point of view, and then from Vernon's. Any shift away from either Vernon or Clive breaks the comfy routine. For example, Part IV opens with Rose's point of view. Rose Garmony is the wife of Julian Garmony, British Foreign Secretary, the subject of Molly's photos, which were taken in her prime, when she was cheating on her husband. Rose is a medical doctor, very solid and not afraid of the TV cameras. She is methodical and heroic. Her days are filled with healing and good works. When she looks at her husband, Rose sees a pitiful man, a silly teenaged boy, a child in need of a mother. The switch to Rose's point of view in Part IV, Chapter 1, sets up her appearance on television three chapters later – in Part IV, Chapter 4, when she makes light of the photos of her husband and attacks Vernon.

Because point of view has the camera-eye power of our time (the age of television and screens), Rose's onscreen curse gets Vernon fired from the editorship of *The Judge*. In the next chapter, George Lane, who sold the photos to Vernon, accuses Vernon of bad timing, but the timing was controlled by George.

In the next chapter, the point of view shifts to Frank Dibben, a subeditor, who takes over a meeting to assign articles to the writers. When Frank takes over Vernon's slot, the reader knows that Vernon has lost his job over Molly's photos.

The most telling point-of-view shift comes at the end of the book – Chapter 6 of Part V – where George Lane goes calling on Mandy Halliday, Vernon's widow. As George presses Mandy's doorbell, he is smiling. The book, which began on a bone-chilling day in February, ends on an evening in early spring. The writer has saved the biggest secret for last: *Amsterdam* is a murder mystery and George Lane is the killer. With the sale of Molly's photos, George cleanses himself of cuckoldry, wiping away the memory of Molly with her deadly photos. The photos do away with Vernon, who loses not only his job, but also his life and his wife. That same wife, Mandy Halliday, is behind the door waiting for George Lane to ring the bell.

For a surprise ending, you manipulate the point of view to control the information that you give to the reader. In our world, point of view works like the TV screen.

It is all we know.

Plotting with more than two protagonists

In *White Teeth*, Zadie Smith uses three main protagonists – Archie, Samad, and Irie. When you use more than one protagonist, you need to connect them. In *Amsterdam*, Clive and Vernon are old buddies from the past. Their main connection is Molly's body. But Molly is dead and now here comes her ghost.

Smith connects her three main protagonists like this:

- Archie and Samad are old Army buddies from World War II. They both carry wounds from that war: Samad's dead hand and Archie's thigh.
- Irie is Archie's daughter. Irie's grandmother's name is Hortense. Hortense's mother's name is Ambrosia. In Chapter 13, 'Irie, 1990, 1907', Ambrosia takes over the point of view to tell the story of the birth of Hortense.
- In Chapter 14, Millat, son of Samad, shares the point of view with Irie, who is now 16, which advances 1990 into 1991.
- In Chapter 15, Irie shares the point of view with a number of other voices.

The blood connection holds the narrators together. If you can, visualise a chorus of singers, with three major soloists. In the first two parts of the presentation, Samad and Archie have the stage. In Part III, Irie has her solos, and then she is replaced by other singers.

If you are writing a novel with multiple voices – and more than one protagonist – then you would be smart to sketch out your plans before you spend too much time writing. Start with a list of protagonists. Block out special locations on your structural diagram. Give a section to Protag 1, another section to Protag 2, and so on. Then add the other voices that you would like to have tell part of the story. Keep adding names to your architectural sketch until it gets too messy, and then switch over to the grid.

The grid below shows the different shifts in the points of view in Smith's *White Teeth*.

Chapter	Name	Setting	Time	Point of View
Part I: Archie, 1974, 1945				
1	Peculiar Marriage of Archie Jones	London	1974	Archie
2	Teething Trouble	London	1974	Clara
3	Two Families	London	1974	Clara/Samad
4	Three Coming	London	1974	Clara/Alsana
5	Root Canals of Alfred Archibald Jones and Samad Miah Iqbal	Greece	1945	Archie/Samad

Chapter	Name	Setting	Time	Point of View
Part II: Samad, 1984, 1857				
6	Temptation of Samad Iqbal	London	1984	Samad
7	Molars	London	1984	Samad/Irie
8	Mitosis	London	1984	Samad
9	Mutiny!	London	1987	Alsana/Samad/ kids
10	Root Canal of Mangal Pande	London/India	1984/ 1857	Samad
Part III: Irie, 1990, 1907				
11	Miseducation of Irie Jones	London	1990	Irie
12	Canines: The Ripping Teeth	London	1990	Joyce, Marcus
13	Root Canals of Hortense Bowden	Jamaica	–	Ambrosia
14	More English Than the English	London	1991	Millat/Irie
15	Chalfenism versus Bowdenism	London	1991	Irie and others
Part IV: Magid, Millat, and Marcus, 1992, 1999				
16	Return of Magid Mahfooz Murshed Mubtasim Iqbal	London	1999	Marcus, Irie
17	Crisis Talks and Eleventh-Hour Tactics	London	1999	Alsana, Millat, Irie, Author
18	The End of History versus the Last Man	London	1992, 1985	Author, Irie, Joshua, Joely, Crispin
19	The Final Space	London	1999	Joshua, Millat, Ryan, Irie, Author
20	Of Mice and Memory	London	1999	Archie, Millat, Samad

TABLE 6: SHIFTING THE POINT OF VIEW IN *WHITE TEETH*

To make this grid, we started with the Table of Contents, where the author uses dates to control the sweep of the story; this covers the last 25 years of the 20th century, with flashbacks to Mangal Pande in 1857 and Ambrosia Bowden in 1907. With her wordplay on teeth, molars, teething, root canals, and mice, the author has some fun with her chapter titles.

The title of Chapter 20, 'Of Mice and Memory', is a pun on the title of John Steinbeck's 1937 novel *Of Mice and Men*, the story of George and Lenny, whose fate (plans gone wrong) haul the reader back to Scottish poet Robert Burns, a stalwart beacon in English literature, who hatched the phrase in a poem called 'To a Mouse', when he wrote 'the best laid schemes o' mice and men/gang aft a-gley'. If the reader doubts this allusion, check out Chapter 20, where Marcus reads a scientific paper on the study of a mouse.

Before we leave *White Teeth*, you should note the tooth in the title.

Then note the title of Chapter 5: 'The Root Canals of Alfred Archibald Jones and Samad Miah Iqbal.'

Then note the title of Chapter 10: 'The Root Canal of Mangal Pande.'

Then note the title of Chapters 12 ('Canines: The Ripping Teeth') and 13 ('The Root Canals of Hortense Bowden').

This is the symbolism of wound – pain of the root canal, pain of getting shot, pain of giving birth, pain of growing up, pain of leaving home, pain of gaining a foothold in a new land – all embodied in the title, also filled with symbolism: *White Teeth*.

As you work through your plotting sections, pause to jot down titles for your work-in-progress.

Exercises

1. Consider your purpose

Why use the double protagonist? Look at *Leaving Las Vegas*. It answers the question: What happens when a drunk falls in love with a prostitute? Answer: The drunk dies; the prostitute lives to tell the tale. The purpose of plot is to let the reader get chummy with the main character. Get inside the head of. Understand. Feel with and sweat with. Want the same resource-base as. Cinderella, the protagonist of her own fairy-tale, wants the castle on the hill. The reader wants her to have it; wants Cinderella to succeed, to climb and not fall. If your protagonist lacks the sterling qualities of Cinderella – pluck, guile, tenacity, a slender foot – rethink as you rewrite.

2. Character list

If you have more than one protagonist, then you have more than one plot.

If you have more than one plot, take the time to list your characters. Make the list from memory; see what you can pull from your head. Then go back to the section on character work. Did you plan for more than one protagonist? Or did the second protagonist come from a character transformation in the writing process?

3. Character and point of view

Gather your characters into a grid and work out the changes in your point of view. When does the point of view go to Protag 1? When does it pass to Protag 2? Who else gets a point of view? Follow the model grid we used for *Amsterdam*.

4. Architectural blueprint

Once you are certain of your larger rhythm – the tectonic shifting of the point of view from one character to another – sketch a diagram that shows movement through time. Use the circle or the line – whatever works for you.

The novel-in-progress: *Trophy Wives*

As we have mentioned, today's writer is influenced not only by stories on the screen – TV and film – but also by the cinematic form. *Thelma and Louise* has two protagonists; *Friends* had six. To handle more than one protagonist, the writer must shift the point of view. To shift point of view and not distract the reader with the clanking machinery of your novel, you need to practise. One excellent way to practise is to keep writing about your story. Here is the writer of *Trophy Wives* using the startline, 'This is a story about...' As you read, circle the names of the characters.

This is a story about power. Paul was born with power. Veronica gains power when she marries Paul and finds herself in the blue-blooded hills of Nob Hill, San Francisco. She is the belle of the ball. From a penniless graduate student, she has become the entertainer and homemaker for the Chairman and CEO of Phoenix Investments. Paul has old money, and he teaches Veronica to fit into the lifestyle. At first, dizzy with money, she takes to it. Paul lives the lifestyle of his father: luxury, indulgence, infidelity. When Paul's mother dies,

Paul's world changes. He wanders. His company suffers. Barbara, his older sister, sees her chance. Barbara wants control of the company.

Veronica is shocked when Paul's mistress is found dead after a failed test for the military. Speculation lands on Paul's shoulders, and he spirals into depression and solitude. For solace, Veronica moves into the arms of Gwyn, her girlfriend since college. With Gwyn's help, Veronica tries to escape from Paul.

San Francisco Police Detective Anderson, a blue-collar cop who hates fat-cat rich boys, uses the power of the police department to bring Paul down. He searches the estate on Nob Hill. He plants evidence. He leaks information to the press, causing Paul to battle with the board of his company.

At the midpoint of the novel, Veronica discovers Barbara's hand in the murder of Paul's mistress. She capitalises on the opportunity to leave a shameful marriage. Veronica chooses money over Gwyn, and the wheels are in motion for a jealous lover to bring the power-struggle to an end.

In the climax, Gwyn finds Paul at his desk with a Heckler and Koch pistol. They struggle, Gwyn pulls the trigger, and Paul falls down, bleeding onto the thick, plush carpet of his father's den. Detective Anderson arrives just as the gun goes off. He runs into the den, catching Gwyn with the gun. She panics, and Detective Anderson shoots her down.

The novel closes with Barbara buying Veronica's stock options, the only part of Paul's fortune not covered by a prenuptial agreement. As the two women walk away from the Phoenix Investments office, Paul's silver Maybach (one of his cars in the five-car garage on Nob Hill) stops alongside Barbara. The door opens and Detective Anderson reaches from the car to help Barbara inside.

If you recall the first few weekends, *Trophy Wives* began as a sexual triad: a rich man, his mistress, his wife. The characters went through the motions. They dressed, they talked at each other, they moved from room to room, scene to scene. Veronica, the wife of the rich man, sprang to life in the car park in the rain when she dropped her shopping in a puddle. She became a more solid character when she pulled out her battered copy of *Jane Eyre*. As the novel progresses, she could also unearth a keepsake from her past, something from her mother that links Veronica to her Native American heritage. Veronica's ugly childhood situation surfaced in her dream, when her mother left her alone with a strange man – a tense back-story situation that sets up the possibilities of child abuse and sexual slavery.

Veronica's other object, her leaky raincoat, sets her apart from the world of Paul Watson – his Porsche, his fancy shoes, his expensive raincoat. Paul's dream uses objects – the watch and the pistol – to connect Paul to his father. The father is important because he founded the company that keeps Paul in fancy shirts. The dream elevates Paul to protagonist status, and this weekend we travelled with Paul to the police station as other characters planted their feet in the story. Gwyn takes more action. The policeman, Anderson, has hooked up with Barbara. Ashleigh Bennett is dead. Did Paul kill her? Did Barbara and the detective frame Paul?

The two characters that need more work are Ashleigh Bennett and Barbara Watson. The fast way to learn about both characters is to bring them together in a scene. Use their wardrobes to show how different they are. Or how alike. Set the scene in a public place, a café or restaurant, where they look like two women having lunch, but where the subtext writhes with intrigue. Questions always surface in the writing: What does this character want? What will she do to get what she wants? At the end of the book, will she be dead or alive?

As the scene rises to a climax, you can interrupt lunch with a third character – an intruder like Anderson, the policeman. Use gesture to show that he is connected to Barbara. If Ashleigh has the point of view, then we find out how smart she is by how fast she catches on to Barbara and her detective. To build this story, the writer will need to make lots of choices. One of the first choices is the number of protagonists, which determines how much you want to shift the point of view. If you can stop and look at the writing you have done, using the TWN checklist to isolate story elements, you can use what you write today to generate what you write tomorrow.

Weekends 19–20:
Plotting with the working synopsis

A story is a competition for the resource-base, the object of desire. In fiction, 'object of desire' means what the characters want, what they need, what they will die for, what they will kill for.

The key word is 'object' – it is something visible, something the reader can see, rather than some abstract concept inside the writer's brain.

Tell your story with a visible resource-base and you have a better chance of becoming famous.

Telling your story

Cinderella wants the castle on the hill. The Wicked Stepmother wants the castle on the hill, too. Clashing agendas produce dramatic conflict. The castle is a visible resource-base. As a symbol, the castle represents not only power and wealth – attached, in this story, to the King and the Handsome Prince – but for Cinderella, a poor orphan girl, the castle represents safety, warmth, comfort, and a home for the baby she will produce with some small donation from the Prince. The plot is all about Character A (Cinderella) climbing the economic ladder. This ascent happens so often that it has its own shorthand name: Rags to Riches.

Jane Eyre, a 19th-century British Cinderella, wants Thornfield, a country house in rural England. Thornfield is safety, warmth, three meals a day, a bedroom of her own, a library, a piano. To get her hands on this Victorian resource-base, Jane must marry the owner of Thornfield, Mr Edward Fairfax Rochester. Mr Rochester, a man of property and wealth, is a womaniser. He proposes to Jane in high summer, in the garden, and Jane accepts. She has climbed the economic ladder, and is about to enter the portals of Upper World, when she discovers that Mr Rochester is already married. He invites her to hang around as his mistress. Jane says no. She wants the resource-base: to get it, she must become Mrs Rochester. Jane's ascent from Rags to Riches is halted by the spectral figure of Mrs

Bertha Mason Rochester, who is kept locked away in the tower at Thornfield. Jane's plot – think about this as you craft your own synopsis – is Cinderella's Rags to Riches with twists: Rochester, the Handsome Prince, is twice Jane's age and he is married; the Wicked Stepmother figure is a madwoman in the attic; unlike Cinderella, Jane has cousins, a blood connection that saves her from the workhouse, the streets, 19th-century oblivion.

Jay Gatsby, a 20th-century American male Cinderella, wants to be accepted by East Egg, a rich man's enclave on Long Island in New York State. Jay Gatsby is a fake name; he was born Jimmy Gatz. His profession is that of bootlegger – he sells bathtub booze from storefronts called 'drugstores' in the big cities of America – and he uses the dirty money to rent a big house in West Egg, across the bay from East Egg, so he can spy on the helper who can get him across the threshold, into the land of gold, elegance, and old money. The helper's name is Daisy Fay Buchanan. Daisy – her flowery name is meant to deceive – is married to Tom Buchanan, the male dragon who guards the gate to East Egg. Gatsby, a poor boy from Out West, shares the same Rags to Riches plot as Cinderella and Jane Eyre. Jane Eyre had one dragon. Cinderella had one dragon. Jay Gatsby has at least three (Tom Buchanan, Daisy Buchanan, and George Wilson) and still he is wide-eyed with innocence as he approaches his own execution.

Using your synopsis

Once you identify the object of desire for your characters, the synopsis will write itself. The key word is a verb: 'want'. Cinderella wants. Jane wants. Jay Gatsby wants. Your protagonist wants. If you have more than one protagonist, your protagonists want.

The dictionary definition of synopsis is something like 'a brief summary or outline'. A synopsis is more than that, though. It does not have to be brief. The longer it gets, the more it can guide your writing. The longer it gets, the more structure a synopsis needs. If your synopsis runs over a page, you'll need to divide it, split the writing into parts. You can use these same parts when you write the novel.

If you are writing a synopsis for a straight-line plot, you'll work in three acts: One, Two, Three. If you're working with the Heroic Cycle (see Weekends 3–4), you'll work with three phases: Departure, Initiation, and Return. If you're working with the Mythic Journey (see the same Weekends), your synopsis will have five sections, or phases, and will begin with your protagonist, Character A, trapped in some kind of container: Cage, Escape, Quest, Dragon, and Home.

The key to the synopsis lies in the last part of the word, 'opsis', which comes from the Greek, meaning sight or view. *Ops* is the Greek word for eye. *Op* is the Greek verb, the infinitive 'to see'. *Syn*, the prefix, means 'together'. 'Synopsis', therefore, means 'a viewing all together'. That's what you do when you write a synopsis – you view the parts as a whole.

A synopsis for Cinderella: a three-act structure

Act One sets up Cinderella's problem; her hopeless situation as she slaves all day cleaning her stepmother's house. News of the royal ball worsens her situation: she has nothing to wear; if she did, and if she could escape the house, she still has no transportation, no way of travelling to the castle. Cinderella wishes for help, which appears in the catalytic character of the Fairy Godmother, a dimpled, absent-minded sorceress who crowns the wardrobe with a pair of glass slippers as, with a wave of her wand, she turns a pumpkin into a coach. The curtain falls on Act One as Cinderella rides off in her fancy vehicle. She does not hear the clock ticking towards midnight.

Act Two, marked by a dramatic scene change, takes place in the castle. It is light here – candles, lanterns, torches – the symbolism radiant in contrast to the gloom of Cinderella's situation in Act One. Suspense builds in the first half of Act Two as Cinderella and the Prince keep missing each other's arms. At last, they dance. At the midpoint, the point of no return, the Prince is smitten (Cinderella, with the intuitive wisdom of a fairy-tale heroine, is already commit-ted), and now the magic of the Fairy Godmother runs short on time, suspense building again as the clock strikes midnight. Cinderella, fearful of losing face, races away from the Prince and down the steps, with the coach already changing back into a pumpkin, and loses one glass slipper. The Prince, clutching the slipper, is bewil-dered. The curtain falls on Act Two.

Act Three is dominated by one scene: the trying-on of the slipper. The Wicked Stepmother is ready to chop off toes to make the shoe fit one of her daughters, but Cinderella, helped by her helpers, tries on the shoe and it fits.

The plot ends with a Royal Wedding. The Royal Wedding, a ritual of connection, opens the gate to Upper World. Cinderella is safe. She has traded her fertility – and her precious virginity – for the Good Life. She has won the hearts of millions of readers by climbing the economic ladder. Her successful climb gives us courage and hope.

Cinderella sets the example for upward mobility. Reminders: the resource-base for Cinderella is the royal castle. Her fate at the end of the story: Cinderella lives.

Write the ending first

Begin your synopsis with a simple phrase like, 'This is a story about...' To keep going, write under the clock, aiming your words at the end. Before you start writing, you might remind yourself about the way your story ends: who lives, who dies, who gets married, who goes to jail. If you're not sure about your ending (climax plus the wrap-up), now is the time to explore it again.

Let's look at some examples of endings from *The Namesake*, *The Alchemist*, *Amsterdam*, *The Amazing Adventures of Kavalier and Clay*, and *White Teeth*.

At the end of *The Namesake*, the protagonist reads a short story from a book of short stories written by a dead white writer. The protagonist is Gogol Ganguli, a Bengali male born and raised in America. The dead white writer is Nikolai Gogol (1809–1852). The short story, called 'The Overcoat', was published in 1842. The protagonist, a timid clerk in an office in a bureaucracy, loses his overcoat to a thief. The police refuse to help. The clerk dies from exposure. His ghost returns to steal overcoats from the living. The book of short stories is a legacy from Gogol's father, Ashoke, who was saved from a train crash because his hand clutched a page from 'The Overcoat'.

At the end of *The Alchemist*, the protagonist finds the treasure in a hole beneath a tree that grows from the ruins of a deserted chapel. The protagonist is Santiago, the shepherd boy who sells his sheep to get money so he can travel to the pyramids in Egypt, where he will find his treasure. Instead of treasure, he finds truth, magic, and true love. The magic comes from the Alchemist, a Dantesque helper-figure who pushes Santiago forwards, close to the edge, close to the wall, until the shepherd boy who talked to his sheep can talk to the wind. Armed with this knowledge, Santiago finds the treasure waiting for him back at the starting point – the ruined chapel in Spain – and now he heads back to North Africa to find Fatima, the girl he left behind. The journey opened Santiago's mind.

At the end of *Amsterdam*, a man goes calling on a married woman. The place is a residential suburb of London. The woman is the widow of Protag 2, who has just died in Amsterdam, City of Death. Protag 2 dies when he takes poison administered by Protag 1, who also dies. The reason for their deaths is a mutual death-pact joined in Part II. As each protagonist expires, he gets a visit from Molly's ghost. At their deaths, both protagonists have visions of needles and doctors trained in the fine art of euthanasia.

At the end of *The Amazing Adventures of Kavalier and Clay*, Protag 1 replaces Protag 2 in the life (and warm bed) of Protag 3. The replacement ritual at the end reverses the replacement ritual at the end of Act Two (Part IV), where Protag 3, pregnant with Protag 1's child, marries Protag 2. The golden key – a symbol in *Kavalier and Clay* – is the child from this pregnancy, Tommy Clay, who is named for the dead brother of Protag 1, Josef/Joe Kavalier, an immigrant to America from Prague, Czechoslovakia. Tommy brings the three adults together.

At the end of *White Teeth*, Protag 1 catches a bullet meant for Protag 2, while Protag 3 watches. The bullet is a sacred object. It travels through the book, connecting the war wounds of Protags 1 & 2 (1945) from Part I to the bullets packed in grease from the Sepoy Rebellion (1857) in Part II to the assassination attempt of the crazed killer in Part IV (2000).

Guidelines for writing your synopsis

Examine the architectural sketches for your novel.

Scan your down-the-page writings. Circle objects, characters, and action verbs like fall, slap, slice, mince, chop, sew, stitch, smooth, stretch, etc.

Jot down a list of characters' wants.

Write three sentences about the ending of your novel, the fate of your characters.

You are priming the pump, loading your unconscious.

Writing your synopsis in three acts helps to organise your work. Act One, your set-up for the novel, is where you introduce characters who come onstage to work out their agendas. In Act Two, the agendas clash and the action gets complicated as your protagonist encounters greater obstacles. Apparent solutions fail, forcing the protagonist to keep trying alternatives. Act Three is your resolution. With the protagonist weary and the goal fading from view, your protagonist makes a decision to give it one last try (Joe Kavalier wants to know his own son; Santiago asks the desert wind to make a sandstorm; Cinderella shows a last burst of courage as she tries on that slipper before it's smashed by the clumsy stepsisters) and succeeds. In popular fiction, your synopsis ends with the problem solved.

Act One

In writing your synopsis for Act One, you should focus on introductions – bringing the characters into your story – and on character connections. The main character connections in fiction and in life are blood and money. Cinderella's widowed father marries a woman who turns into the Wicked Stepmother, an instant disconnect. The royal castle is a metaphor for money – wealth, power – and what it can buy: safety for a powerless, virgin, poor-girl, orphan fairy-tale heroine. To get help, Cinderella calls on her dead mother (blood connection) who sends a surrogate mother called the Fairy Godmother. Let's look at some examples of Act One tactics in our model novels.

In Act One of *The Namesake*, a mother goes to a hospital to give birth to a son while the father has a flashback about a near-death experience. These three characters – mother, son, father – are connected by blood. The big rituals in Act One are moving into a new home; coming of age (for the protagonist); and travel. Moving into a new home cements the importance of money – the father and mother are Bengali immigrants – and the travel in Act One takes the parents back to India to tighten their blood connections with other family members left behind.

In Act One of *The Alchemist*, a shepherd boy named Santiago hears the call to adventure, refuses the call to adventure, and then keeps meeting mythic helpers who point him down the trail to Africa, Egypt, and the Pyramids, where he will find treasure. The connection is money. To get money for his journey, he sells sheep. To get information for his journey, he gives up one-tenth of his flock (sheep are money). When he reaches North Africa, a thief steals his money, forcing Santiago to work as a crystal polisher.

In Act One of *The Amazing Adventures of Kavalier and Clay*, Josef leaves his brother Tommy behind (blood connection) and heads for America, where he hooks up with Sammy Clay, a cousin (blood connection). Sammy is an ideas guy with dollar signs for eyeballs and he sees his artistic cousin Joe as the key to making money in comic books.

In Act One of *Amsterdam*, Protags 1 and 2 are connected to Garmony and to the newly widowed husband by the death of an old love, Molly Lane. Garmony insults Protag 1. Protag 2 decides to get revenge on Garmony, who was caught on film by Molly Lane before her death. The husband has the photos; for money, he offers to sell her photos to Protag 2.

In Act One of *White Teeth*, Protag 1 connects to Protag 2 through wounds contracted in World War II. The story of their connection –

they are bound together by the wounds – climaxes Part I and ends Act One.

Act Two

Act Two gets complicated when the plot collides with subplots. A smart writer uses the midpoint – the point of no return – to sort out the rhythms of plot and subplot. In some novels – *Jane Eyre*, for example – the midpoint can stretch over several chapters and several days. The midpoint of Brontë's book is the marriage proposal. Jane is a girl who wants to get married, but her economic station is so far down the food chain from that of Mr Rochester that she cannot believe her ears. In fictional terms, Jane's disbelief means that Mr Rochester must sweat to convince her. He also sweats because of the secret hidden upstairs: in the tower of Thornfield, Mr Edward Fairfax Rochester keeps a mad wife under lock and key. Subtext thickens Act Two.

In Act Two of *Amsterdam*, while the photos Molly took of Garmony make their way from the husband to the hands of Protag 2, Protag 1 escapes London and heads to the Lake District, where he must find the golden key that unlocks the symphony that has been stalled by Molly's death, followed by a heavy intake of alcohol and a death-pact with Protag 2.

Scribbling away on his script, Protag 1 hears a cry for help. Tearing himself away from his work, he witnesses a rape. The victim looks like Molly Lane. Molly is already dead and the work must go on, so Protag 1 fails to race to the rescue. Meanwhile, back in London, Julian Garmony's wife prepares to defend her children and her home (and, incidentally, her lout of a husband) against Protag 2, who is about to publish Molly's photos showing Garmony dressed as a woman. Act Two ends with both protagonists in deep despair – Protag 1 is called to the police station to identify the rapist; Protag 2 has been fired from his job as editor – as they head for Amsterdam, city of death.

When you write your synopsis, make sure the action at the midpoint sets up the end of Act Two. As we pointed out in the architectural sketch for *The Namesake*, Act Two for Gogol Ganguli starts when he calls himself Nikhil, changing his name to impress Kim the College Girl when he gatecrashes a university party. This brave pretence – assuming another name without the permission of his parents – cuts the umbilical cord and sets Gogol off on the Journey of the Four Females (Ruth, Maxine, Bridget, Moushimi), which results in a midpoint that stretches over several pages.

The midpoint for the book peaks when Maxine meets Ashoke and Ashimi, Gogol's parents. Maxine is educated, urbane, smart, sexy, well-dressed – the very picture of a modern American female. Her parents live in Manhattan. They have a summer place on a lake in New England. They live well: good food, good wine, lots of books, good conversation – and they accept Gogol because Maxine loves him. Gogol's connection with Maxine makes him ashamed of his parents. The shame makes him feel guilty. He cannot change where he came from, cannot rip up his Bengali roots and replant them in American soil.

The midpoint breaks off when Gogol's father dies.

The death of his father shuts Maxine out.

She wants to keep going, stay with Gogol, get married, pull Gogol deeper into America.

The midpoint ends. Gogol takes up with Bridget. Later, he meets and marries Moushimi. Act Two ends when Moushimi starts her affair with a Frenchman. In Act Three, Gogol heads home for Christmas, where his mother is waiting. The power of the movements of the protagonist – he connects with Ruth, who breaks the connection; he connects with Maxine, but the death of his father breaks the connection; his mother connects Gogol to Moushimi, but Moushimi breaks the connection with her affair; Gogol heads home to his mother – can be expressed with a series of character triangles, or triads:

Ruth + Gogol + Maxine
Gogol + Maxine + Father
Maxine + Gogol + Moushimi
Gogol + Moushimi + Dimitri
Moushimi + Gogol + Mother

As you dig into Act Two, you can use little triangle diagrams to help you keep track of the increasing complexity created by the interlacing of plot and subplots. In *The Namesake*, for example, Maxine's subplot intersects the plot when she meets Gogol. When she meets his parents, her subplot collides with their separate subplots. Maxine, girl of the west, meets Ashoke and Ashimi, parents of the east, at the midpoint. The triads above track Gogol's path from character to character, world to world. Gogol wants to find himself, so he bounces between two cultures – America and India, West and East. Maxine wants a mate who can keep up with her. She chooses Gogol, tries to pull him all the way, over the threshold, into the culture of the West. When Gogol's father dies, duty – as expressed by the mother – pulls Gogol back to the East.

For another example, let's look at the sexual triad in *Jane Eyre*, published in 1847 and still on bookshelves today. In Act Two, Jane joins Rochester and Bertha, his mad wife, to form a sexual triad. Jane is unaware of Bertha and the marriage, but Rochester, a man of property, knows what he's doing when he connects with Jane, when he proposes, and when he takes her in his carriage to buy the wedding dress. Jane discovers the sexual triad in the wedding chapel, near the end of Act Two, when Richard Mason, Bertha's croupy brother, accuses Rochester of being an incipient bigamist. Because of her innocence, Jane goes into shock. Suddenly, in this moment of revelation, she is linked to Bertha through Rochester, who wants Jane because she is strong, sturdy, bright, young, not crazy like his wife, courageous (she saves him from death by smoke and fire), and, like Cinderella, still a virgin. Jane wants Rochester because he is handsome, older, and he has resources. As Mrs Rochester, Jane can escape the miserable fate of thousands of poor girls in Victorian England. This guy has cheek; when he finds he cannot marry Jane, Rochester offers her the position of mistress, to make the sexual triad a permanent fixture in her life. Jane's answer is to escape the horror of the sexual triad by leaving Thornfield. As Act Two closes, Jane exits Thornfield. She has no money, no place to go, no friends waiting to take her in. She has lost the love of her life. She could die from exposure on the heath. Suspense builds, and the reader rushes on to Act Three.

Act Two of *Kavalier and Clay* stretches across 250 pages – longer than either *Amsterdam* (193 pages) or *The Alchemist* (167 pages). A long Act Two means a thick midpoint; lots of subplots colliding with the plot or plots. When the writing gets complex, the writer must clarify the subtext. There are two levels here: the surface text seen by the reader; and the lower layer beneath the text, known only by the writer and kept secret from the reader until the time comes to let it out. Subtext is powerful and mysterious. While the characters talk about the weather, the writer works with emotions like anger, fear, lust, greed and hate. Let's use an example from *Jane Eyre*. Jane, an innocent orphan girl with grit, has the plot. She is unaware of Rochester's crazy wife. The writer buries the secret of the crazy wife in the subtext. Jane, locked into her rags-to-riches plot, does not know about the crazy wife. The same thing happens to Jay Gatsby, who is unaware of Tom's affair with Myrtle Wilson – a secret buried in Tom's subplot. The reader meets Myrtle early, when

Tom introduces the narrator, Nick Carraway. Good writers bury secrets in their subplots, hiding them from the protagonist until the right dramatic moment. Let's see how this works in Act Two of *Kavalier and Clay*.

First, we do a quick sketch (Figure 11):

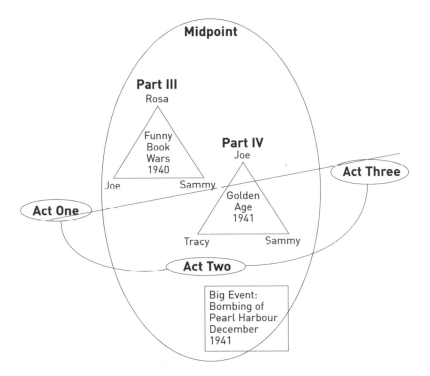

FIGURE 11: ACT TWO OF *THE AMAZING ADVENTURES OF KAVALIER AND CLAY*

Rosa loves Joe. Joe loves Rosa. Sammy loves Joe, but not in a sexual way. These three characters form a powerful sexual triad that dominates the subtext of Part III. Tracy Bacon, a male radio star who plays a superhero, loves Sammy. When pursued by Tracy, Sammy reciprocates. Because Sammy loves Joe, these three males form a second sexual triad that dominates the subtext of Part IV. Act Two covers two years (1940–1941) in the lives of Sammy and Joe. Together, these two boy geniuses use comics to attack the Nazis in Europe, acting like prescient, far-seeing patriots before war is declared. Act Two ends with the Japanese attack on Pearl Harbour. Joe joins the Navy. Tracy Bacon leaves New York for a film career in

Hollywood. Sammy marries Rosa, who is pregnant with Joe's child. The sexual triads in Figure 11 are a graphic representation of heart-power at the centre of Chabon's book. While the world goes to war, the writer balances the horrors of war with the pangs of love.

You can learn this much from studying *Kavalier and Clay*: how to hold your reader in suspense. The characters talk about money. Joe goes after a suspected Nazi saboteur. Sammy falls in love with a beautiful man. Takes the man home to meet his mother. How much does Sammy know? We don't know, but the writer does: in Act Two, near the midpoint, Sammy burns his fingers on a cigarette lighter. To heal his wounds, Tracy Bacon takes Sammy's burnt fingers into his mouth. The flame on the page explains the subtext – Sammy's unspoken love for Tracy Bacon.

This is the lesson: When in doubt, use symbols to tell your story. Write scenes where characters take action. Don't explain the action. Shove the explanation you are dying to write under the surface, into the subtext. If you were writing this book, you would jot a note on your architectural diagram: Sammy loves Tracy. In a hetero-sexual culture, these two lads are outlaws, as demonstrated by an anti-gay raid near the end of Act Two. The date of the raid is 6 December 1941 – one day before the bombing of Pearl Harbour. Act Two closes with Sammy buried in shame and Joe headed for the Naval Recruiting Office.

Kavalier and Clay has two plots – one for Protag 1; one for Protag 2 – and you can only present one plot at a time unless you bring them together in a scene. So when Tracy sucks Sammy's fingers, Joe is not there. And when Joe makes love to Rosa, Sammy is not there. When you have two protagonists and two plots, take the time to work out the action in simple sentences, like this:

Joe joins the Navy.
Tracy heads for California to become a film star.
Sammy was set to go to California with Tracy.
But Rosa is pregnant with Joe's baby.
And the baby needs a name.
And a father.
So the two heroes – Joe and Tracy – head off into adventure.
And Rosa and Sammy get married.
And a new triad is formed.
Father + Mother + Child.
And the sins are washed away by the writer.

Act Three

Let's stay with *Kavalier and Clay* as a guide to writing a synopsis for Act Three. If you recall the architectural diagram, Act Three contains Part V ('The Escape Artist') and Part VI ('The League of the Golden Key').

At the end of Act Two, Joe joins the Navy. At the opening of Act Three, he is trapped in a Navy listening station in the snowy wastes of Antarctica. His life is saved by a dog – a mythic helper – and then Joe and a crazy bush pilot take to the air in a plane made of leather hides (one of these hides is the skin of the mythic helper dog who saved Joe's life). Their destination is an enemy encampment. The plane fails – revenge of the mythic dog – and the crazy pilot is killed, leaving only Joe to attack the enemy encampment.

The only enemy survivor is a German geologist. Joe shoots the German, his only kill of the war, and then he waits to be rescued by a US vessel. The lesson from Act Three is change of setting. Act Two closes in New York, an urban metropolis with streets and traffic signals and cars and skyscrapers. Act Three opens in an icy Hades peopled by men driven insane by isolation, cold, and no female companionship.

As your protagonist crosses the threshold from Act Two into Act Three, try a change of setting. Relocate the landscape of Act Three to let your reader know that you are moving to the last phase of the book. Act Three of *Amsterdam* moves the two protagonists from London to Amsterdam. The distance is short – London to Amsterdam is 30 minutes or so in the air – but the new setting is important because neither protagonist will make it back to London alive.

There are variations on the location change. For example, Act Three of *White Teeth* opens in a new section – Part IV of four – and a shift in the point of view. Act Two ends in Irie's point of view, as time rolls towards the year 2000, the dreaded Y2K, and there is talk of the end of the world; Hortense invites Irie back to Jamaica to witness the end in a prettier place. Act Three opens a new section in the point of view of Marcus, one of the three Ms, who has come to the airport to meet Magid, who is returning to England after spending time in the Old Country. Like the other immigrants to London, and like Gogol Ganguli from *The Namesake*, Magid straddles two worlds. The writer uses her chapter title to emphasise the pomp and ceremony of Magid's return – Chapter 16: 'The Return of Magid Mahfooz Murshed Mubtasim Iqbal' – while using the point of view of Marcus to explain to the reader, through an interior monologue, all about the paper Marcus is writing on the seven years of a mouse, which is picked up in Chapter 20, 'Of Mice and Memory', as the book ends with that bullet.

The two bullets in Act Three – one in *Kavalier and Clay*, the other in *White Teeth* – suggest a nod to violence. Even in the most literary of contemporary novels, the gun reminds us of what Anton Chekhov said: If you plant a shotgun on the mantelpiece, make sure it goes off in the story. Chekhov echoes Aristotle, who said: Don't waste anything in your storytelling. To paraphrase the great philosopher: If you plant an object in Act One, make sure you dig it up in Act Three.

For example, in Act One of *Kavalier and Clay*, Josef Kavalier escapes Prague in a coffin. The object is planted. In Act Three, as we approach the climax, the coffin reappears in New York, at the home of Sammy, Rosa and Tommy (son of Joe).

Suspense hangs here.

A package is delivered to the house. The package is a crate, a box, a coffin, a casket. It weighs a ton, says the delivery man. The package is addressed to Joe, who does not live there. Joe arrives at the house. With Tommy and Rosa watching, he opens the crate to find mud, silt from the Moldau.

The mud is soft. All that remains of the Golem statue, which Joe takes as his other brother. This is a miracle. The coffin has followed Joe from Act One into Act Three. The coffin is a holding place for lost souls and now it has come home; and because of this returning object – a symbol of escape and finding release and coming back – the climax is near.

Like these sharp professional novelists, you can capture the art of Act Three by using these techniques. Plant an object. Let it grow. Bring the object back.

The object in *The Namesake* is the book of Nikolai Gogol's short stories. Planted in Act One in a flashback, the book returns to nail down Act Three, with Gogol reading Gogol.

The object in *The Alchemist* is the treasure. Planted in Act One beneath the sacred tree, it returns in Act Three when Santiago finishes his quest, when he has gained the secret power, when he has talked to the wind and brought sandstorms to amaze the Bedouin. Like any archetypal wanderer, Santiago the shepherd boy returns home to find that what he went looking for was right under his nose – or his feet. His journey started at the ruined chapel. His journey ends at the ruined chapel. The gold treasure was there all the time. The lesson of the book is: 'Open your eyes. Look around.' Readers love this kind of simplicity. They also like stories with happy endings, like Orphan Girl Gets Handsome Prince, or Shepherd Boy Gets Treasure. Maybe that's why *The Alchemist* has sold upwards of 5,000,000 copies worldwide.

With the right object in Act Three, you can use your fiction to teach, guide, lead. As you write your way through your rough draft, keep jotting notes on your synopsis. Think of it as your working synopsis – not only a guide, but also a tool for exploration and discovery. Write a synopsis now. Write another one when you're lost in the middle of Act One, writing that rough draft. Write another one in the middle of Act Two. At the end of Act Two. Allow your writing to shape the contours of your story. If you have done your character work, and if you have used sketches to depict the architecture of your novel, you can use the synopsis to gather all these bits of information together. Remember the definition of synopsis – a gathering view of the whole.

Getting help from other writers

Before we move on to this chapter's exercises, here's a quick working synopsis of Anne Tyler's *The Accidental Tourist* (1985). The parts are: Wants List, The End, Opening Scene, Act One, Act Two, and Act Three. Read it fast. Then go back with a red biro and circle nouns and verbs. They tell the story.

Wants List
Sarah wants Macon to share his grief.
Macon wants to stay buttoned up.
Muriel wants a man to pay the bills.
Julian (Macon's boss) wants a family.
Rose (Macon's sister) wants order in her life.

The End
Macon lives.
Sarah lives.
Muriel lives.
Macon chooses Muriel.
Sarah is left alone.
The object is rain.

Opening Scene
Macon wants to hide. Sarah wants him to open up, share his grief. They bicker. Sarah asks for a divorce.

Act One

Sarah moves out. Macon wanders the house. Edward the dog attacks people. The old kennel won't put up with Edward, so Macon tries a new place where he runs into Muriel, a single mum who's attracted to Macon. For a fee, Muriel offers to train Edward. Macon, locked in his shell, refuses. Edward and the cat team up to break Macon's leg. At home with Rose and the boys, Macon stays isolated while his leg heals. A dinner with Sarah shows her to be happy. She's seeing a man. Macon's still lost. Edward's rage, plus family pressure, forces Macon to agree to Muriel as a trainer for Edward.

Act Two

Muriel comes onstage to help Macon train Edward with a choke chain. Muriel wants Macon, so she invites him to dinner. As he delivers his refusal note, Muriel scares him, saying she's got a shotgun. He confesses to her about his dead son. Muriel lets him sleep. They make love. Redemption begins.

Macon stays the night. He pays attention to Muriel's son, Alexander – a kid with bad allergies. He moves his writing gear to Muriel's apartment. He helps out with money. When he takes a research trip, gathering travel tips for his *Accidental Tourist* series, Muriel asks to come along. She's getting closer, introducing him to her family, sharing her back story. At Rose's wedding – she's marrying Julian – Macon is charmed by the women in his life: Mother, Sister Rose, Wife Sarah, Mistress Muriel. Musing on how comfortable this feels, he backslides, away from Muriel, into his old ruts.

Act Three

Macon's a compulsive guy who likes his ruts, so he goes back to Sarah, settling into the old house and leaving Muriel. When he heads for Paris on a business trip, Muriel (who asked in Chapter 7 to be taken along) now tags along. After all that's happened, she still wants Macon. In Paris, Macon hurts his back, a mirror injury to the breaking of his leg in Act I, and Sarah arrives to take over the research part of his trip. The symbolism is clear: Sarah wants them to get back together again. She keeps Macon punchy with pain pills. If he's to get away, he's got to face the pain and avoid the pill.

The Big Decision: Macon palms the pill.

He leaves Sarah in his bed and creeps out of the hotel and hails a taxi and lo, on the sidewalk is Muriel.

The taxi hurtles along. Macon can get away clear if he wants but instead he tells the taxi to stop. Muriel climbs in, radiant with love.

The curtain falls.

This is Macon's story, but Muriel is Cinderella.

Exercises

1. Wants List

Make a new Wants List for your characters: this refreshes your mind about character agendas. If, during the making of this list, your hand feels like it wants to write sentences and paragraphs, don't stop it. That desire is your synopsis trying to get out.

2. Writing the ending

Take some time to write out the fate of each major character. Then make sure that your protagonist and antagonist collide at the climax. If you have more than one protagonist, they need to arrive at the climax to receive – or to participate in – their separate resolutions.

3. Rough draft – Act One synopsis

When you write Act One, focus on character connections like blood and money, and make sure you get all the main characters into your story. Write about the objects of desire: what the characters want, what they will kill for, what they will die for.

4. Rough draft – Act Two synopsis

When you write Act Two, focus on the midpoint of the novel – the point of no return – and the end of the act, where the protagonist crosses the threshold into Act Three. If you have introduced all your main characters, as suggested above, then Act Two is a working-out of agendas.

Because Act Two is complicated, you would be smart to use little triangle sketches to keep track of the sexual triads. Here is a short list of stories built with one or more sexual triads:

Maxine + Gogol + Moushimi (*The Namesake*)
Gogol + Moushimi + Frenchman (*The Namesake*)
Jane + Rochester + Bertha (*Jane Eyre*)
Gatsby + Daisy + Tom (*The Great Gatsby*)
Oedipus + Mum + Dad (*Oedipus Rex*)
Almasy + Katharine + Geoffrey (*The English Patient*)
Charles + Emma + Leon/Rodolphe (*Madame Bovary*)
Sammy + Rosa + Joe (*The Amazing Adventures of Kavalier and Clay*)

Tracy + Sammy + Rosa (*The Amazing Adventures of Kavalier and Clay*)

5. Rough draft – Act Three synopsis

When you write Act Three, focus on the end – the last page, the final image – and then focus on the climax, the point of resolution. A smart writer brings in a sacred object at or near the climax. Gogol Ganguli has his book of short stories. Santiago the shepherd boy has the treasure buried under the ruined chapel. Joe Kavalier has the coffin that got him out of Prague in 1935. Objects in Act Three help the writer to control time. The bullet in *White Teeth* reaches all the way back from the year 2000 to the year 1857; from London to India.

6. Startlines

From their workshops on writing, Jack Remick and Robert J Ray have developed a set of startlines to get the stalled writer from the opening page to the climax. Use these startlines with joy in your heart:

I am writing a story about…
Act One opens when…
Act One ends when…
Act Two opens in a scene called…
At the middle of my story, my protagonist…
Act Two ends when…
Act Three opens when…
My story climaxes in a scene called…
My story ends with this final image…

The novel-in-progress: *Trophy Wives*

Earlier – using the startline ,'This is a story about…' – the writer of our novel-in-progress combined back story with an overview. This writing, which contained character connection, point-of-view shifts, and action (rituals of the working world, sibling rivalry, mate selection, adultery, takeover schemes, secret plots), prepared the ground for developing a more detailed working synopsis. Like the rest of us, the writer of *Trophy Wives* uses the working synopsis for two purposes: 1) to gather up the scattered pieces of the plot; and 2) to explore the story as it keeps shifting ground.

Working synopsis

This is a story about power. Paul Watson inherits control of Phoenix Investments when his father dies. He and his sister Barbara keep the company growing. Barbara is the nuts and bolts – she runs the operations. Paul has the vision.

Paul is married to Veronica, a poor girl who has no power. She was born an illegitimate child of a cowboy and a Blackfoot Indian woman. Her mother named her for '40s *film noir* star Veronica Lake. Veronica meets Paul on the day his father dies. After a stormy courtship, Paul marries Veronica. Paul's mother is embarrassed by his dark-haired, dark-skinned wife. She is a stain on the family's social status. Veronica signs a prenuptial agreement taking away all her rights.

Veronica and Paul are married and move into Paul's parents' house when his mother moves out to Napa. While Veronica lives in two worlds – her old academic world and her new world of riches and wealth – Paul wanders. He's a womaniser, and Veronica knows it. Veronica is smart. She is also deep in despair. Her world is thrown into turmoil.

When Paul's mistress, an employee of Phoenix Investments, is found murdered in her apartment, Paul is the prime suspect.

Act One

Act One opens at Veronica's mother-in-law's funeral. The funeral takes place at Veronica and Paul's home on Nob Hill. The guests come to pay their respects, but Paul spends the day in his den – his father's old den. At the funeral, Barbara catches Paul with his mistress, Ashleigh Bennett. Barbara sees her opportunity to wrest control of the company from Paul. Act One ends at Ashleigh Bennett's place. The passion driving their affair leads Ashleigh to press Paul to leave his wife. Ashleigh goes too far when she threatens to rat Paul out to the SEC about the illegal after-hours trading that's making money for both of them. When she threatens to expose him, Paul slaps Ashleigh, cutting her face with his father's Breitling watch. As Paul walks out of the building, leaving Ashleigh crying, he passes Gwyn Perez. He walks right by her and climbs into his vehicle. Gwyn and Ashleigh are on-again, off-again lovers from Scripps College. Gwyn finds Ashleigh sobbing. Ashleigh is ashamed of her affair with Paul, but Gwyn tries to help. Gwyn confesses her love, and Ashleigh throws her out, telling her never to come back.

Gwyn leaves and heads to the country club for a tennis lesson.

The following morning, Detective Anderson arrives at the Watson house to question Paul. Detective Anderson tells Paul that Ashleigh

Bennett was murdered last night, and Paul was the last one to see her alive.

Act Two

Act Two opens when Paul and his lawyer, Snyder, arrive at the police station to answer questions about the murder of Ashleigh Bennett. Detective Anderson knows about the affair, and he knows they argued: a neighbour admitted hearing loud, angry voices. Detective Anderson also sees scratches on Paul's arms and blood on his watch. When the questioning gets intense, Snyder calls a halt to the interview.

A reporter outside the police station snaps pictures of Paul and shouts questions. Snyder and Paul slip into the Maybach and drive away, but Paul is worried. Barbara calls Paul and demands that he come to the office for an emergency meeting. Paul refuses and heads home to talk with Veronica. Veronica sits on the veranda overlooking the tennis courts. She and Gwyn share a glass of wine.

Paul arrives home. Veronica wastes no time in berating him for his affair and for ruining her life. He begs for Veronica's help. He needs her to support him. He swears his innocence: on his mother's grave, he's innocent. Veronica sees her chance to end the imprisonment. She wants out.

Act Two ends when Paul is exonerated from murder charges. Botched evidence-gathering and Veronica's concrete alibi for Paul leave him feeling smug and untouchable. Gwyn walks in on Paul and Veronica arguing. Paul promised Veronica the moon for her help with an alibi, and now he won't deliver. She can leave him, fine – but she'll get nothing.

Act Three

My story climaxes in a double-murder scene. Gwyn, defending her new lover, lunges at Paul. He draws his father's Heckler and Koch 9 mm. The gun goes off, killing Gwyn. Detective Anderson crashes through the front door after hearing the gunfire. He's at the house on Nob Hill to return Paul's father's watch. He sees Gwyn's dead body, Veronica hunched in the corner crying, Paul behind the desk with the gun still pointed at Gwyn. Detective Anderson draws his .45 Glock and warns Paul, but Paul just stands still. Detective Anderson fires and kills Paul.

Paul is arrogant about his freedom. He ignores his deal with Veronica and casts her out into the cold. When Gwyn goes into a fit of jealousy and attacks Paul, he kills her. Detective Anderson arrives just in time to protect Veronica and kill Paul. His timing is planned.

In the end, he helps Barbara seize control of the company; he helps her seize power, and Veronica and Barbara reap the rewards.

My story ends with Veronica and Barbara sitting in Barbara's office at Phoenix Investments. Barbara makes Veronica an offer for Paul's shares earned as the Chairman and CEO. The shares he earned while Paul and Veronica were married are the only assets not covered by the prenuptial agreement. Veronica reminds Barbara about the house. Because Paul and Barbara's mother died while Veronica and Paul were married, Paul inherited the house – so the house now belongs to Veronica. Barbara agrees. Veronica signs documents and Barbara arranges for the transfer of funds.

As Veronica walks out, Barbara accompanies her down in the lift. The silver Maybach waits out in front of the building. Veronica walks by the car, but Barbara stops at the back door. The door opens, and Detective Anderson offers Barbara a hand into the car.

Veronica drives home to Nob Hill. As she cruises up the long stone drive, workmen scramble around the estate. Painters work on the exterior, craftsman walk out the front door, gardeners plant new roses.

My story ends with the final image of Veronica walking into her house and remaking her home. She has money. She has independence. She has power.

The goal of the first working synopsis is *writing* your way to the end. Not thinking your way to the end, not talking your way to the end, but writing a synopsis out in three acts, using the startlines that pull you forwards through the key scenes.

It is great fun to chat about writing, books, writers, the writing life, style and character, plot and theme. But if you are a writer, you must stop thinking and stop talking and do the work of writing because writing is the source of fun and power and the glory of creating a storytelling structure with your words.

The trick of creating a big piece of writing – novel, screenplay, memoir, epic poem, stage play – is to start small. Build the pieces, then fit them together. For example, before you wrote this synopsis – perhaps the longest piece of writing you have done so far – you started with a basic plot diagram and then gained momentum by writing down the page; short lines, truncated prose, not fussing with paragraphs. After the first plotting exercises, you did a brief character sketch, followed by back story, dream, and wardrobe. As you added significant detail, your characters changed from stick-figures into people with problems and lusts. By doing the character work for Veronica Watson, the protagonist of *Trophy Wives*, the writer was able to write a solid First Encounter scene. Veronica's First Encounter with Paul Watson follows a very simple pattern of problem and solution, which is one way of moving through the story. Veronica's problem is poverty. The apparent solution is marrying Paul Watson, a rich man. But Paul, like Mr Rochester in *Jane Eyre*, is a man with secrets. Paul is a womaniser who has affairs; and he is a white-collar thief. So the apparent solution turns into an ugly problem which will drive Veronica to make some tough decisions about her life – and when you write your scenario, you can use the same problem-solution structure to boost your writing into overview:

- Problem: Veronica is poor
- Apparent Solution: Veronica marries a rich man
- Hidden Problem: Rich man is a monster
- Tough Solution: Kill the monster? Tame the monster?

As you write your synopsis, you'll be doing two things at once. First, you'll be gathering the pieces of the story – plot, character, places, objects, dialogue, action – that you have already written into scenes, turning them into a narrative overview that works like snapshots that freeze your story as it is on Weekend 20. If you had written your synopsis during Weekend 10, it would look different. If you write another synopsis during Weekend 30, it will look different again.

Second, at the same time that you freeze the story, you will be making new discoveries that will change the shape of the plot as you know it today. Characters grow in stature and, while you don't let them take over, you can still step aside and let them take action that reveals character. In *Trophy Wives*, for example, there are two characters – Barbara and Gwyn – who have grown in importance. Barbara Watson, Paul's sister, enters the story early, brushing past Veronica in the Nob Hill house on her way to Paul's study, where she encounters Ashleigh Bennett just leaving. Barbara lurks in the shadows, scheming with the police detective, Anderson, to wrest the company away from Paul. She is a good character who needs more work.

The other character who needs more work is Gwyn, an estate agent who seems, at this point, to be bisexual, and who stays in the story long enough to die at the climax. As Gwyn grows larger, she will demand her own back story, which will stop the forward momentum as the writer takes a dive into her past. What happened to Gwyn before page 1 that makes her act the way she does? Because this is a rough draft, Gwyn and Barbara may operate from the shadows until the rough draft is done – three acts and a climax – on Weekend 49.

Time-management is the problem of novel-writing. Do you keep going? Or do you stop to fix a hole in the road? There is no easy answer. If you stop, you might learn something valuable about one of your characters. If you keep going, pushing ahead, writing your way to the end, you will feel the heat increase as you reach Act Three (here the novel heats up), and you'll know even more about your characters if you keep writing. An action, a smell, a sound, a gesture, a dialogue line – and the insight blossoms in your brain. And you get still more insights in Act Three.

The best reason for stopping is back story. What's in the back story of *Trophy Wives* that makes Barbara want to take the company away from Paul? It's not just bad management and cooking the books; it's something deeper, probably rooted in their childhood. Why docs Gwyn throw herself at Ashleigh? At Paul? At Veronica? And remember this: when the back story coughs up trauma that delivers a motive that creates an agenda, then you have to write enough scenes to give the character room to work, because this is could be the character who makes you famous.

When a character grows, you're looking at another subplot. What do Gwyn and Barbara do offstage? When we see Mr Rochester riding off on his horse, we know he's escaping Thornfield. He could be headed to the fleshpots of London or Paris. Or he could be trotting off to a week-long party on one of the neighbouring manor houses, where he will drink wine and flirt with beautiful Blanche. When he returns, we feel Jane's stiff-lipped jealousy as she competes with the women who lurk in the shadows of Mr Rochester's subplot. What happens when Barbara drives off? What happens when Gwyn enters a doorway and vanishes into Ashleigh's apartment?

When you finish your synopsis, let it sit for a couple of days before reading it over. When you read, make lists – character, place, object, and scene – and then ask yourself which of the characters merit a subplot.

You don't have time to develop a bunch of subplots while you're writing the rough draft because your main job is plotting the novel. Subplots, however, are the main focus when you rewrite, and – a word of warning here – you should not start rewriting until you have a manuscript of 200–300 pages. Rewriting shakes the bones of the manuscript.

With your synopsis done, it's time to get serious about scene and scene-sequence.

part 5 Weekends 21–28:

Writing Scenes and Building the Scene-Sequence

The novelist in our time competes with visual media. Competition is fierce between the word and the image, the page and the screen. In the 19th century, the novel with its bound pages brought theatre into the living room. In our time, however, a black cable brings the world-on-a-screen into the living room. Instead of finding our entertainment in books, we rent a DVD at the corner video store or we hit the Pay Per View button on the TV remote. 'Movies' are here to stay, and if you are a budding weekend novelist, you can use your movie-watching to hone your storytelling craft, because screenwriters and novelists draw from the same well: character, dialogue, action, object, structure, dramatic conflict, and scene.

If you grew up watching *Sesame Street* on TV, then you grew up watching scenes. A character delivers a monologue or sings a song. Along comes a second character. The two characters engage in a dialogue, and the dialogue connects them. Along comes a third character – an intruder – who breaks in, changing the dynamics. The setting changes, and the characters are in another place. In the simplest language, there has been a scene-change on your screen. As a viewer, you are experiencing the raw power of using scenes for storytelling. By shifting the place, the setting of a scene, you can shift the actors forwards or backwards in time; you can shift the geography from one room to another, one city to another, one country to another, one universe to another. By writing in scenes, you can make use of all those interior journeys – dreams, visions, out-of-body experiences, delusions – that give your writing added depth and dimension. The great thing is, once you start using scenes instead of those large prose passages of narration and exposition, you'll not only be a better writer (a scene has its own built-in time limit), but you will also be writing novels that are cleaner, sharper, and, yes, more 'movie-like'.

So what is a scene? A scene is a single action or a series of connected actions taking place in a single setting in a finite time-period. If you alter the setting, from the living room to the back yard, consider that a scene-change. If you change the time, from the present to the past, letting your character fall backwards into a flashback, consider that a scene-change. If you're careful about changing scenes, you'll bring the reader along to the next scene with a new stage set-up – what film people do with an establishing shot. You've probably seen establishing shots in film scripts. They're written in capitals:

EXT: THE PATIO – NIGHT

and they tell the director, the actors, the camera operator and the crew which scene this is so that the camera can inform the viewer. One of the most common shots is the cityscape. In Chicago, for example, you see the Sears Tower, the Wrigley Building, the Navy Pier. In New York, you see the Empire State Building, the Chrysler Building, the Brooklyn Bridge. In Paris, you see the Eiffel Tower or the Arc de Triomphe. In London, you see Trafalgar Square with Nelson's column and the lions. In Seattle, you see the Space Needle, Pike Place Market, the ferry terminals.

As filmgoers, we're accustomed to establishing shots that take only a few seconds onscreen. Behind those few seconds, however, might be days of set-preparation and lots of film shot to get the right lighting, the right angle. In a novel, the establishing shot is made with word-pictures. As readers with attention spans truncated by watching films, we might read over these passages of description because we're in a hurry to see what happens first and what happens next. But as writers, our role is reversed. We have an obligation to let the reader know the setting for each scene, the time, who's onstage, what they're doing, and who's coming on. One of the tricks of novel-writing is to make these stage set-ups do double the work. Not only do you set the stage, you also establish a mood with your descriptive detail.

Exploring reasons to write scenes

Scenes are the elements of drama. You create scenes to fill a novel and tell a story: a sequence of connecting events, flashes on a timeline. In those scenes, characters act and create drama, and move your plot forwards.

There is surface action in scenes: Character A says to Character B, 'I'm going to kill you,' and she shoots Character B. Surface action is straightforward. There is also action beneath the surface – action that's not seen, but felt; subtext. Subtext is tension between what is said and what the character does: Character A says to Character B, 'What a lovely day it is,' while sizing up the firing distance between her and her cheating lover. It's called subtext because it's located a layer under the text.

You write scenes because they impose a structure that helps you to write with efficiency. A story's structure has a beginning, a middle and an end. An alarming number of scenes begin with the sound of an alarm clock going off. Scores of scenes end with the closing of a door. Think about how to begin and end your scenes. If you rely on familiar ways to open and close scenes, concentrate on eccentric details. If you open and close scenes with unique actions, include familiar details to help your reader stay connected to your story.

Determining the end of a scene can be difficult. If you're not sure whether your scene is over, ask a friend to read the scene out loud. Your ear will tell you if all the action is wrapped up. If your ear doesn't, your friend will.

Establishing rhythm in your novel

Rhythm is patterned alternation. It's as simple as your heart beating, two feet marching, the one-two motion of the tides. If you're in tune with the cosmos, you notice the patterned alternation of night and day, night and day, where the ones and twos are spaced further apart to make a larger rhythm. As you expand time, stretching days into weeks, you tap into the rhythm of the year – the patterned flow of spring, summer, autumn, winter – with all its inherent symbolism. Spring suggests rebirth after the graveyard of winter; summer suggests the heat of life before the colourful death of autumn. To sense the rhythm of the seasons, it helps to step back. Then you see, on a wide canvas, the slow one-two of spring rolling into summer. You see the faster one-two of a cold morning in June that feels so crisp you expect to see autumn leaves falling. Rhythm is there. We don't think about it. But when someone says, 'Life is a fast-track movement from womb to tomb,' squeezing 60 or 70 years into a single sentence, we sense that one-two movement (one: womb; two: tomb) which is enhanced here by rhyme.

How do you establish the rhythms of your novel? At the largest level is structure, a movement of large actions through key scenes which rise to a high point which we call the climax. To begin, open and close your novel with key scenes that echo one another. In *The Art of Fiction*, John Gardner compares the overall structure of a novel to a symphony, with the end of the work echoing the key images introduced at the beginning. In Chapter 1 of *The Great Gatsby*, narrator Nick Carraway sees his neighbour, Gatsby, stretching out his arms – a hieratic gesture loaded with worship – towards the green light at the end of Daisy Buchanan's dock in East Egg. As the book closes, with Gatsby dead and buried, Nick suggests in a passage of exposition that the green light symbolised Gatsby's innocent belief in the future.

By repeating the green-light image, Fitzgerald tightens the structure of his novel, framing the scenes that tell Gatsby's story. As you discovered in the plotting sections of this book, strong scenes control turning points in your manuscript, the twists and hot spots and pinnacles of power in your prose that keep the storyline moving. Cooler, calmer scenes deepen character and function as transitional links between the strong scenes that are packed with power. Establish the rhythms of your novel by alternating strong, active scenes with weaker scenes to produce a rhythm in words: strong movements, crammed with power and symbolic thrust, alternating with weaker movements that are subtler, smoother, and sometimes sweeter. As we'll discover in the next eight weekends, a scene has its own rhythm. Rhythm inside the scene comes when you alternate dialogue with action, action with description. On an even smaller scale, you can also develop rhythm in a scene by alternating speakers in a dialogue:

Voice A: The police were here.
Voice B: Was it the police who messed up my study?

If Character B doesn't answer, and if Character A keeps talking, the rhythm changes. Now you're writing not a dialogue, but a monologue.

In fiction, the simplest rhythm is the one-two. If you have an action, you follow it with a reaction. If Voice A speaks, Voice B responds. If your character looks at something, show the reader what she sees; novice writers tend to leave it hanging, often like this: 'Maria scanned the chalkboard. She thought of yesterday with Brick, watching him eat. She wondered where…' The rhythm is gone, lost in a flashback to yesterday, and with it the chance to echo the larger structures of your novel. So on the rewrite, you try again:

Maria scanned the blackboard. Black Bean Soup, Cornbread, Grandma's Rhubarb Pie. Yum. She was starved.
'What looks good, Mum?'
'Nothing.'

When you show the reader what the character sees, actually writing down the detail, you pick up the stitch that you could have dropped. You don't know how important a single detail can be until you write it into your scenes. Until you write Mum's dialogue line, 'Nothing,' you don't know what a lousy mood she's in. You could tell the reader in an explanatory line, something like this: 'Maria's mum was in a really bad mood today, she thought, before she thought about Brick.' But it is much more efficient to reveal it in dramatic dialogue, and not break your one-two rhythm. As Mum speaks, Maria

148

gets a problem. And when Maria gets a problem, she must make a choice, must take action. Action and reaction propel the scene.

A novel's rhythm is determined by the choices the writer makes when constructing individual scenes and when arranging those specific scenes to tell a story. If you keep practising, you will write your novel as a series of rhythms (word, sentence, scene, scene-sequence, chapter) that echo each other at different levels of the work. Rhythm begins with sentences, but don't let that make you uptight when you write. When you write a sentence in writing practice, you let the rhythm happen. If it doesn't, no problem; you can always rewrite later, after you've pulled back for a look at the overall structure.

To write a novel, you must see structure: the arrangement of parts. The parts of a novel are character, place, resource-base, object, plot, subplot, scene, description, narration, exposition, dialogue, texture, and subtext. If you thumb through a novel, you see a structure of chapters. A chapter can be one page or 100 pages. A chapter can be all narration; narration and dialogue; all dialogue; dialogue and exposition (in fiction writing, exposition means stopping the story to explain the story); or all exposition, the author nattering on. A chapter can be one scene or many scenes strung together.

Here is the first lesson on structure: the chapter has no structural integrity. It's too floppy, too loose, too expandable. Although the chapter is the visible structure – the unit or organisation that readers see on the page – the chapter itself has no dramatic unity. To build a novel, you must punch through the thin veneer of that chapter structure and discover what lies beneath. You must grapple with the invisible.

Smart writers like Robert B Parker (*Spenser for Hire*) and Raymond Chandler (*The Big Sleep*) use one scene to make one chapter. Other smart writers like Anita Shreve (*Fortune's Rocks, The Pilot's Wife*) use three or more scenes to make one chapter. Read good writers. Study their technique. Use them as models for your scenework.

Before you can use scenes to build chapters, you must learn to love scenes. Love of scenes in our time begins with feature films and ends with TV, and that's where you go for a quick education in scenes. Here's how: watch an hour-long TV drama and time each story-segment. A story-segment is the stuff in between the commercials – character, plot, subplot, setting, dialogue, story – which runs before your eyes as a sequence of scenes. The definition of a scene is a single action or a series of connected actions taking place in a single setting in a finite period of time. A scene on TV can be ten seconds or three minutes or any amount of time in between. When the setting shifts from a glittery lift to a dimly lit car park, you know you're watching a new scene. Location, location, location.

If *you're* smart, you will tape a couple of shows – the hour-long dramas like *ER* and *NYPD Blue* and *Law and Order* give you a good return on your time investment – and make a List of Scenes containing the following information: scene name, setting, characters, action, dialogue. The List of Scenes, in turn, will provide you with a skeleton for story. The List of Scenes from TV or a feature film will shine a bright light on the structure of your novel.

As you study your tape, you should time each story-segment as you try to feel the rhythm of drama. At the end of an hour, you'll have six segments and five commercial breaks. The first segment is the Fish Hook. The last segment is the Link, shot like a harpoon into the future, to grab your attention for the next episode. The four segments in between are four acts. To see structure, draw segments and commercials as a diagram, using a line that shows the rising action inherent in all dramatic structures (see Figure 12).

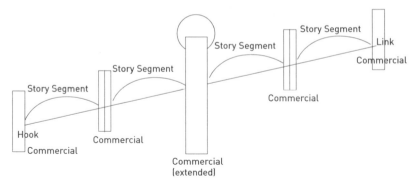

FIGURE 12: COMMERICAL BREAKS AND STRUCTURE IN TELEVISION DRAMAS

If you watch network television, it should come as no surprise that story content is squeezed in between commercial breaks. In most television dramas, the structure looks like this:

Prologue: a hook to grab the audience
Commercial Break
Act One: characters with a problem
Commercial Break
Act Two: problem gets worse

Commercial Break: this is the midpoint of the story; no going back
Act Three: obstacles to the solution gather
Commercial Break
Act Four: action rises to a climax
Commercial Break
Trailer: the hook is set for next week

Noting key scenes on your TV screen

The commercial breaks on your TV screen coincide with the key scenes in a dramatic structure that has lasted for 24 centuries. Old Aristotle should be happy. If you have seen this structure before, you should also be happy. And keep working. If you have not seen this structure before, take heart. Flick on your TV. Watch an hour-long drama. Deploy your trusty timer and time the scenes. When you find a scene that runs three minutes or more, study that scene.

It is time to do some writing. Your characters are ready. They're dressed, expectant, developed. They wait offstage, ready to drop into a scene you create. Your characters have direction, hidden vulnerabilities; they have motivation. Like you, they dream. They're human. They need a place to work out their agendas.

They need scenes.

And scenes work best in a sequence.

Weekends 21–23:
Building scenes and the scene-sequence

You're beginning the 21st week of writing on your novel. You've worked hard. You have loads to show for the hard work. On your hard drive, you have a hundred pages of prose, lists, grids, graphics that show the architecture of your novel. On your shelves sit notebooks bristling with material. You have lists and diagrams and charts. You have a plot, roles for your characters, wardrobes, agendas. You know the climax. You have written sections of your rough draft. You have written scenes and made scene-lists. Now it's time to learn about scene-sequence.

The scene-sequence is a series of three or more connected scenes. Your scenes can connect in time: Scene 1 is early morning; Scene 2 is mid-morning; and Scene 3 climaxes the sequence at high noon. Your scene-sequence can also be connected by characters. In Scene 1, Character A meets Character B; in Scene 2, Characters A and B meet Character C for a drink; in Scene 3, Characters A and C ditch Character B, then they go on to Scene 4, where they hook up with Characters D and E.

In a mystery novel, the detective interviews witnesses and follows clues that lead to suspects who need to be interrogated, because they can lead him or her to the thief or killer. A workable scene-sequence in a mystery might alternate these kinds of scenes – for example, witness interview 1, witness interview 2, clue A, witness interview 3, clue B, suspect interrogation, clue C, sleuth gets beaten up, sleuth to hospital, cops enter.

Scene-sequences give the writer control over a specific span of the novel. You can, for example, use a scene-sequence to extend the action past page 1, and you can use another scene-sequence to build a ramp up to the climax. The easiest scene-sequence starts with a First Encounter scene (we'll study the First Encounter in the next chapter) that develops into a torrid tale of love.

Constructing a scene-sequence

The scene-sequence is a linear construct made by hooking one scene to the next. The scene-sequence has its own logic. This logic comes from the cause-and-effect sequence that we experience in real life. For example, let's say you are out hunting for a connection: someone to talk to, someone to love. The time is night. You have arrived at a place where you might meet someone. Even though you are with friends, you are feeling lonely. Your parents have watched you grow up, and now they are watching you choose a mate. So far, you have not found the Right One. You say you are not looking, not hunting, but your eyes scan the room. You reject several possibles. Your basis of rejection is automatic, but if you have read your Darwin, you know that you are using a three-part measuring device:

- good genes
- good resource-base
- good behaviour

Let's break that down. Good genes translate as symmetry – good shape, good proportion, not too fat, not too thin, pretty for girls, handsome for boys, curves for girls, muscles for boys, good dancer, obvious fertility, no deformities – that will be transported to the next generation. Even though you are not thinking of marriage, the power of coupling controls your search.

Good resource-base means money. Money is represented in our time by objects: cars, clothing, jewellery, the big house on the hill, the family heirlooms. Dialogue is helpful here. Small talk, like where your Target Mate went on summer vacation. Maybe the family has a place on Martha's Vineyard. It's been in the family for ages. There's the smell of money. Or maybe the family name adorns a well-known business firm. Or perhaps one of your friends touches your arm, says: 'Have you seen where he/she lives?' And then that same friend drops the address. Only it's not a number; it's a well-known neighbourhood, dripping with acreage, big fences, huge houses, mansions.

Good behaviour is an immediate measure, a green light or a red light for your choice of a mate. Is the Target Mate too loud? Too drunk? Too forceful? Not forceful enough? Does he/she talk dirty? In the old days, in the time of Doris Day, a female on the prowl could reject a male for using foul language. In the old days, foul language used to be called 'language of the locker room', a hangout for men only. In our time, in the Age of Screens, pretty starlets with the faces of angels use four-letter words that writers are forbidden to use in books.

Good behaviour, associated with dialogue and conversation, shifts gears with the times. And that's the way you define your times – by describing behaviour that attracts, and behaviour that repels. Green light, red light. If, for example, your character arrives at a sweaty disco joint, and there is this person doing a sexy dance, there is a chance for some clever writing about behaviour. Is your character a dancer? Or an observer of the dance? Does your character wait for a chance to dance with the Target Mate? Or does the character turn his or her back on overt behaviour? Is your character a drunk? A drug addict? Does your character seek another addict? A denizen of the Underworld, where coins rattle in slot machines, where the casinos never close.

That's what the author of *Leaving Las Vegas* did. Two underworld characters – one drunk and one prostitute – meet for the first time in the city that never sleeps. From that First Encounter, a love story grew. And you can use the same structure (with modifications for your story) as you build your novel. In this book, you have seen the power of down-the-page writing; how it follows a sequence that moves from moment to moment, room to room, scene to scene. The scenes that follow the First Encounter run in a sequence too. You can use as much of the sequence as you like. Here's a quick list of scenes and ritual actions to choose from:

- First Encounter: A meets B. They do their measuring. The subliminal yardstick: good genes, good resources, good behaviour. There is dialogue, not much touching.
- First Sighting: the first glimpse following the more formal first encounter. It could be passing on the street, seeing the Target through a door, a window. Writer, use that imagination. Load with significant detail to make judgements. Looks better in the light. Great walk. Forceful for males. Sassy for females. Use First Sighting to develop your point-of-view control.
- First Words: the first words following the first encounter. 'Hello.' 'Oh, hello.' 'Didn't we meet at the Bone Crusher?' 'Oh, you're the friend of Q.' 'That would be me.' Use First Words to practise writing dialogue.
- First Touch: the first touch (a sense perception) following the first encounter. Target falls. 'Here, let me take your arm.' Target falls. Asks for help that involves touching. 'Here, grab my arm.' Use First Touch as a strength test, an intimacy test. Electricity flows, bringing heat to face, neck, ears, elsewhere. First Touch is a good place to arrange a First Date.

- First Date: a form of commitment. Two incipient lovers willing to spend time to get to know the Target Mate. First Date is a good place for a full scene or even a scene-sequence. Use the TWN checklist: Time, Place, Ritual, Object, Dialogue.
- First Kiss: this is a big deal. How do those lips taste? What smells usher forth from the mouth? Is it tongue time? What's happening in the Pelvic Arena? First Kiss is a good place to write one long sentence with no punctuation no full stops no commas no quotation marks no dashes just one long breathless kiss-holder sentence while the rapture builds. First Kiss is a test. Another measuring device. Does your Protag want to kiss those lips again? How many times? Once? Twice? A thousand times? A lifetime? An interesting exercise (see Exercises) is Last Kiss.
- First Foreplay: follows First Kiss. Great time for a scene here. Use the TWN checklist: Time, Place, Ritual, Objects (add body parts), Dialogue.
- First Sex: this does not have to follow foreplay in time. Use your judgement here. What would your lovers do? Delaying the first-sex-scene is handy for building suspense. When you write the scene, use the TWN checklist and run another long sentence – and be sure to have fun. Sex in fiction is comic.
- First Fight: this is a lovely scene in the sequence because it brings conflict to the surface. First Fight, no matter when it takes place in your story, demands a scene and the TWN checklist.
- First Making Up: this could be two minutes after, the morning after, two weeks after, 20 years after. Another chance to play with suspense.
- First Proposal: First Proposal is the big step towards marriage, the coupling bond, making a family, getting in line with Society. Check your favourite novels and films for placement. In *As Good As It Gets* (a 1997 romantic comedy that won Oscars for Jack Nicholson and Helen Hunt), there was a promise of a proposal as the lovers entered a bakery at three in the morning. The audience wanted a proposal of marriage. But there was so much work to do, so much for the female to teach the male, that the proposal would have to come in *As Good As It Gets: The Marriage*. For a nice suspenseful proposal, see the midpoint of *Jane Eyre*.
- First Engagement: follows First Proposal and introduces its own scene-sequence. Time is important here. Do the lovers drive to Las Vegas, get married at midnight? Drive to Mexico, get stopped at the border? Drive to a motel for the joys of First Sex? Does the time spin out while the groom tests his male powers with old

girlfriends? While the bride extricates herself from a sticky love affair? While the bride's mother builds a monster guest-list? Lots of good stuff here.

- First Wedding: if you have a choice between writing a wedding and not writing a wedding, go for the wedding. The wedding is a threshold-crossing. From a single entity, the character bonds into a coupled entity. If you know your cultural anthropology, you know that mated couples generate the offspring that keep civilisation chugging along. First Wedding is a good time for conflict if the balance is out in one of the three measuring devices – good genes, good resources, good behaviour. For example, in *Trophy Wives*, our protagonist is a poor girl, an illegitimate child born out of wedlock, a half-breed female whose father deserted when she was a baby. Her Native American blood is written in her genes – dark hair, striking cheekbones, athletic body, brilliant white teeth – but Veronica's good genes do not compensate, in the eyes of the groom's mother and sister, for her lack of good resources. No money, no family, a shoddy pedigree. Lots of conflict here. First Wedding is a dynamite place for an intruder. Remember that wedding-chapel scene in *Jane Eyre* where Richard Mason calls Rochester an incipient bigamist?

- First Wedding Night: follows inexorably from First Wedding. A chance here for some fine writing, as the husband and wife couple for Society. You have a chance to work subtext if you bury some secrets in a subplot: Lover B has an illegitimate child; Lover A has a criminal record. First Wedding Night is also a great place to bring in an intruder. Something like this: the bride and groom are sweaty in bed, doing you know what, when there is a pounding on the door. Not just a gentle tapping, but a loud pounding, as if a giant had a sledgehammer, and there is the sound of wood in splinters, and Lover A grabs under the pillow for her Beretta Nine, and then...

- First Baby: First Baby comes after First Wedding Night, but not always (think of Veronica in *Trophy Wives*), and the key here is how long after the lovers tied the symbolic knot did the baby arrive, screaming and kicking and red-faced, onto the story's stage? One handy plot device is to rethink parentage. What if the groom got hammered, then zapped out on Ecstasy, and what if the bride ran for help, and what if she encountered her father-in-law, and what if the father-in-law took her back to the room where his lout of a son slept, leaving his beautiful bride in her sheer green negligée, and what if they had a drink, and what if the bride cried, and what if her tears led her to... more suspense?

- First Baby Trauma: First Baby Trauma has much power. It shows who cares about the baby and who's faking it. First Baby Trauma for our *Trophy Wives* protagonist was her father deserting the family. No money, no prospects, so what does Mum do? In *Kavalier and Clay*, the trauma comes when Tommy Clay goes to the magic shop to hunt down his real dad.

- First Baby's Sibling: introduces conflict into the family. No spotlight for the first-born. To see this competition in action, check out the birth of the sister in *The Namesake*.

- First Divorce: First Divorce is a traumatic time, especially if your protag is getting rejected. First Divorce opens the door for First Affair, one of the plotting devices for *The Namesake*, where Moushimi, a Bengali bride, initiates contact with a male from her past and starts an affair that blows her marriage apart. In the book, the protag is Gogol Ganguli, a Bengali boy born in America of Bengali parents. His discovery – that a female from his own culture can cheat on him – comes close to stopping his heart from beating, and sends him back to the bosom of mother, sister, what family is left, and a book of short stories, a gift from his dead father. *The Namesake* shows the awesome power of divorce.

- First Encounter with Ms/Mr New Person: a second first encounter does not depend on marriage alone. This is a replacement ritual that is part of the courtship dance, where the protag keeps the mate-search going, a quest for the perfect match, and the quest turns a new corner with each new first encounter. We can see this working in *The Namesake*, where Jhumpa Lahiri uses a series of first encounters to structure Act Two. Let's see how this replacement technique works.

First Encounter (College Dorm): Gogol introduces himself as Nikhil to Kim, the college girl.
First Encounter (Train): Gogol replaces Kim with Ruth.
Rejection: deserted by Ruth, Gogol replaces her with Maxine.
Dad Dies: Mum calls Gogol, the eldest son, to fetch the body back home.
Goodbye Maxine: Dad's death cracks the bond with Maxine; Mum wants Gogol to replace Dad.
First Encounter (Bar): Gogol replaces Maxine with Bridget.
Mum's Iron Fist: Gogol replaces Bridget with Moushimi.
Darwin and Evolutionary Biology: Gogol likes Moushimi's curvy body (good genes) and her resource-base (she's a fellow Bengali),

but lurking in the subtext is…
Treachery: Moushimi has a secret.
Clue to Her Secret: in Paris for a conference, Moushimi shuts poor Gogol out; she smokes, she's hip, he's bored and outclassed – no foothold in her world for the sad-faced protagonist.
Secret Revealed: Moushimi, veteran of many love affairs, replaces Gogol with Dimitri.

This ritual of replacement takes an ironic turn when Gogol the Replacer is himself replaced. Act Two of *The Namesake* stretches out more than a decade – from that college visit when Gogol was 18 to Moushimi's secret affair, when Gogol is 30 – and Lahiri is wise to build her Act Two on a series of first encounters to represent the boy coming of age.

Getting help from other writers

When she wrote *Jane Eyre*, Charlotte Brontë built her Act Two on the love story of Jane and Mr Rochester. If you recall the book, the first ten chapters cover eight years. At the age of ten, Jane is ejected from Ferndean by nasty Aunt Reed – a Wicked Stepmother figure – and sent off to Lowood School, where she witness intimidation, corporal punishment, disease, and the death of her best friend. At the age of 18, Jane answers an advertisement that brings her to Thornfield Hall, where, after time passes, Jane encounters Mr Rochester, an antagonistic man of property. They meet in the dead of winter on an icy causeway. Mr Rochester, like the causeway, is a man of ice and steel. Through the long spring, Rochester thaws. Jane rescues him from a fire set by crazy Bertha Mason Rochester. The fire helps to thaw Rochester and by the time of the summer-house parties, he is taunting Jane with his alleged engagement to a rich and handsome country belle, Miss Blanche Ingram.

As the novel's midpoint approaches, Jane escapes Thornfield to spend a month at the deathbed of Aunt Reed, the Wicked Stepmother. It is high summer when Jane returns to Thornfield; Rochester, after more flirtatious dallying, asks Jane to marry him. The marriage proposal is sealed with a kiss. To explore the power of scene-sequence, let's take a close look at one of the film adaptations of *Jane Eyre* (this one starring William Hurt as Mr R and Charlotte Gainsbourg as Jane). The technique here, developed for screenwriters by Robert J Ray and Jack Remick, is called Minute-by-Minute.

Ritual of courtship in Jane Eyre

Minute 38 –   First Sighting: Jane sees a man thrown from his horse.

Minute 39 –   First Words: the fallen man interrogates Jane.

Minute 40 –   First Touch: Jane helps the man to remount the horse.

Minute 41 –   First Separation: the man rides off, followed by the dog.

Minute 44 –   First False Accusation: the man, aka Mr Rochester, blames Jane for the fall; she 'bewitched' his horse.

Minute 46 –   First Power Trip: Rochester interrogates Jane about the 'furniture' in her brain.

Minute 47 –   First Test: 'Do you consider me handsome?' Jane says, 'No, sir.'

Minute 48 –   First Closeness: Jane sketches Rochester, captures his image for herself.

Minute 50 –   First Revelation: Rochester the paper man calls for the eraser of India rubber.

Minute 54 –   First Fight: Jane confronts Rochester about his treatment of Adele.

Minute 57 –   First Rescue: Jane saves Rochester from Bertha's fire.

Minute 61 –   First Apology: Rochester holds Jane's hand. 'I am in your debt.'

Minute 64 –   First Doubt: seeing herself in the mirror, Jane says, 'You are a fool.'

Minute 66 –   First Competition: seeing the beauteous Blanche Ingram, Jane feels outclassed.

Minute 69 –   First Withdrawal: watching Rochester dance with Blanche, Jane exits.

Minute 70 –   Second Confrontation: Rochester orders Jane back to the party.

Minute 73 –   First Request for Help: Rochester tells Jane to bandage Mason, who is bleeding from a knife wound.

Minute 76 –   First Separation: Jane leaves Rochester, visits Aunt Reed.

Minute 84 –   First Reunion: Rochester welcomes Jane back with his usual sarcasm.

Minute 88 –   First Proposal: Rochester kisses Jane; proposes.

Minute 93 –   First Wedding: lawyer stops wedding.

Minute 96 –   First Ugly Secret: Jane sees Bertha.

Minute 98 –   First Barter: Rochester asks her to stay. Jane exits.

Minute 106 – First Real Hope: at Helen's grave, Jane hears Rochester calling.

Minute 109 – Final Reunion: Jane finds Rochester at Thornfield.

When you watch a film, study the story elements. Minute-by-Minute is a tracking device that helps you to concentrate on the specific details. When Jane leaves Rochester to visit Aunt Reed, she is gone for eight minutes of film time. To Rochester, she is gone for an eternity. He conceals his pain under a mask of sarcasm in minute 84. Four minutes later, Rochester proposes. If you compare the same scene-sequence in the novel, you will see that it takes several pages. Using Minute-by-Minute, you can watch films without wasting time – you'll be working at your novelist's craft. Later on, when you write your rough draft, you should study the architecture of Act Two in *Jane Eyre*, which is much stronger than Act Three. Charlotte Brontë wrote a strong Act Two by using scenes linked to Jane's First Encounter with Mr Rochester.

Plot and subplot in the scene-sequence

Plot runs on the surface, where the actions of the protagonist are visible to the reader. Subplot – *sub* in Latin means 'under, beneath, down below' – runs under the plot. In *Jane Eyre*, for example, Jane has the plot and Mr Rochester, antagonist and master of Thornfield Hall, has Subplot 1. While Jane enters in Chapter 1, the writer delays Mr Rochester's entry until Chapter 12, when his horse skids on the icy causeway, throwing its rider, pinning his leg, giving Jane her chance for First Touch as she rushes to help.

Like most antagonists, Mr Rochester enters the story in a First Encounter scene. Also like most antagonists, Mr Rochester has a secret, buried in his back story, kept hidden in Subplot 1. Like most protagonists, Jane does not know, or cannot even guess, the antagonist's secret: a crazy wife locked in a tower.

Jane Eyre is told in the first person. When we read the novel, we stick tight to Jane. Because we see the antagonist through Jane's eyes, we think her thoughts about him, we feel about him what she feels. Hooked into Jane's point of view, we are limited to what she knows. Until Jane learns the secret, we are kept in the dark. The housekeeper, Mrs Fairfax, knows the secret. So does Grace Poole, the jailer of Bertha – the mad wife. But Jane does not know, and if we flip ahead, fast-forwarding to the wedding chapel where Jane learns Mr Rochester's dastardly secret, we disrupt the fictional dream and lose our willing suspension of disbelief – something that separates great stories from everyday reality.

But when you write a novel, whether it is in the first person like *Jane Eyre* or in third-person multiple like *The English Patient*, you must know more than the reader knows. You must know Subplot 1:

where it starts, where it ends, where it came from. Where it came from means back story, planting seeds in the past, before page 1, making sure the seeds sprout on schedule. Mr. Rochester's ugly secret, for example, is scheduled to sprout near the end of Act Two. The moment of sprouting is an explosion, where Jane's wedding, the sacred ceremony that will give her access to Thornfield, blows up in her face. Like a dagger, the secret buried in the subplot pierces Jane's code of honour, her determined honesty, her heart, her livelihood, her soul. And it happens on schedule because the writer has control of Subplot 1.

The trick to controlling plot and subplot is the scene-sequence. Scene-sequence lets you spin the story while you maintain suspense. Suspense means keeping the protagonist in the dark about the secret. Jane does not know about Bertha until her wedding day. Nick, the protagonist of the film *Body Heat*, does not know about Mattie's husband until after he is seduced by her wiles. Mattie uses her sex appeal – her good genes – to recruit Nick as an amateur hitman.

Exercises

1. Deep breathing

Find a quiet place. Get comfortable. Close your eyes and let your brain roam across the span of your novel. Focus on characters entering the story for the first time. What are they wearing? What are they eating? Driving? Doing? How does each character enter the story? Doorway? Tunnel? Cave? Beamed down? Taking a bath? Lost in the forest?

2. Firsts and Lasts

Firsts and Lasts work like bookends – my first birthday party, my last birthday party; my first funeral, my last funeral – and rituals contain emotion. Kick your protagonist loose by writing about Firsts and Lasts. Use the pronouns he/she and also the name of your protagonist. Set your timer. Write for two minutes on each of these startlines:

The first time s/he made love...
The first time her/his mother told him/her...
Her/his first day of school...
At her/his last birthday party...
The last time s/he wore...
The last time s/he saw her/his mother...
The last time s/he kissed...

3. First Encounter and Then

First Encounter is a threshold-crossing that opens the door to a series of logical follow-ups that can develop into major scenes that can structure a large section of your novel. Using the list below, select half a dozen scenes from the First Encounter sequence. Then write three-minute summaries of each scene.

First Encounter
First Sighting
First Words
First Touch
First Date
First Kiss
First Foreplay
First Sex
First Fight
First Reconciliation
First Proposal
First Engagement
First Wedding

Weekends 24–25:
Writing the First Encounter scene

The First Encounter scene is the first meeting of your protagonist and your antagonist. For novelists and screenwriters, the scene is inevitable and mandatory. It must be included, and you should write it early. Take heart: this is your story, written in your personal style, sung in your own voice, and you are free to play the First Encounter tune your own way. Here are some examples:

The season is summer. The place is Louisville, Kentucky, USA. The year is 1918 and a young soldier headed for the Great War meets a maiden wearing white. The soldier calls himself Jay, last name Gatsby. His real name is Jimmy Gatz, and he is a poor boy clawing his way up the economic ladder. The maiden in white is named Daisy Fay, and she motors around town in a cute white roadster.

Jay and Daisy meet in the back story of *The Great Gatsby*, and we view their meeting through the eyes of Jordan Baker, Daisy's Louisville buddy, as she convinces Nick the Narrator – Nick is Gatsby's neighbour and Daisy's cousin – to act as connector and get them back together, even though Daisy is married to Tom and Gatsby is a bootlegging criminal. Jordan unveils the back story to Nick in the summer of 1924, six years after Daisy meets Gatsby. Because the First Encounter happens to us in real life, we can imagine the Louisville summer heat, love thick in the air, the soldier buttoned up in his dress uniform, the maiden cool in white.

Because the First Encounter scene is so powerful, and so loaded with promise (as you saw earlier, a scene-sequence started by the First Encounter can carry an entire act or a large chunk of the novel), we advise you not to bury it deep in the back story. Don't make the reader imagine that first meeting between the protagonist and antagonist, or between two sworn enemies, or, in a mystery, between the sleuth and the killer. If you do shove it back there, however – if you don't take our advice – you're still in good company. For example, Melville planted the leg-biting scene in Ahab's back story, a perfect example of trauma in the back story driving an agenda in a big novel like *Moby-Dick*. In *Hamlet*, Shakespeare planted the First Encounter between the protagonist, Hamlet, and the antagonist, his deadly, father-killing uncle, in the back story. When the uncle kills the king (Hamlet's father), Hamlet spends five acts on a quest for revenge and the two characters who met in the back story die at the climax.

In *As Good As It Gets* – an Oscar-winning film with a flawless three-act structure – the director, James L Brooks, plants the First Encounter of Jack the writer and Helen the waitress in the back story. They have already met, and the enmity runs deep enough to make them shout in public. Jack wants his eggs. Helen hates serving him. But serving customers is her job, and she has a sick child, and not enough money to pay for first-class health care. Jack has money, so he sends a doctor to her apartment on a house call. At the end of the film, the waitress gives the crazy writer one more chance, as they enter a local bakery to buy bread.

Writing tip: if you must set the First Encounter way back there in the back story before page 1, make sure you pack it full of emotion.

Film-makers know the power of the First Encounter. When William Wyler (*Roman Holiday, The Best Years of Our Lives, Mrs Miniver*) turned *Dodsworth* (a 1929 Sinclair Lewis novel) into a film, he moved the First Encounter between Dodsworth, an automobile tycoon, and the sensitive socialite Mrs Cortright from way back in the rear-end of the novel to a scene nearer the opening of the film. Moving the First Encounter scene shifted the film's emphasis.

Lewis's novel portrays an already disintegrating marriage breaking up between the protagonist and his shallow, youth-crazy wife, with Mrs Cortright sailing in at the last minute like a *deus ex machina* from Greek theatre. (*Deus ex machina*, you will remember, means 'God from the machine', and covers any miraculous rescue at the climax – whether it's a cavalry charge to save the besieged wagon train or the appearance of a larger-than-life figure to rescue the protagonist.) Because Wyler and Howard moved the First Encounter forwards in the film version of *Dodsworth*, we root for the lovers to stay together.

Anthony Minghella did the same thing by moving the First Encounter between Almasy and Katharine Clifton in *The English Patient*. In the book, Katharine enters as an anonymous naked woman who leans out the window of an apartment in Cairo to wet her body with sudden rain. In the film, she enters in Act One.

And, as we will see in the next few pages, Mike Figgis did the same thing with his movie adaptation of the John O'Brien novel

Leaving Las Vegas. He moved the First Encounter from Act Three in the novel to Act One in the film, with a stop-off in Act Two in the script. The script, published in book form, is a must-read for any aspiring weekend novelist.

The First Encounter in *Leaving Las Vegas*

As you can see from the architectural sketch that follows (see Figure 13), taken from a study of *Leaving Las Vegas* in its novel and film incarnations, the first six key scenes - climax, midpoint, opening, closing, curtain one, curtain two - are fixed in place. The First Encounter, however, is movable. Born in Act Three in the novel, the First Encounter moves to Act Two in the script, and then to Act One in the film that grabbed those Oscars. As the scene moves forwards in the structure, the details of the scene - place, time, ritual, objects, dialogue - stay the same. Another good reason to write scenes instead of narration: when you move a scene, the contents stay the same. Try moving a passage of narration, and what happens? You have to work hard, rewriting, to reintegrate the narration. Let's look at the sketch that reveals the architecture of *Leaving Las Vegas*, and then, as a guide for your work, we can examine the contents of the scene.

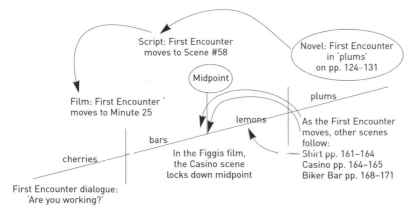

FIGURE 13: MOVING THE FIRST ENCOUNTER SCENE IN *LEAVING LAS VEGAS*

As already mentioned, the novel version of *Leaving Las Vegas* has four chapter titles, all in lowercase letters, that gather together the fruits and symbols from the world of slot machines: Chapter 1 is 'cherries', Chapter two is 'bars', Chapter 3 is 'lemons', and Chapter 4 is 'plums'. Both the novel and the film develop a doomed love story between a drunk and a prostitute. The First Encounter opens Act Three of the novel, in the chapter called 'plums'. This placement compresses the love story, squeezing it into the last 68 pages. If you check out the list below, you will see the love story in compressed form:

Novel Pages	Chapter	Scene	Film Position
121–124	4: plums	Whole Year Inn	Act One
124–131	4: plums	First Encounter	Act One
131–132	4: plums	Al/Gamal Alone	Act Two
132–134	4: plums	Sera Analyses Ben	Act Two
134–135	4: plums	Sera's Wound (back story)	Act Two
138–139	4: plums	Al's Lair	Act Two
139–142	4: plums	Sera Takes Ben Home	Act Two
142–146	4: plums	Getting Acquainted	Act Two
146–148	4: plums	Paying Al Off	Act Two
148–151	4: plums	Ben Moves in With Sera	Act Two
151–153	4: plums	Stripping Away	Act Two
153–155	4: plums	Al Exits	Act Two
155–159	4: plums	Trouble at the Threshold	Act Two
159–160	4: plums	Two Flashbacks	Act Two
161–164	4: plums	The Shirt (Gift-Giving)	Act Two
164–165	4: plums	Casino: Night Out	Act Two
165–168	4: plums	Recapping the Night Out	Act Two
168–171	4: plums	Blood in the Biker Bar	Act Two
171–172	4: plums	Home Again, Bleeding	Act Two
173–174	4: plums	Earrings: Ben to Sera	Act Two
175–176	4: plums	Sera Dresses for Work	Act Three
176–182	4: plums	Desert Motel	Act Three
182–184	4: plums	Sera Feeds Rice to Ben	Act Three
184–186	4: plums	Ben Cheats on Sera	Act Three
186–189	4: plums	Ben Dies; Sera Presides	Act Three

In the novel, Sera's pimp is named Al. In the film, the pimp, played by Julian Sands, is called Yuri. In the film, Yuri exits early in Act Two, freeing Sera to give Ben shelter. More evidence that moving the First Encounter gives the love story time to grow.

Because the film director understood structure, pacing, rhythm, and scene-sequence, he could breathe new life into a dead book by shifting the First Encounter scene from the rear-end of the story to the front-end. What a good lesson for the weekend novelist. You can write the scenes whenever you feel the heat of creation, place them into the structure, and then move them later, when you step back for a look at the structure, preparing for your rewrite.

Let's check the diagram (Figure 13 on page 165). The First Encounter builds with the same pattern as most First Encounters. First there is the setting: night on the Las Vegas Strip. Lover A spots Lover B, and we see Sera from Ben's point of view. The sighting is followed by action, as Lover A exits his car. And action is integrated with dialogue: 'Are you working?' The dialogue introduces a pattern called the Language Lesson, as Lover B says: 'Working? What do you mean, working?' This is tight writing: nine words of dialogue, and one of them gets repeated three times, as Sera asks him, in a defensive tone, to define his terms. Lurking under the subtext is the label of 'working girl', which translates as hooker, whore, or prostitute. Note that Lover A does not say, 'Are you hooking?' That would be too overt, too obvious, too invasive, and Ben is a clever drunk.

So the First Encounter shifts from Act Three in the novel to Act Two in the script, to Scene 58. And then the First Encounter shifts for one last time, to Act One in the film, Minute 25, just in time for the lovers to move to the Whole Life Inn, where the clock on the wall has stopped ticking.

Leaving Las Vegas is a story of thwarted love, and the love cannot get going until the First Encounter takes place.

With the shifting forwards of those scenes from 'plums', the director made room for rituals like gift-giving, which means objects. Sera gives Ben a shirt that is orange – a beautiful, sunny colour – and the orange shirt pulls together the scenes that form the midpoint of the film. The object at the midpoint of the novel is fire, the flames licking up to consume Ben's memorabilia, furniture, photos of his past, etc., as he cleanses himself of the past. As Ben burned his past, Sera killed time waiting for Ben, walking the neon streets of Las Vegas.

The fire burns out and Ben heads for Las Vegas – Act Two in the novel, Act One in the film – leaving a slot for a new object, the orange shirt that Ben wears to the casino on his first real date with Sera. The orange shirt lights up Ben's shadowy, booze-haunted life. In the novel, the shirt was an ugly jungle-camouflage thing. The colours were pink and green.

The lesson of the orange shirt is that the right architecture – by 'right' we mean artistic, efficient, crowd-pleasing – coughs up objects that become symbols. You have to get the architecture right before you hang the pictures. The orange shirt carries several scenes in the novel. It is an emblem of Sera's love for Ben. She wants him to live. He wants to die. But he looks good in the shirt. And the light goes out for Ben in the biker-bar scene in Act Two, when he fights a burly biker and his nose bleeds, ruining the orange shirt.

This strong scene-sequence – from the casino, where Ben goes crazy while wearing the orange shirt; to the biker bar, where he gets blood on the orange shirt; to the shopping centre, where he wears a white shirt; to the desert motel, where he and Sera cling to each other in the pool; to the dressing scene where Sera dresses for work – bridges the long stretch between midpoint (Ben and Sera in the casino) and the Act Two Curtain scene, where Ben betrays Sera by bringing a rival prostitute into her bed. If the director had not moved the First Encounter, it would have been impossible to build that powerful scene-sequence. The novel, published in 1990, died on bookshelves. Five years later, director Mike Figgis turned the novel into an Oscar-winning film. On the screen, the story, pulled from the ash-heap, had a rebirth. Like so many novelists who reject the idea of structure, the writer waited for the writing to get hot, and the writing did not heat up until Act Three.

Don't wait around to write your First Encounter.

Getting help from other writers

The protagonist of *Fortune's Rocks*, by Anita Shreve, is Olympia Biddeford – bright, fulsome, and well-cared-for, a woman ready to mate but trapped in the body of a girl of 15. She stands on the edge of her 16th birthday when she runs into Mr Right. The First Encounter – Olympia is Lover A; John Haskell, MD, Lover B, is 42, married, and has three children – takes place in Olympia's father's summer house, called Fortune's Rocks. There are other characters around to clutter up the scene, but the raw power of love drives Olympia forwards to First Sex, First Secret, and First Separation, which comes about when her parents discover her locked in a sexual embrace with her married lover. The discovery, a turning point in Olympia's life, happens at midpoint. Following the discovery at midpoint, she has a baby; her parents drug her with laudanum, and, while she is unconscious, they steal her baby away.

But true love runs deep in this coming-of-age tale, and Olympia likes what she sees. Haskell is educated. He rescues poor people with medicine, dedication, and skill. He attacks slum housing in his essays. His three children display good genes, which bolsters Olympia's confidence in Haskell's genetic donation to her.

The author develops a series of Firsts that carries her heroine from First Encounter to First Words to First Touch to First Separation to First Sex, all the way to First Baby Delivered deep in Act Two, where Olympia wakes from a morphine sleep to find that her baby has been stolen away. Shreve uses First Encounter to set up the sociobiological sequence of sexual selection, fertilisation of the egg, reproduction, and birth. By removing the baby from its mother, Shreve sets up the second half of her novel: a quest for the stolen child. The quest leads to another First, a nasty public trial where Olympia uses the law and her father's money to get her lost child back. She is the mother, the creator of the egg, the birth-giver. It is her job to nurture the egg to adulthood. The child has been adopted by a working-class couple. Olympia, a product of the affluent class of Bostonian Brahmins, can offer more resources for raising a child. Her lawyer uses the argument of available resources to win his case. The novel takes place at the turn of the century, when working-class children were exploited by the horrors of child labour. In the court-room during the First Trial, the lawyer for Olympia uses labour statistics to forecast a bleak future for the adopted child. If he stays with the working-class parents, argues the lawyer, then he will surely go to the mills. Once in the mills, there is a good chance he will die of some lung disease. If, on the other hand, he goes back to his natural mother, the child will flourish. It is a harsh argument, but Shreve is an incredible writer. Read the book to find out what happens. What does the judge decide? What does Olympia do? How does the story end?

Guidelines for writing your First Encounter scene

First Encounter can be a single scene in which the protagonist meets the antagonist for the first time. (In mystery tales, First Encounter is the first meeting between the sleuth and the killer.) Or it can be the first in a series of scenes: First Sighting, First Touch, First Words, etc. Each First is a threshold-crossing. Threshold-crossing is a ritual of transition, not only from one physical location to another, but also from one psychological state to another. Once your character crosses a threshold, that First is over. A character is a virgin before having sex for the first time. During First Sex, the character moves from a state of innocence to a state of experience. During Second Sex, the character is no longer a virgin. Life is filled with Firsts: First Birthday Party, First Baptism, First Bad Disease. We look back on a fondly remembered First and feel the wonder of innocence. And the transition – from innocence to experience – is the very stuff of fiction.

If you add time to that list of Firsts, it's easy to develop a structure for writing your novel. Time (minutes, hours, days, months, years) helps you create clusters of Firsts. For example, First Sighting and First Words and First Touch could occur in sequence:

Lover A spots Lover B from a distance – First Sighting
They talk – First Words; they make a connection, but one of them has an appointment
They shake hands – First Touch
The lovers part – First Separation

If you add time after First Separation, you create suspense. When will Lovers A and B get together again? In *The Great Gatsby*, the lovers meet in the back story, in Louisville. Jay Gatsby is a young officer who sails off to war, leaving behind Miss Daisy Fay, a golden girl who dresses in white. After First Separation, the writer adds time: from 1918, when Gatsby sails away, to 1924, when he reappears in his West Egg mansion, across the Sound from Daisy, who lives in super-rich East Egg. The six-year hiatus creates fire in the loins of these lovers. The fire gets Lover A (Gatsby) killed.

As you structure your Firsts, don't forget to add real time. First Pregnancy for human gestation is nine months. If you create a small-town setting, you can use this unit of real time to define your characters. Let's say you have a newly married couple and the woman delivers a baby five months after the wedding. Gossipy people in your story – our version of the Greek Chorus – can have some fun guessing the identity of the sperm donor. Once the baby is born, delivered into the world, the Chorus can deliberate on genetics and body parts – that baby, now, he's got ears just like the postman – and then you can spin time and suspicion into more scenes:

The husband comes home from the office. The wife's on the phone with the postman. She hangs up fast. Her face is red. The baby is crying. 'Who was that on the phone?' 'My mother, dear.' The wife meets a Chorus member at the supermarket. A smirk, a smug shrug of the shoulders, a sly comment about eye colour or the curve of the baby's mouth or those large ears, just like the postman's. The wife exits, cold sweat on her face. As she unlocks her car, she sees the Chorus member chatting with the checkout girl.

Add complication: the checkout girl is the girlfriend (or wife) of the postman.

If you juggle the order of events in your scene-sequence, you can dislocate fictional time without destroying the story, because the steps following First Encounter are so well known – so much a recognisable ritual of courtship – that they arrange themselves in the reader's mind. In *The English Patient*, as already mentioned, Lover B appears at midpoint in a classy image: 'A woman in Cairo curves the white length of her body up from the bed and leans out of the window into a rainstorm to allow her nakedness to receive it.' The woman is Katharine Clifton, wife of Geoffrey Clifton. The narrator is Count Almasy, a desert explorer. Katharine is naked. First Sex is over. First Sex implies the Firsts that have come before: First Sighting, First Words, First Touch, and First Separation. Several months pass before the lovers are together at a party in Cairo and Katharine says six words – 'I want you to ravish me' – that will destroy all three members of this sexual triad: husband, wife, lover. With a close reading of the novel, you can track Katharine's words, a form of First Overt Invitation, from the midpoint to the climax, where her husband tries to kill her lover with a yellow aeroplane. Another First here: the climax is marked by First Murder Attempt.

Exercises

1. Architecture of your novel
Study the sketch of your novel and locate the First Encounter scene. Is it in Act One? Act Two? Act Three? Is it buried in the back story? If your First Encounter is in the back story, rethink your plotting. Will you bring the First Encounter into the story in a flashback?

2. Spinning the scene
Before you work on the parts of a scene (time, place, characters, objects, ritual, dialogue), spend half an hour spinning the scene down the page. Let your keys fly. If you write in your notebook, let your biro rip down the page. Sentences are okay. Fragments work. Snippets of dialogue are good.

3. Scene-profile

Take ten minutes to run a scene-profile using these categories:

Novel Title
Scene Name
Location (Acts One, Two, Three)
Time, Place, Temperature
Characters (Protag, Antag, Helper, Antag 2)
Ritual/Action (What are the characters doing?)
Dialogue (What are they talking about?)
Objects (What objects do they carry?)
Symbolism (What symbols carry over from earlier scenes?)
Hook (What scene comes next?)

4. Write the scene

Start writing your scene using this startline: 'This is a scene about...'
Write for a couple of minutes and let your characters talk. When you
write dialogue, you're out of author voice and ready to write the
scene.

Writing tips: Lock down your point of view and write a description of the setting. Use a startline that contains sense perception:
'The time was... The place smelled like...'

From the same point of view, write a description of a second
character: 'Her/his hairdo looked like...'

Pick up your dialogue again with an easy startline: 'What are you
looking at?' or 'Give me some money.'

Using a strong action verb, write some action: 'Her hand dipped
into the urn. I could hear her fingers scratching at something inside.
Her hand came out holding...'

To give your scene a climax, write a long sentence with no punctuation, using connectors like B and, then, so, and then, and so, and
when, but, B and B but then B. Let go and have fun while you write.

The novel-in-progress: *Trophy Wives*

A man drives a vintage Porsche.
The Porsche belonged to his father.
The man wears a Burberry trench coat.
Under the Burberry is a black suit.
Black tie, black dress shoes.
The man needs cigarettes.
The Porsche pulls into a supermarket car park.

The rain pelts down, biting the windshield.
The car park is crowded.
Old cars, beaters, dented pickups.
Not his neighbourhood.
Through the windshield, he spots a running figure.
A female, a girl, black hair, a dark face.
Body thin under the pea-green raincoat.
She carries two shopping bags.
Her foot splashes water.
She keeps going.
Reaches a grey Honda with a broken tail-light.
Drops one bag, leans against the Honda, digging in her handbag.
The man passes by.
Her face in the rain. Wet, shining.
He parks the Porsche in the slot across from the Honda.
Exits the Porsche. Walks towards the Honda.
She's inside, cranking the engine.
The battery is dead.
He waits outside the window.
She looks up, sees him, shakes her head.
He waits until she rolls the window down.
He offers to help.
She looks from him to the Porsche.
Then back at him.
Decision time. She nods okay.
Back at the Porsche, he phones his garage.
'A 1982 Honda,' he says. 'Dove grey, with a broken tail-light.'
'Keys in the ignition,' he says.
'Fix the tail-light. Run a check. Send me the bill.'
The woman sits in the Honda.
Incredible cheekbones, lips ripe, hair black as night.
The man feels the urge.
Walking to the Honda, he grins to himself.
Back at the Honda, he explains about the garage.
'How long?'
'Tomorrow.'
'I have no money,' she says.
'Taken care of,' he says.
'So then I owe you?'
'You look cold,' the man says. 'How about some coffee?'
'Tea,' the woman says. 'I gave up coffee.'
'So did I,' the man says.

'Nerves?' the woman asks.

'I have nerves, yes.'

'There's a café on the way to my place.'

'Let me help with those bags.'

'Something got broken,' the woman says. 'A jar.'

'Smells like mayonnaise,' the man says.

'Damn,' the woman says. 'Damn, damn, damn.'

The First Encounter above takes place in the back story. Because the writer is using the scene to get to know Paul Watson, Paul has the point of view. He is Character A; in this scene, Veronica becomes Character B. The weather is still rainy, a force of nature that pulls them together. Rain gets us wet. Rain drives us to seek a dry place. The old clunker car is an object that shows Veronica's moneyless state. The contrast in vehicles – her ancient car; Paul's vintage Porsche, a legacy from his dead father – shows the gap between their worlds. She is Lower World. He is Upper World. If we use the measuring devices from sociobiology – good genes, good resources, good behaviour – Paul sees a beautiful female (good genes, arty-looking, student of literature), who drives an old clunker (bad resources), who laughs at his jokes and who does not look like a drug addict.

Veronica's plight opens the door to Paul's power. She needs money. He has a job waiting. Her car is dead. He orders up a tow truck. Paul is a womaniser. Veronica looks like prey. Part of the story is their courtship: How long is it? What are the moves? To write this courtship, you would use the First Encounter scene-sequence – the subject of this chapter.

The important thing to remember when you are writing a novel – whether it is your first effort or novel number ten in a successful writing career – is to stay fluid. Each character who enters your story will change the dynamics. Each scene that you spin down the page will make shifts in the structure. This First Encounter, for example, contains the raw power of rich and poor, male and female, loneliness and sadness. These two people belong together in this story. They might love each other forever. They might kill each other. There are other characters with other agendas.

But this First Encounter sets up a love story that turns into something ugly.

It's an excellent way to open the book.

Weekends 26–27:
Writing your climax

The action of your book rises toward a climax – the high point, the culmination, the moment of resolution in your story that explodes while it reveals and releases. This is climax for your reader, a purging of emotion because of your expert handling of theme and symbol and character.

At the climactic high point of *Moby-Dick*, as Captain Ahab plunges-in his harpoon ('Thus,' he grunts in italics, 'I give up the spear'), he realises, and we realise with him, that his harpoon, dripping with vengeance and green with bile, is just one more mosquito bite in the thick white hide of the great white whale. Ahab dies, the crew dies, the good ship Pequod is lost to the deep. Ahab has been aiming at this moment long before he stepped onstage in Act One. To arrive here, at his big moment of revenge, he crushes all obstacles in his path. Then he dies.

Build your novel in an upward-sloping structure, represented on your drawing of Aristotle's Incline as a line of rising action with hot spots and turning points controlling the story. The novel's climax is the highest point and the hottest spot and from here you can look back over your shoulder at the storyline. Writing the climax now helps to anchor your novel and will help your unconscious to track the book.

As a reader, you read to see what happens, to see how the story comes out, to see how the dragon/ogre is dispatched and who winds up with whom in a relationship. As a writer, you sweat to create a climactic moment with your imagination.

Constructing a chain of events

In Tyler's *Accidental Tourist*, the novel's high point caps a chain of events that builds as it gathers momentum. In your writing, you work towards a fundamental decision made by the protagonist: a decision to resolve conflict. The decision must have consequences. Macon drops his pain pill; the consequence is pain. In *The Great Gatsby*, Jay Gatsby, thinking it will smooth Daisy's delicate East

Eggian nerves, decides to let her drive his yellow car back from the city; the consequence is the death of Myrtle Wilson.

Practise constructing this chain of events by studying professionals. Let's reconstruct the chain of events in *The Great Gatsby*. The protagonist (Jay Gatsby), faced with a multitude of obstacles (Western innocence, bootlegger past, Tom, Old Money, East Egg), grabs the prize (Daisy, who represents Old Money), taking the consequences (Daisy kills Myrtle Wilson, Tom's mistress, with Gatsby's yellow car; Tom deflects Wilson away from Daisy to Gatsby; Gatsby does not rat to the cops on Daisy). After the collision which killed Myrtle, Gatsby keeps watch outside Daisy's house, waiting for Daisy to return to his side. When Daisy fails to appear, Gatsby returns to his house, where he is killed by George Wilson, who then then commits suicide. On the day of his funeral, the irony of Gatsby's arduous pilgrimage from Out West to Back East is highlighted by his dad's words: 'Jimmy always liked it better down East.'

Guidelines for writing your climax

Let's look at the chain of events in *The Accidental Tourist*, beginning with Macon's trip to Paris.

Problem: Muriel tags along
Solution: Macon hurts his back
Problem: Sarah arrives to take over research chores
Solution: to avoid pain, Macon takes pills
Problem: Macon feels the heat from the Muriel-Sarah struggle
Solution: Macon must choose; refuses the last pill
Problem: Paris taxi, driving fast, Muriel alone on the curb
Solution: Macon tells the taxi to stop

To create momentum, you can follow the model we used for Gatsby, compressing your chain of events into a couple of sentences. Let's try that now for Macon Leary. The protagonist (Macon Leary), faced with a multitude of obstacles (Sarah, pain, fear of change), decides to push ahead (drops the pill), taking the consequences (increased pain, Sarah's ironic ire), which leads to his decision (he's going back to Muriel), made personal by a character trait that is still part of his problem (the old Deflector Reflex): 'I didn't want to decide this.'

Sometimes the hardest part is getting your hand moving, so take the time to copy down part of your storyline. Pretty soon, you'll be writing.

Your scene-sequence creates a chain of events that builds up to the climax of your book. Remember that it's just a list – it doesn't have to be perfect or even smooth – and no one will see it but you. Play with scenes and events as if they were coloured building blocks, moving them around to see where they might fit.

One key to discovering climax is to reach back to your character work to find the motive that works itself out in actions that produce conflict. Macon Leary's conflict, for example, is between the Old (Sarah, family, suffocation in the glass box) and the New (Muriel, Alexander, chance for change). At the moment of climax, he chooses the New (a fundamental decision). Because change is hard work and because we avoid it, we like to see change at work in our stories. Change gives the reader hope.

Exercises

1. Chain of events
In your notebook, copy out a piece of your storyline from your working synopsis. From that passage, following the model we used for *Tourist* and *Gatsby*, create a chain of events leading up to your climax. Try this model, expanding the parentheses to fit your own detail:

the protagonist (   )
faced with a multitude of obstacles (   )
grabs the prize (   )
taking the consequences (   )
made personal by (   )
as he/she acts/reacts/awaits (   )
and the final twist is (   )

2. Identify the parts of your climax
Take a few minutes to jot down notes on the parts of your scene: What's the setting (time, place, temperature, lighting)? Who are the characters? What are they wearing? What objects do they bring to the scene? What actions do they take? What words do they say? How does the scene end? Make certain that your protagonist is present. Make sure that each character in the scene has a clear agenda.

3. Timed writing
Write the climactic scene in a 15-minute timed writing. Keep the hand moving and let your imagination go. Remember that this is a discovery process in which you explore with sentences.

4. Rewrite

After letting your scene cool, read it over, jot a few notes, and then rewrite it. Start by copying a few lines from what you have written in Exercise 3 (above), and allow your sentences to dig deeper.

The novel-in-progress: *Trophy Wives*

The example below is in two parts – an action sequence followed by dialogue. The characters are Veronica, her husband Paul, and her lover, Gwyn.

Action

Veronica jerks open the French doors.
Paul sits behind the massive oak desk.
On the desk is a briefcase packed with money.
Gwyn hits Veronica in the head with a gun.
They handcuff her to the high-backed leather chair.
She wakes up and Paul and Gwyn are arguing about what to do with Veronica.
Gwyn points the gun at Veronica.
Paul moves, and Gwyn points the gun at Paul.
Sirens scream up the drive.
Police cruisers stop in front of the house.
Detective Anderson steps out of the car.
He takes out a sniper's rifle.
Men fan out across the front of the house, taking cover behind the cruisers.
Gwyn shoots at Paul.
At the same instant, the big window explodes.
Gwyn's bullet hits Paul.
The bullet that broke the window hits Gwyn.
Police officers break through the front door.
Detective Anderson runs into the house after the police officers.
They clear the house and converge on the den.
Detective Anderson leans down, unlocking Veronica's handcuffs.
Paramedics run to Paul and Gwyn.
Paul is bleeding.
Gwyn is already dead.
Paul dies looking at Veronica.
Detective Anderson picks Veronica up.
She clings to him.
He carries her outside to an ambulance and stretcher.

He lays her on the stretcher.
She thanks him.
Just doing his job.
He walks about 20 feet away and pulls out his mobile phone.
He dials.
Barbara answers the phone.

Dialogue One – Gwyn as the 'bad guy'

She's awake, Paul.
Time to go.
Don't tell me we're leaving her big mouth here.
Take the bag, wait in the car.
You talk like we're married.
Take the bag, Gwyn.
You told me you were finished with her.
Wait in the car, I said.
Step aside, Paul.
Are you crazy?
You're weak, Paul. No balls.
This is not the pistol range, Gwyn.

In this dialogue, the writer explores Paul's connection with Gwyn. Gwyn wants to kill Veronica, but Paul stops her. Gwyn has a gun. And she expresses her jealousy when she says: 'You told me you were finished with her.' From this line, we conclude that Paul has lied to Gwyn as well as to Veronica. In the next dialogue, the writer explores Paul as the bad guy.

Dialogue Two – Paul as the 'bad guy'

Ready, Paul?
One last thing.
Leave her, Paul.
This bitch ripped my heart out.
It's over, Paul. We've got what we…
Ripped it out, you hear, and dropped it into the dustbin.
They'll know you did it.
She's the bad-luck girl.
Paul, please.
Take your hand off me.
Paul!
How was it with her in bed?
It was nothing, Paul. It was…

What's with the tears?
Oh, God, Paul, please put the gun down and let's...
This bitch of yours, she almost killed me.

In this dialogue, Paul is a straight guy and his dialogue line, 'How was it with her in bed?' reveals his anger about a lesbian relationship between Gwyn and Veronica. With the words 'bad-luck girl', Paul dooms Veronica to die, but Gwyn intervenes with logic: 'They'll know you did it.' Because dialogue is so efficient, so quick to write, you can use it to explore character. The idea that arises out of this dialogue is that of serial killer. For example, what if Gwyn kills Ashleigh, and then she comes to the house to kill Veronica? And what if Paul takes the bullet for Veronica? By sacrificing himself, he would save Veronica and have a chance at redemption. If Gwyn is sent by Barbara, then there is some work to do on character connection: Barbara wants Paul's share of the company; she hires Gwyn to kill Ashleigh and frame Paul. When you play what-if, you get pulled into the back story to find motive.

Dialogue Three – Veronica as the victim
Mrs Watson, are you OK?
I'm... I'm OK.
Let's get you out of here.
Sir, the woman is dead. You hit her in the chest.
What about Watson?
He's losing blood. She got him in the neck. He's a goner.
Let Forensics handle it.
Mrs Watson, I'm going carry you out, OK? It's over now. You're going to be OK.
OK? I walked in here and found...
You're in shock. These people will look after you. We'll need to talk later. I'll come to the hospital.
Can you stay with me?
I'll be right back.
Don't let go.

In this dialogue, Veronica is helpless and innocent. She faints and the detective picks her up. Their connection prompts another what-if: What if Veronica and the detective get chummy earlier in the story? What if Barbara sends the detective to find dirt on Paul and instead he finds beautiful Veronica and what if Barbara wants to frame Veronica for the murder of Ashleigh? Remember that this is early in the writing and the writer is poised in the gap between midpoint and climax. What better place could there be to play what-if?

By spinning the climax, the writer of *Trophy Wives* gathers together objects and characters in a setting. Let's run the TWN checklist:

Time: late afternoon

Place: private study of Paul Watson, husband of Veronica; a big room with a great view on San Francisco's Nob Hill

Characters: Veronica (Protagonist), Paul (Antagonist), and Gwyn (Helper turned Antagonist)

Objects: gun, desk, briefcase with money, police car, sniper's rifle, window, handcuffs, ambulance, stretcher, mobile phone

Actions: quick and decisive – they handcuff Veronica; they aim the pistol; Gwyn shoots the pistol; the cop shoots the rifle; Detective Anderson plays hero when he carries Veronica to the ambulance

Let's look at the symbolism of this scene. Paul's study is a sacred space, a closed circle of masculine objects. If you remember, the study appeared early in Act One, at the funeral of Paul's mother. Readers like familiar ground. They like it when a story keeps coming back to a familiar place. The study is Paul's sanctuary, his private lair. When she approaches the door of Paul's study, Veronica always knocks, like a beggar knocking at the gate of a castle. When she crosses at the climax, Veronica does not knock. She becomes the intruder. The question for Paul and Gwyn is how to deal with the intruder. To explore this question – how to deal with the intruder – the writer of *Trophy Wives* writes three dialogues: one that shows Gwyn as the Evil Person; one that shows Paul as the Evil Person; and one that shows both of them dead and Veronica the Innocent in the arms of the detective.

At this point in the story, there is more work to do. But we have our climax. And that final phone call that the detective makes to Barbara, Paul's sister, is part of a subplot that will get a lot more work. For now, the writer has locked-in a climax. There is just one more scene to write before the writer loops back to Act One and starts writing. That scene – it will probably become a scene-sequence – is the midpoint.

Weekend 28:
Writing your midpoint

The quicker you lock down your midpoint, the sooner you will stabilise the structure of your novel. If you are working in a three-act straight-line structure like we developed in Part II of this book, then you know that the midpoint divides Act Two. If you are working with the Mythic Journey – a five-part structure – then the midpoint is located near the centre of the Quest. If you balk at using the three-act structure (Act Two is twice as long as Act One), then you can adapt your structure to a four-act one where all four acts are roughly the same length. The four-act structure for a novel mirrors the four-act structure of popular television dramas like *ER*, *NYPD*, and *Law and Order*. In the architectural sketch below (see Figure 14), you can see the midpoint inside an egg-shaped enclosure. In the middle of a four-act structure, midpoint separates Act Two from Act Three. To emphasise the importance of midpoint in your writing, we have made the egg really big and the typeface really bold.

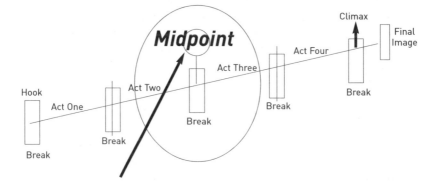

FIGURE 14: MIDPOINT IN A FOUR-ACT STRUCTURE BORROWED FROM TELEVISION

Midpoint is the point of no return. From here, there is no going back; all the writer can do is move forwards. By midpoint, you should have introduced all your main characters into the story. If you still have characters to bring on, make sure you connect them to the thrust of the story. In *The Namesake*, the midpoint stretches from the party in New York City, where Gogol Ganguli, the Bengali protagonist, meets Maxine, who represents the essential American female (liberated, Western, educated), to the phone call that informs Gogol of his father's death in a distant place. Maxine is an antagonist. She wants Gogol to propose. But he waits too long. And he is ashamed of his parents. And he is torn between two worlds. And death is more powerful than love. If you are writing a novel like The *Namesake* – where the protagonist struggles to survive between two worlds – then you should study the scene where Gogol brings Maxine to meet his parents. The writing there is brilliant, a model for us all.

Seeing midpoint on the big screen

In his *Screenwriter's Workbook*, Syd Field calls midpoint a pit stop, a beacon, a point of no return. In Chapter 11, for example, Field tells the story of his discovery of midpoint. Students in one of his early screenwriting workshops wrote wonderful first acts, Field says, but went off the tracks when they arrived at Act Two. When Field asked for help, veteran screenwriter Paul Schrader came up with this tip: 'Something happens,' Schrader said, 'at about page 60, which is midway through a script of 120 pages.' Chasing that elusive something, Field explored three films: *An Unmarried Woman* (1978), *Manhattan* (1979), and *Body Heat* (1981). At the end of that chase he discovered midpoint. Let's take a quick look at those films.

In *An Unmarried Woman*, Jill Clayburgh's therapist advises our heroine to experiment with her life. She can't tell Clayburgh what to do, she says, but: 'I know what I would do… I would go out and get laid.' That line, advice from the therapist, is close to minute 60: midpoint. At minute 85, enter Alan Bates, the Mad Artist. After Clayburgh is released at midpoint, she is free to fall for him.

In *Manhattan*, Mary (Diane Keaton) and Ike (Woody Allen) move from being friends to being lovers. Their love scene, at minute 60, is the midpoint.

In *Body Heat*, Ned (William Hurt) kills Hubby (Richard Crenna) aided by Matty the Wife (Kathleen Turner). The murder takes place at minute 60, halfway through the film. As the action peaks in Act One, Ned Racine breaks through the glass doors to get close to Matty, who recruits him to kill her husband at midpoint. The husband's body is barely cold by the end of Act Two, when Ned learns that he is the main suspect in the killing. In Act Three, Matty goes free and Ned goes to jail for the killing.

Notice how midpoint determines (or is determined by) the type of film. *An Unmarried Woman* is a rebirth story; the midpoint is a dialogue line by a therapist that triggers action in the protagonist. *Manhattan* is a relationship story; midpoint is a love scene, a turnstile that transforms friends into lovers. *Body Heat* is a *film noir* mystery thriller; midpoint is an act of violence that digs the protagonist's grave another three feet down.

There are two keys to writing a solid Act Two, which is the key to writing a solid novel. First, using your midpoint, you should divide Act Two into two equal parts, thus removing the awesome pressure of writing a huge, sprawling thing. Second, you must forge a connection (action, character, motive, symbol, or theme) between Plot Point 1 (Act One ends and Act Two begins) and Plot Point 2 (Act Two ends and Act Three begins). When you lock down the midpoint, you stabilise the novel.

Novelists can learn from screenwriters because novels and films use the same Aristotelian architecture – beginning, middle, and end – and because screenwriters and novelists encounter the same problems: a sagging somewhere near the middle of an extended work. A solid understanding of midpoint could save your novel.

Getting help from other writers

Midpoint is a good place to dive into the past. Your protagonist has made it halfway through the plot, and by midpoint you have written all of your major characters into the story, with objects attached. Each character has an agenda that comes from trauma in the back story. Back story, as you recall from Weekends 9–10, is what happens to the characters before your book opens on page 1. Back-story events can be an hour before page 1, two hours before, one day before, one week before, or one month, one year, five years, ten years, or even 25. At the midpoint of *Gorky Park*, for example, a sleuth named Arkady Renko discovers the trauma that drives the killer to kill: a traumatic event buried 25 years ago in the bloody snow of Leningrad. By midpoint, your reader is hooked into the story and you can use the midpoint to reveal important details from the past. We'll be looking at three midpoints here: one from *Oedipus Rex*, written by the Greek playwright Sophocles and first performed in 430–426 BC; one from the novel *All the King's Men* (1946), by Robert Penn Warren; and one from Anne Tyler's *The Accidental Tourist* (1985).

At the midpoint of *Oedipus Rex*, Oedipus and his mother, Jocasta, compare back stories as both recall details that deepen the grave for Oedipus. Jocasta recalls dumping her newborn baby with his ankles pinned together because of the curse (the son will murder the father and marry the mother) that drives the story. Jocasta recalls that Laius, her husband and King of Thebes before Oedipus, was killed at a place where three roads meet. Oedipus, who, as a grown man, still walks with a limp from having his ankles pinned, recalls leaving Corinth because of the same curse that made Jocasta dump her newborn baby, thereby saving him from Laius, who was acting under the same curse. Now, as Oedipus recalls having killed a rude old man at a place where three roads meet, we can see he's trapped himself. The rude old man was Laius. With the blind strength of youth, Oedipus murdered his dad and three faithful retainers. That is some midpoint.

At Plot Point 1 of *All the King's Men* by Robert Penn Warren, the Governor (Willie Stark) orders Jack Burden to get some dirt to use as blackmail on the Judge. The Judge is Old Money and the Governor, who wants to be President, needs the Old Money support to win the next election. To get this dirt, Burden dives into the past. Finding the dirt at midpoint, in a series of journeys into the past, he brings it back to the present. The dirt, a smirch on the past, shows that the Judge was not totally upright in his back story. Burden shows the dirt to the Judge; the Judge commits suicide because of it and that's the Act Two curtain. Act Two, the best place in your structure for flashbacks and back story, contains Burden's journey into the past.

If you think in scenes, you can practise your craft all day long. Say you're sitting in a coffee shop watching a man and woman arguing. You jot down action and dialogue. You list the items in the room. A scene builds in your mind. The woman leaves in a huff. The man turns, catching the eye of the waitress, who gives him a sympathetic smile. You block out the scene on your storyboard, not thinking about where it goes until you've written it out, until the woman climbs into her car and drives away. Would it make a good opening? A good ending? A good midpoint? The answer rests in the writing. Keep writing scenes and you'll write many novels.

Something must happen at midpoint. Record that happening with action. If you're writing a mystery, there's a good chance you'll have a violent act around midpoint. If you're writing a rebirth novel – a man, newly separated, foundering, refuses Help from Without – you should initiate a change in direction at midpoint.

The midpoint of *The Accidental Tourist*, for example, occurs in Chapter 11 (the book has 20 chapters). Muriel (Help from Without) has invited Macon to dinner and he fusses about, writing a note declining her invitation. It's the day of the dinner, too late for the post, so Macon braves the city streets to deliver the note in person. After threatening him with a fake shotgun, Muriel lets Macon in, and he burbles out a confession about Ethan. Whispering, 'Sleep, sleep, sleep,' Muriel leads Macon to bed. In response to Macon's question, 'Will you take this off?', they make love. Their relationship is transformed from business – dog trainer and dog owner – to a level of deeper intimacy. At midpoint, having changed course through action, Macon begins to heal.

Guidelines for writing your midpoint

Focus on action that initiates a big change in your characters. If they're in love, they fall out of love. If they're friends or have a business connection, they become lovers. Things change at midpoint.

Macon's action in Chapter 11 of *The Accidental Tourist* is confession. He's come almost 200 pages since the opening scene in the car, when Sarah badgered him about not caring (with the heavy subtext of Ethan's death like a rancid pool between them), and now, at midpoint, he chooses to confess – not to Sarah, but to dizzy Muriel Pritchett. Confessing to Sarah could have ended the book.

Midpoint anchors two other chains of events: one leading up to the midpoint action; the other leading away from it. These chains of events dramatise the change in direction initiated at midpoint. For example, events leading up to the midpoint in Anne Tyler's book include: training Edward to curb-sit while Macon shops; a dinner invitation from Muriel; Macon, uncertain, in Full Deflector Mode; Macon meeting Alexander; Muriel continuing to push her invitation, shoving it in his face; midpoint section (Macon declining the invitation to dinner and ending up confessing his sorrow). Events leading away from the midpoint include: Rose badgering Macon about his new schedule (part-time at Leary House, part-time at Muriel's); Macon delivering pizza to Muriel and Alexander; Macon having new energy for his work; Macon taking Muriel on a business trip.

Think about Tyler's technique. Before the midpoint, your character withdraws; after the midpoint, your character charges ahead with new energy. At the midpoint of his story, Macon Leary makes a good effort to leave the confines of the glass box. Think about what your protagonist does. Study what you discovered about your characters in your character work. Line up their motives, their fears, their strengths, their weaknesses. Check your Wants List. What do they want? How close are they to getting it? What decision do they make that takes them deeper? You want to construct a midpoint that transforms them.

Exercises

1. Chains of events
Develop two chains of events: one leading up to midpoint; the other leading away from it. Write long lists for both chains of events. Lists are easy. They don't commit you the way paragraphs do.

2. Blocking your midpoint
Take a few minutes to list the scenes that make up your midpoint. Jot notes about action and dialogue and setting. Make sure that each character coming onstage has a clear agenda.

3. Timed writing
Write the midpoint scene (or scene-sequence) in a 15-minute timed writing. Keep the hand moving and let your imagination go. Remember, this is a discovery process during which you explore with sentences.

4. Rewrite
After letting your scene cool, read it over, jot notes in the margins, and then rewrite it. Select a key phrase from Exercise 3 and, using that phrase as a startline, write for five minutes. When the timer beeps, select a second phrase and write for ten minutes. When the timer beeps, select a third phrase (dialogue is fun!) and write for 15 minutes. When the timer beeps, write your way to the climax in one long sentence – no stopping to think, no punctuation, pushing your way to the end with and, and then, then, but, so, and when, and when as you breathe deeply and fully all the way to the climax of the scene. Have fun with the writing.

The novel-in-progress: *Trophy Wives*

Veronica sits in the dark den.
The shades are drawn.
Veronica's head turns to the French doors as the front door clicks. Footsteps echo off the wood panelling, approaching the French doors.

Paul walks in.

Paul scans the room, his eyes cutting across the papers and rubbish scattered like his life.

His father's gun sits in front of Veronica.

The police came to see you.

About what?

A dead girl.

What happened to my den?

The doorbell rings, the sound reaching into the den, freezing Paul.

The maid steps into the den.

She hands Paul a business card from Detective Grant Anderson.

Show him in.

Anderson enters, sees the gun on the desk.

Your gun?

My father's pistol.

Step away from the desk, please.

At the desk, Anderson uses a biro to pull the pistol away from Paul.

Anderson hits a button on his mobile phone.

Anderson, at the Watson place. Get a forensics team over here.

Anderson pulls a plastic bag from his coat pocket.

See this, Mr Watson? It's an evidence bag. Forensics folks use them for lunch. We fill them up and you land in jail.

Paul reaches for the phone on his desk. He presses a memory button.

He phones Snyder, his lawyer.

Sirens blare outside the home.

Forensics vans pass through the gate and roll up the driveway.

Anderson walks back to the foyer with the Watsons behind him.

The house staff gathers in halls, murmuring.

The drivers park the vans, and the teams spread out across the estate.

Anderson's phone rings.

The voice on the other end says: a nine-millimetre slug killed the girl.

I love it, Anderson says.

Paul walks out the front door.

Veronica follows.

The stone fountain sprays water into the light breeze. Light mist moves across Veronica's face.

Paul stands silent.

A green Cadillac races up the drive and Snyder jumps from the back door.

He's wearing golf clothes.

Snyder recognises Anderson.

Anderson steps down from the front door.

Nice outfit, Mr Snyder.

What the hell, Detective?

Talking to your boy Watson.

Talking about what?

One of his employees. She's dead. We need you and your client at the station.

Who got killed?

Her name is Ashleigh Bennett. She and Watson had a little thing cooking?

Ashleigh Bennett? Veronica says. That woman from work?

Paul takes Veronica by the arm, but she jerks loose.

Veronica jumps up the steps and runs into the house.

Paul scrambles after her.

Paul stands in the bedroom looking out the window at Alcatraz.

Veronica sits on the bed, sobbing.

Snyder knocks. Anderson says you were the last one to see her alive.

Veronica, can you give us a minute here?

Veronica moves into the dressing room. She grabs her handbag.

Where are you going?

Veronica slaps Paul with an open palm across the face. The sound fills the room.

She runs from the room.

Snyder sits in the easy chair. Paul stands at the window.

He's after you, Paul.

Who?

Anderson. He wants your ass.

That's why I hire hot lawyers like you, Snyder.

He caught you playing with Daddy's pistol.

For the burglars.

Anderson knocks on the door.

Ready, guys?

Paul stands straight. How long will this take?

Be at the 19th precinct in one hour.

Anderson leaves the room.

The police vans head out of the gate.

Snyder waits for Paul downstairs.

Paul washes his face.

He walks down.

The two men ride to the police station in Snyder's green Cadillac.

They talk.

Were you nailing that girl?

Off and on.

They ask you a question, check with me.

Right.

The green Cadillac stops in front of the police station.

Two TV mobile units. Two reporters, two cameramen.

Paul walks to the door.

Snyder behind him.

TV crews crowd in.

Anderson blocks the reporters. Then he leads Paul and Snyder to an interview room: metal table, dirty coffee-maker, cigarettes on the floor.

Coffee?

No.

Ashleigh Bennett worked for you?

Yes.

What was her job?

She was my accountant.

Good with numbers, was she?

She was good, yes.

Good in bed, too?

Snyder nods at Paul.

Paul turns to Anderson. We were both adults.

Glad to know that. How long did this go on?

A couple of months.

Did the wife know?

Ask her.

Good-looking girl, your wife.

Are we done here?

Anderson holds up a bag. Inside is Paul's Breitling watch.

We're going to need a DNA sample and fingerprints.

This is over. Snyder stands up. We're not giving anything until you get a warrant.

Anderson grins. Leans back in his chair.

Makes a pistol with his thumb and forefinger.

Aims the forefinger at Paul.

The thumb drops.

Anderson says: Pow.

The writer of *Trophy Wives* uses a scene-sequence to explore the action at midpoint. The scene-sequence starts in the study, Paul's male sanctuary, in the big house on San Francisco's Nob Hill. The scene moves from the study to the bedroom, from the bedroom to the foyer, from the foyer to the green Cadillac that takes Paul and his lawyer to the police station. With our sequence in place, let's run the TWN checklist.

Time: the time is morning, lots of visibility, very few shadows.

Place: there are two fixed locations: one is the big house on Nob Hill; the other is the police station. If the writer wants some secret talk, the characters can chat in the green Cadillac on the way to the station. There are two main places in the house – the study and the bedroom.

Characters: as the characters move from place to place, from room to room, the writer has opportunities to explore the different connections between them. Snyder and Paul are connected by their upper-class buddy status. Veronica and Paul are connected by marriage and by money. She needs money. He uses her need for money to control her. Paul and Anderson are connected by murder. Anderson and Snyder are connected in the back story – they are both officers of the court – and their connection might be explored in the green Cadillac on the way to the station. If, for example, Snyder has a story about Anderson's tenacity, his bloodhound way of sniffing out crime, then Paul could get the shivers. Or, what if Anderson comes from Poverty Row and enjoys bringing down rich cats like Paul?

Objects: the main object is the Heckler and Koch pistol that gets passed down from father to son. With a gun in your scene, you show the power of the object in fiction. The gun is inanimate, but it demands attention from the characters. Is this gun the murder weapon? At this point, we don't know. Because we don't know, we keep writing. It is very smart of the writer to insert an object into the scene, planting it and allowing it to grow in the rewrite. The other objects are the Breitling watch, the search warrant, the plastic evidence bag, and various vehicles like the taxi cab, the police cars, the forensics van, and the green Cadillac. You can see how the writer of *Trophy Wives* is following the lessons on plotting with sacred objects.

Ritual: the main ritual is threshold-crossing. Anderson barges into Paul's house. Then Snyder barges in. Then more cops. Each room (private study, bedroom) is a sacred circle. Each character is an intruder who cannot be repelled. The final threshold for Paul Watson in this scene-sequence is the doorway to the police station. The scene-sequence ends with Paul trapped in the interview room. To exit, he must cross the threshold from the station back to the real world. When he re-enters the real world, Paul will discover that his life has changed.

part 6 Weekends 29–49:

Writing Your Rough Draft

If you drive an unfamiliar road, not knowing the landmarks, no map in hand, there's a chance that you'll make a couple of wrong turns. If you're in a rush – say you have an important appointment, or night is falling and there are potholes everywhere and you're tired and you need a stopping place – you might feel that the road is against you, an obstacle to your progress instead of a helpful corridor leading to your destination. If the road is too long, your joy in exploring new territory will fade, to be replaced by frustration growing out of your need to get somewhere. Next day, however, driving back up the road, retracing your route from yesterday, you will wonder what all the fuss was about. The landmarks are familiar. You're in control of your time.

That's the kind of journey you'll take as you write the rough draft for this first novel. You know your final destination – the climax in Act Three, followed by a brief wrap-up – but won't know every stopping place on the road, because some of the road signs have yet to be painted, and because there are potholes in the road that you'll know when you hit them, when the writing goes 'whump'. Before you headed out, you drew a map. Perhaps it was a straight line rising to climax; perhaps it was a circular line that ended at the same place where it began. On the map you printed character names, objects, landmarks, dates, and names of certain specific scenes, like midpoint and climax, that established waystations for your journey.

If your map describes the Mythic Journey, you start writing your rough draft with your protagonist in a cage guarded by a dragon. You write about constriction as a motivation to escape the cage. You find a helper to aid in the escape. The escape leads to a quest, where the protagonist gathers tools and wisdom enough to confront the dragon at the climax. As you write scenes, keep track of your progress by drawing fresh plot sketches. The quest in the Mythic Journey is analogous to Act Two in the straight-line plot, and to the Initiation phase of the Heroic Cycle. Armed with tools and bristling with wisdom, your protagonist has a face-off with the dragon. This face-off could be an argument or an execution. With the dragon confronted, your protagonist makes the trip home.

When you write the rough draft, don't stop for research. Don't stop to fix a sentence or to monkey around changing words or fixing metaphors. Don't stop to polish-up an image. Don't worry about form. Your internal editor, that voice inside your head, will urge you to stop. 'Listen up, dummy,' the editor will say. 'you can't write a novel this way, without rewriting. It's too messy. Its formlessness makes me sick. Fix your spelling now. Edit your sentences, *now*.'

Don't listen, and don't stop. Sink into the flow of your novel. Settle into the warmth of words. Get to know your characters. Go again into closet and bedroom and desk drawer and mind and memory and poke around. Gather the images. Hold them in your arms. Knit them into your book. Keep filling-up the well of your unconscious.

Try not to worry about what you are writing while you are writing. This is the rough draft of your first novel. You're learning as you go, making discoveries about character and plot that you could never make if you hadn't come this far. You're growing like crazy. Every day of writing increases your writing power.

Write dialogue and attach it to action and watch the scene grow, almost by itself. Build a stage and watch the lights come on and feel the temperature change and bring on a character dressed by your wardrobe people and nail down your point of view with a touch or a sharp smell or the tick-swoosh of rubber wiper blades on the windshield and let your action peak and write an exit line and suddenly you've got a scene which is a bucket for drama which is what audiences pay for.

As you craft the rough draft, stay fluid. Start with your laptop, rolling fragments down the page. Write fast and write hot, and when you come to a stopping place, a cold place, grab your spiral notebook and draw plot diagrams. Where does your story want to go? Keep this fluidity – notebook to laptop, laptop back to notebook – the entire time you are writing your draft.

Filling the notebook or the page will give you confidence so that when you come to the end and choose a direction for your writing life – novel, script, memoir, epic poem, stage play – most of the scenes will be fully formed. When you have finished a section of 10–15 pages, make sure you print the pages and place them in a folder. Label the folder Rough Draft, and then add your working title. Our working title is *Trophy Wives*.

Keep a tracking page at the front of the folder. On the tracking page, write the date and number of pages completed. Recap the characters and check their roles: protagonist, antagonist, helper. If you're writing a mystery, the roles are: killer, victim, sleuth, and catalyst. (For a full description of the catalyst character, with examples, see *The Weekend Novelist Writes a Mystery* by Robert Ray and Jack Remick.)

Writing tips – how to keep going

When you write your rough draft, you need to observe some basic principles:

1. Keep writing. When your writing hits a pothole, don't stop to explore the pothole. Instead, keep your story moving by keeping your hand moving – if you're working the rough draft in a notebook – or, if you are composing on your laptop, hit those keys.
2. When you do stop, draw a sketch to show your progress. On the sketch you might write something like, 'Today I finished scene number 14; only three more scenes to midpoint.'
3. Create a list of scenes. Each scene should have a name and number. The list should be divided into the sections of your story: three acts or three heroic phases or the five stations of the Mythic Journey. To create a really helpful list, you can add character, object, place, time in your story, time of day, what action takes place, and the subject of the dialogue in this scene. You don't need to write complete sentences. Keep it simple.
4. Establish structural landmarks. In our fiction workshops, we use screenwriters' terminology for marking the three-act straight-line structure. You can read more about this in books on screenwriting, like Syd Fields' *Screenwriter's Workbook*. The generic term used by screenwriters to nail down structure is 'plot point'.

- Plot Point 1 ends Act One and opens Act Two.
- Plot Point 2 ends Act Two and opens Act Three.
- Midpoint locks down, not only the middle of Act Two, but also the entire structure.
- Climax is the moment of resolution near the end of Act Three.
- Opening Scene throws open the doorway that beckons to your reader.
- Wrap-up is the end, the last scene, the final image, the doorway closing.

If you feel overly constricted by this screenwriting lingo, then feel free to grab onto what feels good for your own, personalised structural landmarks. Thinking in acts and plot points, however, is good discipline. If you're writing the rough draft for a novel of 300 pages – a recommended length to control the tendency to 'wordy' first novels – then Plot Point 1 should fall near page 75; the dead centre of your midpoint should fall on page 150, but spread out several pages on both sides; and Plot Point 2 should fall near page 225. Working with plot points leaves 75 pages for Act Three. If you write 150 pages and you still have not located Plot Point 1, then you have a choice: you can tighten up the structure; or you can plan on creating a 600-page novel, following in the footsteps of Michael Chabon's *The Amazing Adventures of Kavalier and Clay*.

In our writing workshops, we encounter writers who have not done their preparation. No plot work, no character work, no fistful of objects, no scene list, no targeted climax, and a disdain for structure that is absolute, fanatical, and often fatalistic. Can't do structure, they say. Feels too constricting. Don't need a list of scenes, they say, because this novel is right up here, in the old cranial cavity, all thought-out, word by careful word.

These same writers stall at around page 50. But this won't happen to you, because you have been preparing for the last 28 weekends. So get started with Act One, which translates, as already mentioned, to the Departure phase of the Heroic Cycle, and to the cage-escape waystations of the Mythic Journey.

Weekends 29–33:
Writing your rough draft for Act One

The rough draft is an exploratory piece of writing containing scenes, scene-sketches, and scene-lists. You work fast, writing with short lines, using snatches of dialogue, snippets of action, and stage set-ups that are overwritten on purpose as you root for symbols.

As you write, speeding along, new characters (strangers never seen before) will come onstage. Since they're new, they won't have back stories. Since they don't have back stories, you're not sure of their motivation – where they're coming from – so make a note to yourself: 'During the week: prepare back story on Character F,' and then keep writing.

That's your goal in this rough draft: to keep writing. Give yourself room to grow while you produce a lot of manuscript. Make a list of scenes, keeping it fluid, to give yourself a track – a chain of events to follow. Act One is your set-up, just as it was for Anne Tyler, or for F Scott Fitzgerald, or for Herman Melville. Act One begins with your opening scene and builds to the first structural peak, Plot Point 1. In Act One you introduce your characters, who come onstage brandishing their individual agendas. In Act One you set up your scenes, writing stage set-ups to establish place, time of day, temperature, season, and lighting. As you write these stage set-ups, stay open to symbols and images popping up, stuff you never thought of, so you can develop some of them into central images.

In Act One you allow large actions to spring from the motivations of your characters. Cinderella wants to go to the ball, so she dials the universe for help and, because it's a fairy story, the Fairy Godmother enters from stage right, where she's been waiting in the wings. One of the core actions in Cinderella is her transformation, via the magic of the Fairy Godmother, into the Belle of the Ball. This large action provides a timing clue – where to end Act One.

As you write Act One, bring on those characters you've got waiting in the wings.

Because of the careful preparation you've been doing for the last 28 weekends, you've already assembled most of what you need for writing Act One. Some of your characters are onstage; others, dressed and expectant, wait in the wings.

Your Wants List reminds you what they're after in the story. You've recorded their speech and mentally videotaped their actions and gestures. You've poked around in their closets; you've probed their back stories. You've built stages and furnished them. You've written key scenes built around large actions. A quick look at the problem-solution rhythm of your storyline will remind you of things you need to accomplish in Act One.

Bringing your characters onstage

Bringing your characters onto the stage of your novel is your main job in Act One. And the way you bring them on is determined by your style, what kind of writer you are, the kind of book you're writing, and the time period in which you write.

To bring Captain Ahab onstage in *Moby-Dick*, Herman Melville wrapped his description, of roughly 300 words, around the image of Ahab's scar: 'Threading its way out from among his grey hairs, and continuing right down one side of his tawny scorched face and neck, till it disappeared in his clothing, you saw a slender rod-like mark.' The weight of words, the sheer mass of detail, tells the reader that Ahab is important. Do the same thing with your words. Bringing a character on with 100–150 words indicates a character of more importance than one you bring on with a dozen words.

By the end of Act One, you should have all your key characters onstage. Let's look at how Anne Tyler does this in *The Accidental Tourist*. Macon and Sarah come onstage in the first word, the pronoun 'they', of Act One: 'They were supposed to stay at the beach a week, but...' Macon is the protagonist; Sarah is the antagonist hiding behind the mask of dutiful wife. Muriel, the helper, comes onstage in Chapter 3, when the boarding kennel refuses Edward because he's a biter. A dog trainer who doesn't like dogs, Muriel works at Meow Bow. She enters around the middle of Act One, which has six chapters.

Rose and the boys come onstage in Chapter 5, when Macon moves back to Leary House after Edward, displaying to the world his need for training, breaks Macon's leg in the basement. Rose, Macon's old-maid sister, is important for the Romance–Marriage subplot.

Julian Edge, Macon's publisher, comes onstage in Chapter 6, precipitating Plot Point 1 when Edward trees him in the Leary front yard. Julian joins Rose in the Romance–Marriage subplot.

List of scenes for Act One

Before you start writing, you might take the time to create a list of scenes. This is a quickie list that works as a roadmap for your writing. The creative self creates the list; reading the list calms the editorial self down so that the creative self can keep working.

As an example to follow, here's a list of scenes for Act One of Tyler's *Accidental Tourist*:

1. Inside the Car (Hook): coming home from a trip, after bugging Macon about comfort, systems, and getting out of the rain, Sarah asks for a divorce.
2. Home Alone: Macon wanders the house, which seems to be closing in. Empty spaces remind him of where Sarah's stuff used to be.
3. Phone Call: Sarah bugs Macon about the separation.
4. Running the House with a System: Macon does laundry, washes the dishes, makes the bed – all done with his system. No system could keep Ethan alive, as Macon, in a tense interior monologue, blames the world for his son's death.
5. Phone Call: Sarah, phoning about a rug, vents her anger at Ethan's killer.
6. Meow Bow: when the old kennel refuses to keep Edward, Macon takes him to Meow Bow, where he has a First Encounter with Muriel.
7. Aeroplane: on a flight to London for his work, Macon relives a back-story trip with Ethan.
8. London: Macon surveys hotels and restaurants. He thinks Sarah might meet him in New York. No luck.
9. Meow Bow: Muriel offers to train Edward. Macon hedges.
10. Phone Call: Julian, Macon's boss, wants copy for the new edition of *The Accidental Tourist*.
11. Back Story: Macon remembers meeting Sarah. Dates in Grandfather Leary's long, black Buick. Engagement, marriage, work at the bottle-cap factory. Love troubles.
12. Phone Call: Muriel, her true purpose veiled, asks about Edward. Asks Macon to supper. He says no.
13. Building the System (Mini-Climax): working with a new system of laundry, Macon gets tangled between Edward and the cat and breaks his leg.
14. Leary House: at home with Rose and the boys, Macon defends Edward (he was Ethan's).
15. Back Story: flaky Alicia, Macon's mum, who married an engineer

and sent the Leary children off to live with grandparents. Close-up of a photo on page 66.

16. Decision: since Sarah might call, they decide not to answer the phone. Garner Bolt, a neighbour, informs Macon that mail is piling up.
17. Leary Family Lore: back story on the boys. They play a Leary family card game called Vaccination. The phone rings; no one answers.
18. Leary House: Edward trees Julian, who develops a crush on Rose.
19. Back Story: how Macon and Julian met.
20. Edward Bites Macon: family wants Edward to go.
21. Macon Okays Muriel: this is Plot Point 1, as Muriel takes over in Act Two.

Threads run through this list of scenes, tying events together. Sarah's request for a divorce – Inside the Car (1) – causes Macon to be alone in Home Alone (2), which echoes with the silence caused by Sarah's departure, which gets worse when she calls him up in Phone Call (3). Since Edward won't behave, Macon takes him to Meow Bow (6), where he has a First Encounter with Muriel, whom he hires to train Edward. Macon's decision at the end of Act One opens the door for Muriel, who takes over the stage in Act Two. At Meow Bow, clashing agendas lurk: Macon wants a place for Edward; Muriel, a blue-collar Cinderella, wants Macon. What Muriel wants, so invisible to Macon, seems clear to the reader, providing a nice dramatic irony for Act One.

Edward, onstage with great fanfare in the scene called Building the System (13), is the cosmic agent who gets Macon out of the house by breaking his master's leg. For care, Macon retreats to Leary House (14), where Edward trees Julian (17), who initiates the Julian subplot (Romance with Rose).

You need to tag your subplots early. If you were writing *The Accidental Tourist*, you would have Act One subplots listed for Sarah (Antagonist), Muriel (Helper), and Julian, Macon's boss, who will get engaged to Rose, Macon's sister. The Julian–Rose subplot is a logical use of cause and effect. Rose and Julian's engagement foreshadows the wedding, which brings down the curtain that ends Act Two. Muriel is not present at the wedding, but Sarah is.

The list of scenes, whether it is six scenes or 20, marks the pathway for writing the rough draft. You can now start with the novel's opening scene.

Sketching the opening scene

Your opening scene is a doorway into your novel's story – an invitation that beckons the reader to accompany you and your characters on a journey. With the first lines of your opening scene, you say: Come on along, Reader, and let me entertain you, maybe even enlighten you.

The opening scene establishes tone, mood, situation, problem, and genre. You build the stage of your novel and bring on your characters, who enter with conflicting agendas. What do these people want? Why do they think they can get it here? What's in their way? How will they handle the obstacles?

With your opening scene, you make a promise to the reader, a sort of contract that guarantees you will fulfil in the rest of the book what you set up in the opening scene. Tyler's opening scene in *The Accidental Tourist* sets up Macon Leary as a Man in a Glass Box. His wife can't break him out, so she leaves, creating a vacuum. In Act Two, that vacuum is filled to bursting with the bubbly froth of Muriel Pritchett. At the end of *Tourist*, Macon, a newborn baby chick emerging from his transparent glass egg, chooses Muriel.

One change in your opening can alter the course of your book. What if Macon Leary had died when their car slammed into a trailer in the rain? Then it would have been Sarah's story. What if Macon had choked Sarah to death under the shelter of the Texaco canopy? Then it would have been a murder mystery. If Sarah pulls a gun on Macon, and the author describes it as a Heckler and Koch 9 mm with a 15-shot magazine equipped with a German-made silencer, the detail alone changes the genre: from psychological mainstream to crime thriller.

Open fast. Open with image and action. Because of the preparation you've done, you're in good shape. The plotting exercises, where you stretched your mind out to reach the end, enabled you to know the story. You know the ending, the climax, the turning points. Now, using Tyler as a model, think about writing the key start-up scene.

Beginners in our fiction classes often make the mistake of opening their books slowly, taking a long time to set things in motion. Our advice is to begin the way Tyler begins, with a dramatic scene that sets up the characters and establishes the problem of the novel in a few well-written pages. Since half of Tyler's opening scene is made up of dialogue, pack your opener with dialogue – two characters talking. Use action to build to a climax, close off the scene with an exit line, and move on to finish Act One.

Before beginning your opening scene, sketch out the parts for your scene. For example:

Setting: inside the Leary's car; a sedan, no specific make.

Time/Place: Thursday morning, on the road.

Temperature/Season: muggy heat, late summer.

Lighting/Sounds/Smells: sky darkens as rain approaches; rain hammers roof; mildew, dank smell.

Symbols/Images: rain (water images), car, road, sight/blindness. Sarah implies that Macon cannot see what's happened to their marriage after the death of their son.

Characters/Relationships: Macon and Sarah Leary, a married couple in their mid-30s.

Dialogue Subjects: rain, comfort, systems, the past.

Sub: anger that the child is dead.

Action: Macon drives the car; Sarah asks for a divorce. Outside the window, cars pass in the rain, throwing spray. She grips the dashboard. She sits up straight, rigid with anger and grief. Macon turns on the windshield wipers.

Point of View: The point of view is third-person omniscient, turning like a camera eye on Macon, then on Sarah, then back to Macon.

Climax: Sarah tells Macon she wants a divorce.

Exit Line: the opening scene ends with the car at a dead stop, the rain drumming the roof.

One way to control the rough draft of Act One is to leap forwards, from the opening scene to the end of Act One, and write (or sketch) a scene for Plot Point 1. Plot Point 1 ends Act One. It wraps up the action of your set-up – where you introduce characters and the problematic situations fired by their conflicting agendas – and shoves the rest of the story into Act Two. If there is a big scene-change, say, from a small town in Kansas to the war-torn streets of Beirut, Plot Point 1 functions as a curtain for Act One.

In *Amsterdam*, Ian McEwan ends Act One with Vernon Halliday on the verge of buying Molly's photos from her husband, George Lane. As Vernon leaves George's house, he directs his taxi to stop by

Clive Vernon's home in South Kensington, where he drops off a note agreeing to Clive's mutual suicide pact. As he moves to Act Two, McEwan shifts locations, from London to the Lake District, where Clive goes to escape London, hoping to finish his symphony – scheduled to be performed in Amsterdam in Act Three.

In *Tender Is the Night*, which is divided into three books, Fitzgerald uses his Plot Point 1 to drop us backwards in time. Book One/Act One opens on the French Riviera in 1925. The action of Book One ends with Plot Point 1 in Paris, where Nicole Diver, distraught after seeing a corpse in the hotel hallway and jealous of youthful Rosemary Hoyt, a budding film actress, goes bonkers in the bathroom. Rosemary has the point of view. We see Nicole through her young eyes. The curtain falls.

When the curtain opens on Book Two, we see Dr Richard Diver, aged 26, arriving in Zurich in 1917. In this time of war, he has come to Switzerland to complete his studies in psychiatry. Before she becomes Mrs Diver, Nicole will be a patient of his.

In a long novel like *The Amazing Adventures of Kavalier and Clay*, Act One will take longer – Chabon's runs for 161 pages – and you'll need tighter control to lock down scenes for Plot Point 1. To get control, you can use a grid like the one below.

Chapter	Date	POV	Symbol	Action/Ritual
Part I Escape Artist				
1	1939	Sammy	Cigarette Butts	Sammy meets Cousin Joe/mystery of blood
2	1935	Josef	Train	Joe fails to escape from Prague/needs help
3	1935	Josef	Chain/Moldau	Joe fails to escape from chains/needs help from Tommy
4	1935	Josef	Golem/Casket	Joe's first sex/escapes in Casket with help
Part II A Couple of Boy Geniuses				
1	1939	Sammy	Ink	Sammy & Joe join forces to create funny books
2	1939	Sammy	Radios	S&J make deal with Anapol
3	1939	Sammy	Cigarettes	S&J invade Rathole/intruder inside
4	FB	Sammy	Steam Room	Mighty Molecule deserts Sammy & Mom

Chapter	Date	POV	Symbol	Action/Ritual
5	1939	Sammy	Ladder	Joe flies/escape artist born
6	1939	Joe	Rosa Drawing	Joe gets $3 for drawing of Rosa Saks
7	1939	Joe	Golden Key	S&J brainstorm future of Escape Artist Hero
8	1939	S&J	Golden Key	Adventures of Max Mayflower (Tommy, J's brother)
9	1939	Joe	Cigarettes/Gum	Joe orders his thoughts into comic panels
10	1939	Joe	Ink Blob	S&J recruit Rathole Gang/boy bonding/teamwork
11	1939	Sammy	The Book	S&J create their first book
12	1939	Sammy	Money	S&J barter with Anapol over wages

TABLE 7: LOCKING DOWN SCENES FOR PLOT POINT 1 IN *KAVALIER AND CLAY*

If you check Chabon's table of contents, you'll see that his novel has six parts. Act One contains the first two parts – 'Escape Artist' and 'A Couple of Boy Geniuses' – and the number of chapters increases as the author moves through Act One. To show the movement through time in his novel, we have added dates to the grid. Joe's story starts in Prague in 1935, with his escape in the Golem casket. Sammy's story begins when his cousin Joe arrives in New York City in 1939. Act One builds to a mini-climax when the two boys, joined by their talents (Joe is an artist; Sammy is a writer) in creating superhero comic books, use their art to make demands for more money from Anapol, a hard-as-nails businessman of the late 1930s.

Guidelines for writing your rough draft for Act One

The first step is to create a list of scenes. Number and name each scene. You can use places for the names (e.g. Meow Bow, Leary House). You can link a character name to an action: Macon Hires Muriel. For each scene on the list, you should provide information on character, object, setting (time, place, lighting, temperature), action, and dialogue.

The next step is to review your list of objects. As we discovered when we worked with *Amsterdam* during Weekends 15–16, photos of Julian Garmony taken by Molly Lane in the back story not only destroy Julian's career as Foreign Secretary, but also trigger the mutual suicide pact that leaves the two protagonists, Vernon and Clive, dead in Amsterdam. If we track the object through the novel, we can capture Molly's power in a graphic using a series of inter-linked sexual triads.

Third, check through your scene-list and make sure that all major characters have entered the story by the end of Act One. If new characters are waiting until Act Two, make a note to remind yourself. Make sure that each character has a role: protagonist, antagonist or helper.

As you sketch your scenes for Act One, let your characters talk to each other. Use the handy question-and-answer technique:

'What are you looking at?'
'None of your business.'
'Okay, then hand over the car keys.'
'Didn't you forget something?'

How do the scenes work in time? Do they run sequentially? Do you stop the clock to run flashbacks? How much time are you covering in Act One? Chabon covers several years, from 1935 to 1939. Anne Tyler covers a couple of months: she shows us the weather getting colder. Ian McEwan covers a couple of weeks.

Pay attention to place. *The Accidental Tourist* takes place in Baltimore, Maryland, with side trips to Europe for Macon's guidebooks. *Kavalier and Clay* starts in New York, shifts to Prague in a flashback, moves to the South Pole for Joe's Navy tour, and returns to New York. *Amsterdam* begins and ends in London. Clive escapes to the Lake District. And Clive and Vernon die in Amsterdam. Characters in *The Great Gatsby* shuffle back and forth between East Egg and West Egg; between the Eggs and the City. And there is one long flashback to Louisville, as told to Nick, the narrator, by Jordan Baker, Daisy's best friend.

Place gives your characters a setting within which they can act out their agendas. Place gives them a season to dress for, and locks in a time of day to establish mood and lighting. If you build a stage in Detroit in January, there's a good chance that it's snowing, with a wind-chill well below zero. Your characters, dressing in response to the weather, decide what to wear, and that helps you write detail: parka, long underwear, snow boots, mittens. If you're building a stage in Sarasota in the winter home of a snowbird from Detroit, use contrasting details from the places of the two homes, Sarasota and Detroit, to convey a sense of lifestyle for your characters.

Place helps you, as a writer and as a narrator, to stay objective by using detail to convey information. Instead of telling and explaining, you're showing with careful detail. Showing is more professional – and far more interesting to the reader. It's also hard work. As you train your eye, however, you'll grab onto better details, faster, and the payoff comes when images cluster on the page to form symbols. Symbols add an extra layer of meaning to your story.

Using diagrams to probe subtext

Use a diagram to explore the hidden structure buried in your subtext. In a huge number of novels, the hidden structure is the sexual triad; three characters connected by the elemental force of sex – not only desire and mate-selection, but also possession, loss, grief, jealousy and betrayal. In *The Great Gatsby*, the main sexual triad is formed by Gatsby + Daisy + Tom, with Daisy as the centrepiece. In *The Accidental Tourist*, the main triad is formed by Sarah + Macon + Muriel, with Macon as the centrepiece. In *The English Patient*, the sexual triad of Almasy + Katharine + Geoffrey (Katharine's boy-husband) is echoed in ancient Lydia by the triad from Herodotus: King Candaules + Queen Omphale + Gyges, the spear-carrier.

In *Amsterdam*, there are four sexual triads as Molly Lane, who is married to George Lane, connects to the two protagonists, Clive and Vernon, and also to Julian Garmony, the British Foreign Secretary, who stars in Molly's photos. The diagram (left; Figure 15) is a pictorial representation of Molly and her triads.

As the four triangles tumble down the page, the characters switch corners, and at the end of the book we have three dead people (Molly, Clive, and Vernon). George is about to replace Vernon in

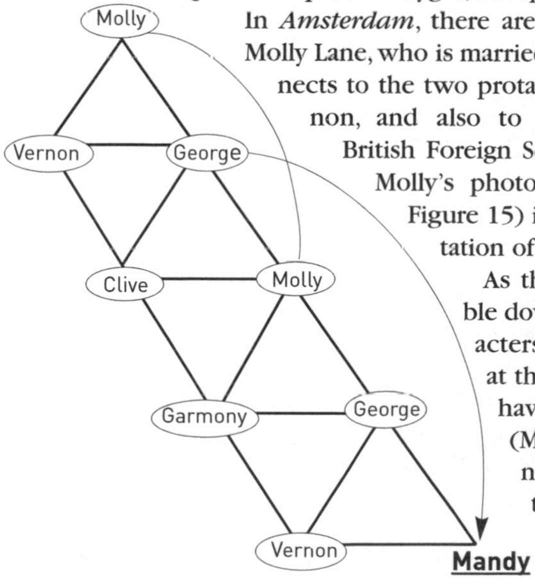

FIGURE 15: THE CHARACTERS CHANGE PARTNERS IN *AMSTERDAM*

Mandy's life. If that happens, Mandy will replace Molly in George's life. We have one Minister in exile, Julian Garmony. As Molly's photos slide through the novel, the reader feels the irony: Molly Lane is dead, but her photos keep her alive. This is another good lesson: the character dies, but the character's object keeps on working. In a finished novel, you have to dig to find the subtext.

With your diagram done, you are ready to sketch the scenes in words.

Exercises

1. Breathing
Close your eyes and pay attention to your breathing, chest rising and falling, as you reflect on the entire expanse of Act One. Allow your mind to play over character entrances, stage set-ups, large actions, central images, long passages of explanation, a line inside the narrator's head that you could change to dialogue.

2. Warm-up
Write for five minutes on 'This is a story about…'

3. Favourite season
Choose your favourite season and describe the weather. Use the startline: 'I love the weather here during Autumn [Winter, Spring, Summer] because…' (writing time: 5 minutes).

4. Least favourite season
Choose your least favourite season and describe the weather. Let emotion enter. Use the startline: 'I hate the weather here during Autumn [Winter, Spring, Summer] because…' (writing time: 7 minutes).

5. Use a diagram to explore your subtext
What's going on in your subtext? Use a diagram to find out. The simplest and most powerful subtext is the sexual triad: two males and one female (*The Great Gatsby, The English Patient, Amsterdam, Kavalier and Clay, Gorky Park, Oedipus Rex, Madame Bovary*) or two females and one male (*Lolita, Jane Eyre, The Accidental Tourist*). Have fun with this diagram.

6. Subtext
Write about the hidden subtext in your work. Use the startline: 'The secret that lurks in my subtext is…' (writing time: 15 minutes).

7. Cast-roster

Build a new cast-roster and include all the characters in your story. Turn the roster into a character grid – name, role, object, wants/needs, entry point, fate – and, if you see several main characters stalling around, waiting for Act Two, try to bring them into the story in Act One.

8. List of scenes

Each weekend, before you start work, jot down the list of scenes for Act One. Making a list is fast, and it gets you back in touch with the scope of the work. A list of scenes charts your progress and gives you a sense of accomplishment. In your list, include pieces of scenes, bits of scenes, snippets – whatever you've written, no matter how tiny it seems. If a scene is complete and whole, write 'Done' in red pencil near your entry. If a scene is incomplete, write 'Still to write' or 'More to come'. When your list is done, examine the story-line (written during Weekends 19–20) for holes. Can an old scene be expanded to cover the hole? Or do you need a new scene? If there are scenes you can cut now, do so. Cutting the excess now can close gaps in Act One.

9. Prepare back stories

Prepare back stories for new characters who come onstage in Act One. For each character, do a quick chronology and then a back story. This should take 10–15 minutes – do it during your lunch break. Doing the back stories now, focusing on childhood trauma that produces motivation, will save you hours of time as you continue on with the rough draft.

10. Spinning your way to the end of Act One

Write as many scenes as you can, using your notebook and your laptop. Write fast and don't look back. Don't worry about the potholes, you can fill them later. Writing in notebooks creates energy because it engages more of your body – not just your head and typing fingers. Sweating the rough draft is good. Sweat means that the writer cooks.

As you write, look up; try to see the end of Act One. In the theatre, that would be the curtain falling. On TV, that would be the first 15-minute commercial break. Writing fast drives you to closure, the end. For some writers, the word processor is a mind tool. Writing in the notebook keeps the writing physical.

11. Saving your work

Print out your scenes for Act One. File the new pages in your folder.

The novel-in-progress: *Trophy Wives*

1. Doorway

A big house on Nob Hill in San Francisco.
Veronica in black.
Veronica stands in the foyer, receiving guests.
The guests fill the big room.
Veronica goes to the kitchen to direct the staff.

2. Den

Paul is in the den, sitting at his father's desk.
Pistol on the desk.
Ashleigh Bennett walks into the den.
She locks the door behind her.
Paul slides the pistol into a drawer.
Are you OK?
My parents are gone.
I'm here for you.
She moves behind him.
She rubs his shoulders.
He stands, turns, kisses her.

3. Drawing room

Veronica moves through the drawing room.
She stops in front of Barbara, Paul's sister.
How are you holding up?
Where is Paul?
He's in the den.

4. Corridor

Barbara walks down the corridor, headed for the den.
She walks through the kitchen and across the great room.
She straightens a picture on the wall. Frowns.
She reaches the den's French doors.
As she turns the doorknob, Ashleigh Bennett exits.
They collide.

5. Den

Barbara enters, smirks at her brother.

Paul walks to the window, stares out.
Do you trust her?
Like I trust you.

6. Bedroom
Veronica sits at her dressing table in the bedroom.
Paul enters, holds out his arms.
Veronica stands and walks to Paul.
She smells perfume, steps back.

7. Pro shop
Morning. Veronica enters the pro shop, big smile from the pro.
Would you help me with that backhand?
For you, I'd even memorise *Jane Eyre*.

8. Ashleigh's office
Paul watches Ashleigh's hands on computer keys.
He nods.
She keeps typing.

9. Court three
Veronica at the Country Club.
She flirts with the tennis pro.
He's young, strong.
She pushes him away, walks off.

10. Paul's office
Barbara opens a printed spreadsheet.
Indicates numbers circled in red.
You're too aggressive.
You think too much.
Are you into something with that girl?
It's over, Babs.
Don't call me Babs.

11. Gwyn and Paul
Gwyn, an estate agent, shows Paul office space. Afterwards, they
make love on his boat. Gwyn went to college with Ashleigh Bennett.
She plays tennis at Paul's club. With long legs, tanned from hours in
the sun, she has shoulder-length hair in tight curls. Her mother was
mixed-race. Gwyn is one-quarter African American, three-quarters
Caucasian. She moves with feline grace around the tennis court. Her

tennis strokes are aggressive and fluid. The racket held back as her feet deliver her to the hitting zone. Her forehand releases a grunt, uh, and Paul knows the grunt. On the veranda, Paul sips a martini. Would you like another martini, Mr Watson? Good, thank you. Smooth, the crushed ice under the stainless strainer, the cold liquid. Boy she's smooth, Veronica says. She is. Paul smiles. Uh. Uh. She has so much power. She does.

12. Bathroom

And in the morning, Veronica slides out of bed. In the shower, the razor slides, glides, sneaks, slinks up her leg. Smooth. Steam on the mirror, fog fills the bathroom, the heated limestone under her feet as she dries her hair. In the dressing room, drawers packed neatly, skirts hanging, blouses under plastic, cashmere folded. A smart suit: black, with black stockings. Hair pulled back, professional. Flats, not stylish, but unique, boutique on the avenue through the Castro district. Where are you headed today? The library. I'm doing the benefit planning committee. How much am I in for? Well, nothing yet. Keep it that way. Your time is enough. We could give a little. You can, out of your allowance. What about the office? Surely the office could use the charity. Not this quarter. Our costs are up. His lips on her forehead: dry, cold. See you at dinner. I might have to work late. His hand, sharp, firm on her behind.

13. Veronica's Volvo

In the Volvo, Veronica's mobile phone. Hello? Mrs Watson? Yes. This is Ashleigh Bennett of Phoenix Investments. From the funeral? Yes, I'm so sorry for your loss. What can I do for you? We've opened an account for you and there are some papers to sign. Oh, Paul will be in the office in a bit, he takes care of that. Yes, I know, it was Mr Watson who set up the account for you. This is for the trust account, you need to sign it in person. OK. Can you give the papers for Paul to bring home? Mr Watson asked for you to stop by. OK, I'll be in tomorrow morning. Today would be better. OK, I'll see you this afternoon.

14. Ashleigh's office – Phoenix Investments

Phone clicks back into the cradle on the desk, black on black. Paul nods. She's coming later today. Make sure she leaves. Walk her out once she's done. Are you sure you want to do this, Paul? He turns his back. The door slams.

15. Library Board conference room

Veronica sits at the back of the library conference room. The meeting is over and she needs a quiet place. Pad and pen, she writes: caterer, champagne, donors' names. The skirt rides up her leg. The lace at the top of her stocking sneaks out, and she feels eyes watching her, looks up to see Gwyn, looking down, staring at the bare skin. Eyes on lace, Gwyn moves to the hem of the skirt, up the line of the black jacket, over the buttons to the neck, the bare skin, the dark skin of the Blackfoot people. The brilliant eyes looking back. The smile.

16. Veronica meets Gwyn

Veronica smiles at Gwyn, hiding the gap between her two front teeth. The lips, Veronica's lips sticking to her teeth. I'm Gwyn, Gwyn Chambers. Veronica Watson. Very nice to meet you. Nod, look of recognition. Paul Watson's wife? Yes. Do you know him? I'm showing him office space. I didn't know they were moving. Paul wants something with taste. Paul has great taste. He does. Does. He does have good taste. Meeting you, I agree. Veronica writes 'taste' on the pad. Are you helping with the benefit? I am. It's a good cause. It's a good place to meet prospective clients. I suppose so. Can I buy you a cup of coffee? Not now. I need to get going.

17. Garage, lift, Reception desk

Back in the Volvo at the Phoenix Investments building, the garage door. Veronica Watson for Ashleigh Bennett. Fifteenth floor. Thank you. The security guard, a black man with pearl-white teeth, a blue shirt, navy trousers, a watchman's hat. In the lift, Beethoven's Sixth Symphony. Veronica taps her foot. Veronica Watson for Ashleigh Bennett. The receptionist glares back. Headset over her blonde hair, solitaire diamond dangling into her cleavage. No, Paul Watson, please. Mr Watson is very busy. What was your name again? Veronica Watson, his wife. Oh, I'm sorry. She slides back in her chair, stands up, extends her hand. I didn't know Paul was married. In the waiting room, a pile of magazines: *Forbes, Money, Newsweek*.

18. Ashleigh's flat

Paul and Ashleigh kiss.
She wants more.
They wrestle.
She takes him to bed.
They argue about money.

Paul exits the bed.
Ashleigh calls after him.

19. Street
Gwyn sees Paul's car leaving Ashleigh's building.
Gwyn finds Ashleigh in tears.
What happened?
It's over.
He'll be back.
How do you know?
I know, okay?

20. Nob Hill exterior
The landscape architect shows up at the house on Nob Hill.
A young woman, Gwyn, walks the grounds with Veronica.
They talk about the Earth.
They talk about growing.
They talk about the power of nature.
Paul's car glides up the driveway as Gwyn is leaving.
Her eyes connect with Paul's eyes.

21. Nob Hill mansion
Alone in the Nob Hill mansion, Veronica is startled to hear the door bell.
The visitor is Gwyn.
Veronica offers Gwyn a glass of wine.
The two women sit on the back patio.
They kill two bottles of Pouilly-Fuissé.
Gwyn stands up to leave.
Veronica walks her to the door.
Gwyn moves close to Veronica.
Presses into her.
Gwyn kisses Veronica.
Veronica hesitates, then kisses Gwyn back.
End of Act One

Notes on *Trophy Wives*

The way of the rough draft is seldom smooth: that's why it's called a 'rough' draft. Constructing a rough draft when you don't have the full weight and bulk and trajectory of the entire novel is like building a motorway through the wilderness. There are gaps, curves, surprises. You have to build a foundation in layers before you can roll on the smooth stuff and paint the lines that mark the edges.

The rough draft might feel incomplete. That's because the subplots keep shifting, changing in importance as the characters change. One reason you write a rough draft is to chronicle the character-changes that appear during the writing. You can see this kind of change happening in the rough draft for Act One of *Trophy Wives* when the writer constructs a new scene-sequence, starting with Scene 11. Gwyn and Paul are together in a subplot, which insulates them from Veronica, who's isolated in the plot. Later in the sequence, Veronica is surprised about the search for office space when she meets Gwyn in the library, after the Board meeting.

When your writing shifts from short, choppy lines into paragraphs, go with the flow. This is one of the secrets of writing under the clock. When your paragraphs get tangled, you straighten out the language with short lines written down the page. The writer of *Trophy Wives* opens Act One with the scene-sequence developed earlier – Veronica in the black dress greeting guests; Paul in his study with pretty Ashleigh. The dialogue is sparse, the characters jab at each other with words. From the midpoint-writing, we know that Ashleigh will die and that Paul will go to the police station for questioning. We know from writing the climax that Paul and Gwyn die, and the rough-draft-writing puts Paul and Gwyn together on his boat, then shifts to Gwyn on the tennis court, where she is watched by Paul and Veronica, who sit on a veranda overlooking the courts. The dialogue is very efficient – two characters talking about a third character – and the Tennis Club/Country Club setting has the earmarks of an Upper World where Veronica feels comfortable.

The Upper World settings dominate this scene-sequence as Veronica, at home now, bathes and dresses, costuming herself for a meeting of the Library Board. Her change in station, from a library information clerk to a member of the Board, is a metaphor for how far she has climbed on the economic ladder since she met Paul Watson in the rainswept car park. Sitting alone after the meeting, Veronica meets Gwyn, who eyes up Veronica with a man's eye. At the end of Act One, Gwyn kisses Veronica. The scene-sequence in paragraphs ends with Veronica about to meet Ashleigh Bennett to sign papers for that new account at Phoenix Investments, which has the hot smell of corporate crime.

The rough draft is a snapshot of where you are with the novel. When new information bobs to the surface, you must quell your surprise, look the universe in the eye, and keep writing – even if the writing raises questions about plot and subplot. The big question in Act One concerns Barbara and Gwyn. For example, when Gwyn meets Veronica in the library, is she already on track to murder Ashleigh? When Gwyn comes to the Nob Hill house to drink wine with Veronica, what is her motive? Is she on a personal errand to check Veronica out for herself? Or is she casing the house for Barbara? There is, you will recall, bad blood between Paul and Barbara. He's running the company; she wants to run it. And Ashleigh Bennett, writhing with jealousy, wants to replace Veronica as Mrs Paul Watson. Lots of good stuff brewing, which is just what you want for Act One.

Weekends 34–43:

Writing your rough draft for Act Two

Act Two is your complication. Here the problems for the protagonist worsen, the holes in the road get deeper, the pathway twists like a corkscrew, the obstacles get tougher.

In Act Two, as you track down the problems, you follow the trail into the past – because problems in fiction have their roots planted deep in the back story. When you write Act Two, you play detective. You return to the past, and there you unearth images that connect to images from Act One. If you need to explore back stories for your main characters, now is the time, and this is the place.

In Act Two you have room to expand your work with myth and symbol. In Act Two, you feel the weight of the subplots. Where you might have started writing about only one subplot, in Act Two you could be dealing with four or five. Because each subplot is attached to a main character, you can number these subplots 1, 2, 3, 4, 5, etc., and use a grid to sort them out.

Act Two is fun to write because you keep gaining momentum as you push deeper into your story. Ideas pop in Act Two the way they never popped before and you realise that this is why you prepared, giving yourself a foundation so that you could arrive at the writing desk ready to write.

Guidelines for writing your rough draft for Act Two

Divide your work at midpoint. Write the first half, then the second half. Put labels on the movement of both halves of Act Two. For example, in the first half of Act Two of Jhumpa Lahiri's *The Name-sake*, Gogol Ganguli, a Bengali boy who comes of age in a Boston suburb, changes his name from Gogol to Nikhil. Gogol, as we have said, is the last name of a Russian writer, Nikolai Gogol, who lived in the first half of the 19th century. Nikhil, the name chosen by Lahiri's wounded protagonist, is a diminutive for anyone named Nikolai. There is irony here. Even though he changes his name, Gogol sticks close to the Russian source. Is this genetic? To find out, we read on.

The official name-change – Gogol goes to court, raises his hand for an American judge, answers questions about his motivation – launches Act Two of the book. When you write your own Act Two, choose a place to start. If you have a clean break between your first two acts, like a curtain falling to signal the intermission, you'll have no problem starting Act Two.

In the same breath that you use to start Act Two, you must look ahead for the scene that ends Act Two. It's like closing doors at both ends of a long tunnel. Your goal is to isolate the three large parts of your novel: Act One, Act Two, and Act Three. That way, you'll know where the key scenes are located in the structure: the turning points, the places in your prose that seethe with emotion, the dark rabbit holes that seduce your characters. Knowledge, for the writer, is power.

As a guideline for writing Act Two, we have chosen to examine the chapter–date structure from Lahiri's book. We use a simple compression device – a one- or two-sentence summary – and list the findings down the page:

Chapter 1: Gogol's mother, Ashima Ganguli, delivers a baby boy. The year is 1968. The Gangulis are Bengalis who live in Massachusetts. In the back story, the author describes the train crash from 1961. Thrown from his Pullman car, Dad clutches a copy of Gogol's short stories. The page reflects the beam from a flashlight and Dad is saved.

Chapter 2: a necessary trip to India forces the Gangulis to choose the name Gogol on the passport for their first-born.

Chapter 3: the year is 1971. The Gangulis live in a Boston suburb, on Pemberton Road. At school, Gogol discards the chance to be called Nikhil.

Chapter 4: the year is 1982; Gogol is 14. His father gives him a fresh new copy of the short stories of Nikolai Gogol. His high-school English class studies Gogol the writer. Gogol Ganguli is embarrassed. While Gogol is still in high school, he meets Kim, his first college girl, and flexes his identity muscles as he introduces himself as Nikhil.

Chapter 5: in 1986, Gogol changes his name to Nikhil. As Nikhil, he meets Ruth and falls in love. She heads for Oxford. They split up. At the end of the chapter, Dad tells Gogol the story of the train crash. Gogol is pissed off at Dad.

Chapter 6: the year is 1994. Gogol lives in New York. He works for a midtown architecture firm. At a party in Tribeca, Gogol meets Maxine, a tall babe with green eyes and dirty blonde hair. Maxine is an art major from Barnard. She introduces him to her parents, a laid-back couple, both educated, who fold Gogol into their family. On a trip to their lake cabin, Gogol introduces Maxine to his parents. Gogol feels torn between two worlds: one Bengali, one American.

Chapter 7: the year is 1995. Gogol is 27. Dad takes a job in Cleveland, where he dies in a hospital. Going to fetch the body, Gogol sleeps in Dad's bed. Death pulls him back into the Bengali culture. He turns away from Maxine. At the end the chapter, in a flashback, Gogol recalls walking with his dad to the edge of America – Land's End symbolism.

Chapter 8: Gogol has an affair with Bridget, a fellow New York City architect who is married to a professor in Boston. Then Mom hooks Gogol up with a young Bengali woman named Moushimi Mazoomdar, a child from his past. They make love. Equip their apartments with stay-over gear like clothes and toothbrushes. Back story on Moushimi focuses on her string of international lovers before Gogol: French, German, Persian, Italian, Lebanese, and American. Engaged to an American who mocks the Bengali wedding ritual, Moushimi breaks it off.

Chapter 9: Gogol marries Moushimi. Cash wedding gifts total more than $7,000. In Paris, Gogol cannot fit into Moushimi's world. At a party in New York, Moushimi's friends make fun of 'Gogol', the name of the namesake.

Chapter 10: the year is 1999. Gogol and Moushimi's anniversary dinner is a flop. Moushimi encounters a man from her past, Dimitri Desjardins, a master chef and the first man who had ever touched her sexually. In a section written from her point of view, Moushimi starts an affair.

Chapter 11: in this short chapter displaying Gogol's ignorance of Moushimi's affair, he climbs to their apartment with a Christmas present in the dark. His darkness is lit in the final chapter.

Chapter 12: the point of view switches to Mom, who is readying the house for her children, Gogol and his sister. In a flashback, Gogol relives the moment of his discovery, a year ago, of Moushimi's affair. She clears out, leaving him in the apartment. At home on Pemberton Road, Gogol recovers the book of Gogol short stories from his father. Alone in his room, Gogol escapes the party downstairs and reads the first story written by his namesake.

Finding Act Two

Finding Act Two is a two-step process. First, you find the second act of your favourite novel, the novel that made you want to write your own book. Second, you apply what you have learned to your own work-in-progress.

When you read through the chapter summaries, what do you see? Where does the story make a turn? Where does the book shift gears? Here are some examples of what you might have noticed when you studied our notes on Act Two of *The Namesake*:

Dates: Lahiri starts most of her chapters with dates. The dates keep the story moving forwards in time, from 1968, the year of Gogol's birth, to the year 2000, when he reads Gogol and starts to accept his Bengali blood.

Time Jumps: in film-making, time jumps are called jump cuts. If you are writing a novel that covers half a lifetime – Gogol is 32 when the book ends – and if you are not planning a sequel (Gogol: 2), then your choice of time span forces you to hop from one year to another. The combination of these first two techniques (dates plus time jumps) marks Lahiri as a savvy writer.

Back Story and Flashbacks: because she is careful about her timing, Lahiri has room for flashbacks. The main flashback is Ashoke's memory of the train crash – India, 1961 – when he was saved by a page from Gogol's short stories. This train crash starts a chain of events that culminates in dropping the name Gogol onto the head and shoulders of Ashoke's first son.

Point-of-View Shifts and Flashbacks: to take the reader into Ashoke's flashback, Lahiri shifts to his point of view. She shifts the point of view before that in Chapter 1, as Ashimi is about to give birth to Gogol. She shifts the point of view again in Chapter 10, when Moushimi reviews her marriage to Gogol; finding it not to her liking, Moushimi connects with Dimitri the Intruder, a Frenchman from her life before she entered the story in Chapter 8. The author shifts the point of view back to Ashimi, Gogol's widowed mother, as she waits for her children to arrive. The year is 2000. The season is Christmas. Her husband is dead. She waits for her son to become the man of the house.

Threshold-Crossings and Mythic Helpers: to get her protagonist from Act One into Act Two, Lahiri uses a mythic helper named Kim. Kim is a college girl from Connecticut with brown hair, red lips, and a thrift-store dress. She is pretty and slender. Gogol meets Kim at the unnamed university where his father teaches. Gogol is a senior in high school, but he tells Kim he's a freshman at Amherst, using the lie to boost his image from high-school boy to college kid. Kim approaches Gogol, tells him her name, lights a cigarette, and asks for his name. At this moment in the story, the world stops turning as Gogol Ganguli prepares himself to cross the threshold. He hates the name Gogol. He wants to impress this college girl. Searching his brain, he remembers another name, buried in deep memory. He calls himself Nikhil. Kim, the perfect mythic helper, honours Gogol's lie by repeating the name – Nikhil. A lovely name, she says. Gogol kisses Kim. She kisses him back. They press bony knees together. His mind swirls with the power of threshold-crossings: by calling himself Nikhil, he has gained the power to kiss this magic girl. The Amherst lie, combined with the name lie, has catapulted Gogol Ganguli into another world. Act One is over. The world of Act Two awaits.

Work, work, work

The lesson here, of course, is to take pains with your threshold-crossings. If you look back through the work you have done, you will see several of them. You use the most important threshold-crossings to mark large sections of your novel. Kim is the mythic helper that spirits Gogol across the threshold from Act One to Act Two. Kim has the same role as the Fairy Godmother in the Cinderella fairy-tale. The Fairy Godmother, if you recall, popped onstage with a makeup kit and a wardrobe that contained the magical glass slippers, one of the most memorable sacred objects in the history of storytelling. Kim has the same role in *The Namesake* that Edward the dog has in Anne Tyler's *The Accidental Tourist*. In *Tourist*, if you recall, Edward conspires with the cat to break the protagonist's leg. Because he cannot walk the dog, Macon seeks help from a dog-trainer named Muriel. In a clever retelling of the Cinderella fairy-tale, Muriel combines the archetypes of Cinderella and the Fairy Godmother. She is poor; but she has magic.

With Kim, the college girl, helping Gogol cross the threshold to Act Two, we can see, from the list of chapters and dates above, that Act Two starts in Chapter 5, where Gogol, having lied about his name to Kim, stands before a judge to change his name under the law.

When you start Act Two, you need to have a 'curtain scene' in mind. One way to find the curtain scene – the symbolic end of Act Two and beginning of Act Three – is to sketch a diagram. If you recall the plotting section, we use a mythic-journey diagram to display the plot of *The Namesake*. When you focus on a particular section of your story, isolating a part from the whole, you can use another diagram, like the one that follows (see Figure 16):

Through repetition, the sketch emphasises the important pieces of information. The protagonist is born in 1968. The book begins with his birth. The book ends in 2000; our hero is now 32. He's alone in his father's house, reading Gogol, the Russian writer who gave him his name.

Writing with power

The story of Gogol Ganguli is that of a quester searching for his identity. But Gogol becomes a quester only in the third stage of his life, represented by Act Three. Before that, he goes through a ritual familiar in divorce courts – replacing one partner with another. The raw power of Lahiri's Act Two comes from this pattern of replacing one female with another. If you did not see the pattern before, go back to the book and track it from page 96 (in the hardback edition), where Gogol meets Kim the college girl, all the way to page 256, where Moushimi, rooting through the post, spots Dimitri's

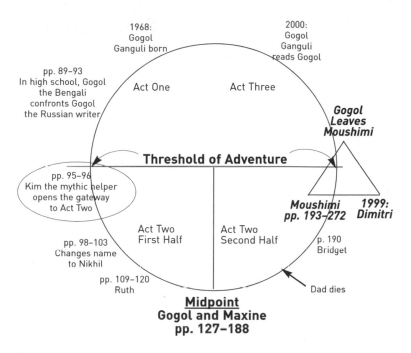

1968:
Gogol
Ganguli born

2000:
Gogol
Ganguli
reads Gogol

pp. 89–93
In high school, Gogol
the Bengali
confronts Gogol
the Russian writer

Act One   Act Three

Gogol
Leaves
Moushimi

Threshold of Adventure

pp. 95–96
Kim the mythic helper
opens the gateway
to Act Two

Moushimi   1999:
pp. 193–272 Dimitri

Act Two   Act Two
First Half   Second Half

pp. 98–103
Changes name
to Nikhil

p. 190
Bridget

pp. 109–120
Ruth

Dad dies

Midpoint
Gogol and Maxine
pp. 127–188

FIGURE 16: USING THE MIDPOINT TO CONTROL ACT TWO

name and return address on an envelope that contains his resumé. At that moment, Gogol Ganguli is on his way to Act Three.

When you sketch your ideas for your own Act Two, pay attention to Figure 16. The basic structure of the Hero Cycle is there, but you should notice that the three phases of the cycle – Departure, Initiation, and Return – have changed to Act One, Act Two, and Act Three. Renaming the large sections early on helps you focus on Act Two, which has two halves, indicated by the vertical line that divides the first half from the second half. Drawing this new diagram and adding the vertical line through Act Two will help your brain deal with the weight of the second act, which, in most books (and in 90 per cent of film scripts) is twice as long as Acts One and Three. This balancing act is important for your schedule, because Act Two is where the book thickens. In Act Two, the past intrudes. A good example is Moushimi's secret history of ill-fated lovers, which means that Gogol is just one more guy in a long line of her replacements. In Act Two, you will need to manage your subplots.

Study Figure 16 again. Five female characters – Kim, Ruth, Maxine, Bridget, and Moushimi – dominate Act Two. The reader sees these women and asks questions: When will Gogol settle down? When will he stop replacing one partner with another?

He stops when his father dies.

The diagram captures the irony of Gogol's decision to marry Moushimi: Gogol Ganguli, split between two worlds, should have married Maxine (the West), but he marries Moushimi (the East) instead, to please his parents (also from the East), and she's the one who deserts him. When you sketch your ideas for Act Two, make sure that you mark the thresholds first. In Figure 16, the threshold from Act One to Act Two in *The Namesake* is marked with a circle, an arrow, and a mythic helper named Kim. The threshold from Act Two into Act Three is marked with an arrow, a triangle and a mythic helper named Dimitri.

The important thing to remember about mythic helpers is that they walk on once, maybe twice. They do their work and then they vanish. Gogol sees Kim only once. He never lays eyes on Dimitri.

In a good novel – the kind you are writing – everyone works. No waste allowed.

Crossing into Act Three

Moushimi's affair with Dimitri is the motivation that drives Gogol away from the five females of Act Two back into the bosom of his family.

In real life, Dimitri is a home-wrecker, a possible womaniser who will have his way with Gogol's bride and then leave her behind when he has had enough of her.

In literary terms, Dimitri is a mythic helper. In Figure 16, Dimitri has been placed across the circle from Kim, who helps Gogol to move across the threshold from Act One to Act Two. Her opposite number, Dimitri Dejardins, helps Gogol move across the threshold from Act Two into Act Three.

In terms of the plot, Dimitri helps Gogol escape Moushimi.

In dramatic terms, Dimitri is an intruder who penetrates the circle of marriage; a third person who forms, with the husband and wife, the sexual triad – one of the most powerful structures for novel writers.

The sexual triad, a three-pointed geometric figure, is represented by the triangle on the right-hand side of the circle. Dimitri hangs out on the lower left corner, Moushimi on the lower right. Gogol, driven from the marriage by his wife's affair with Dimitri, is depicted in a tilted fashion at the top of the triangle. If you can use your sketch to indicate mood or scene or atmosphere or movement – for example, here the tilted typeface could represent the notion that Gogol is out of balance and sliding – then you have another tool to help you manage your characters when the book thickens in Act Two.

In his role as intruder, Dimitri is like the Patient in *The English Patient*, a desert explorer who is invited to have an affair with the wife of a British spy who flies a yellow aeroplane. The sexual triad looks like this on paper:

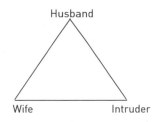

FIGURE 17: THE ELEMENTAL SEXUAL TRIAD

The same triad powers classic novels like *Madame Bovary* (Emma and her husband and her various lovers) and *The Great Gatsby*, where the intruder is the protagonist and the husband and wife team up for a masterful execution. The same triad powers two of our model novels: *Amsterdam* and *The Amazing Adventures of Kavalier and Clay*.

Exercises

1. Deep breathing
Close your eyes and pay attention to your breathing, chest rising and falling, as you recall both halves of Act Two. Allow your mind to play over ritual, the past, wants, obstacles, images, and character agendas. As always, keep a sharp eye out for a line inside the narrator's head that would go better as a dialogue line.

2. Warm up
Use this startline: 'The shape of Act Two looks (feels) like…' (writing time: 10 minutes).

3. Divide Act Two and apply labels
Cut your work in half by dividing Act Two. On your plot diagram, apply labels (e.g. Dancing with Muriel, At Home with Muriel) covering the themes for the first half and the second half. Below the line on your diagram, jot down ideas for scenes.

4. List of wants

Study your characters' Wants List, jotting notes down. For each want, jot down two obstacles in Act Two that stand in the way of the want. In *The Accidental Tourist*, Macon wants to be left alone. His obstacles are Muriel and Edward. Muriel wants someone to pay the bills. Her obstacles are Macon's desire to be alone, and Macon's family.

5. Back-story connections

Connect your characters and their traits to the past, using back-story scenes in Act Two. Macon's odd Leary worldview is inherited from Grandfather Leary, who invents a non-existent Indian tribe, the Lassaquans, whom he plans to visit. In a flashback, Macon and Grandfather Leary hunt without success for the Lassaquans in the encyclopedia.

6. List of scenes

Create a list of scenes for both halves of Act Two. If your goal is to write a book with 40–50 scenes (making the transition from book to film relatively easy), then you'll list 20–24 scenes for Act Two. Draw boxes around scenes taking place in the past.

7. Write the scenes

In timed writings of 15–20 minutes, write the scenes from your storyboards. The easiest way to start is to write dialogue, then fill in with action and stage set-up.

8. Build those subplots

Act Two is the place to deepen the subplots that you tagged way back in Act One. For example, Anne Tyler enlarges Muriel's subplot to deepen Act Two. Muriel's overall objective is to marry Macon. Her objective in Chapter 7, which begins Act Two, is to show Macon what a great person she is by training Edward to obey.

At the end of Chapter 7, Muriel kills her chances by choking Edward. In Chapter 9, her subplot picks up again when Macon is forced to call Muriel for help when Edward traps Charles in the pantry.

9. Getting to midpoint, then to Plot Point 2

Your first goal is to reach midpoint. If you don't finish drafting all the scenes, sketch the rest and stay on schedule. Reaching midpoint should give your momentum a boost. After that, move on to Plot Point 2. Use your notebook first, your word processor later. When new scenes appear, sketch them quickly on your storyboard and keep writing towards the end.

10. When in doubt, dip into ritual

Ritual includes training, teaching, learning, cooking, eating, drinking, shopping, praying, sewing, washing, washing up, applying makeup. Use ritual to deepen your scenes and to connect the chains of events in Act Two.

11. Saving your work

Print out your scenes for Act Two. File the new pages in your folder.

Getting help from other writers

In Chapter 13 of *The Screenwriter's Workbook*, Syd Field explores strategies for building Act Two, writing that all you need is 'one key scene' to hold Act Two in place. In the film *Chinatown* (1974), for example, the key scene is Hollis Mulwray's murder, which occurs in the script on page 45. In *Body Heat*, the key scene is Matty Walker's announcement that she wants her husband dead, also on page 45.

In Act Two of *The Accidental Tourist*, Macon suffers an attack of distance phobia on top of a skyscraper in Chapter 9; he calls home, only to find his brother Charles trapped in the pantry by Edward, which forces Macon to phone Muriel to rescue Charles. The skyscraper scene occurs about halfway between the beginning of Act Two and midpoint.

In *The Namesake*, the key scene is the death of Gogol's dad, which pulls Gogol away from Maxine and sends him to Moushimi, who caps off Act Two when she initiates her affair with Dimitri.

In Act Two of *Moby-Dick*, Melville deepens the symbol of whiteness with two fulsome chapters ('Moby-Dick' and 'The Whiteness of the Whale'), and then weaves the ritual of the whale hunt with a parade of nine ships met by the good ship Pequod on the open sea. These meetings, beginning with the Jeroboam in Act Two and ending with the Rachel just before the climax in Act Three, form a bridge that keeps the story moving as Ahab and crew approach the final and deadly confrontation with the White Whale.

The novel-in-progress: *Trophy Wives*

1. Paul's Office Building – Day

Gwyn rides the lift up.
She waits in the reception area.
Barbara walks out, greets Gwyn.
They walk back to Barbara's office.

Gwyn tells Barbara about new office space to purchase.
Barbara's against it, all Paul's idea.

2. Lawyer's Office – Day
Veronica, in khakis and a cashmere sweater, wants to know about
the prenuptial agreement.
The lawyer shows her in – no secretary.

3. Kitchen – Day
Paul and Veronica stand in the kitchen.
They talk about money.
Veronica hates to ask for money.
Paul doles out money, making her beg.
Paul exits.
Veronica looks out of the kitchen windows to the lawn where they
were married.

4. Flashback – Wedding Day – Day
Veronica wears a white gown.
She walks through the reception, meeting her husband's friends.
No one from her family.
She hears Paul's mother apologise for Veronica's skin.

5. Ashleigh's Building – Night
Ashleigh hugs Paul.
They have dinner, drinks.
She boots up her computer, shows him a spreadsheet.
Paul stares at Ashleigh.

6. Paul's Study – Night
Veronica rifles through the drawers.
In the top drawer is a gun.

7. Bedroom – Day
Paul and Veronica are in bed.
The maid knocks.
Detective Anderson waits downstairs.
Paul tells Veronica to wait in the bedroom.
He walks down to the foyer.

8. Top of Stairs Looking Down – Day
Veronica, in her robe, stands at the top of the stairs.

Detective Anderson asks:
Where were you last night?
Here. Anderson looks up at Veronica.
She nods yes.
What's this all about?
Ashleigh Bennett. She's dead.

9. Kitchen – Day
Veronica, Paul, and Anderson.
Snyder arrives out of breath.
Veronica backs Paul's story.
Snyder ends the meeting.
Detective Anderson leaves.

10. Bedroom – Day
Veronica and Paul in the bedroom.
They make a deal: alibi for the house.

11. Snyder's Green Cadillac – Day
Snyder warns Paul: Anderson, born poor, wants revenge on rich people.
Paul sweats, twitches, laughs.
Strategy is clear: let Snyder talk.
The car stops and a reporter pushes forwards.
A photographer shoots photos.

12. Nob Hill Mansion – Day
Gwyn arrives early with scones and a floor plan.
Floor plan is for Paul's new office.
He's moving?, Veronica asks.

13. Interview Room – Day
Paul sits in the metal chair and scans the dirty room.
Anderson offers coffee, no takers.
Anderson produces evidence: fingerprints.
They argue about Ashleigh's last hours.
Paul agrees to take a gunshot residue test on his hands.
The test yields nothing.

14. Barbara's Office – Day
Barbara watches the financial news.
Corporate scandal, Paul's photo.

The company's stock is falling.
Clients are calling.
Paul enters; they bicker.
Barbara wants Paul to step down.
She will run the company until he's cleared.
Paul walks out.

15. Nob Hill Mansion – Day
Veronica shows Gwyn out of the front door.
They kiss.

16. Palace of Fine Arts – Day
Anderson watches Barbara walk up.
She sits down next to him.
They murmur.
She gives him an envelope.

17. Paul's Yacht – Day
Paul pours a tall scotch.
Gwyn walks up the ladder and onto the boat.
They kiss.

18. Tennis Club – Day
At the edge of Court One, Veronica sips iced tea.
Detective Anderson sits next to her.
From Court One, the tennis pro watches.
When Anderson leaves, Veronica calls Gwyn's mobile phone.

19. Paul's Yacht – Day
The mobile phone rings and Gwyn answers.
Veronica and Gwyn make plans to meet for a drink that night.
Gwyn gets out of bed.
She dresses, kisses Paul.
She leaves the boat.

20. A Women's Only Club in the Castro District – Night
Veronica and Gwyn drink with other women.
Gwyn gives Veronica a happy pill.
They dance, kiss, grind.
Veronica is wild on ecstasy.
They leave in a town car.

21. Gwyn's Bedroom – Day
Veronica wakes up hurting from the drugs.
She can't find her handbag.
Gwyn gives her the cab fare.

22. Nob Hill House – Shower – Day
Paul opens the shower door.
Veronica won't let him in.
Paul slams the shower door.
The sun beats hot through the bathroom window.
Veronica's tears are lost in the shower spray.

Notes on *Trophy Wives*

Act Two of the rough draft of *Trophy Wives* has 22 scenes. Some scenes have been sketched earlier; some were created by spinning down the page; others are just names – place-holders to stabilise the structure, leaving the writer free to keep moving to the climax.

Of the 22 scenes in Act Two, the writer has designated five for the midpoint:

Scene 9 – Kitchen: the characters are Paul, Veronica, and Anderson. The ritual is interrogation. Where were you last night? What time did you get home? Was your wife asleep? When did you last see Ashleigh Bennett alive? What does Mrs Watson have to say? Objects in the scene will be kitchen things: cups, saucers, coffee pot, sugar, cream, perhaps a danish – the detective is hungry – and fancy cutlery. Another object is the detective's little notebook. The scene ends when lawyer Snyder arrives.

Scene 10 – Bedroom: the characters are Paul and Veronica. The ritual is barter. She will trade him one alibi for the deed to the house. If she is smart, Veronica will get a note signed right now. Remember that your characters are evolving. You will keep making changes until the book is at proof stage.

Scene 11 – Green Cadillac: the characters are Paul and Snyder. The ritual is interrogation. If Snyder is nervous (he's a civil lawyer with no criminal experience) then Paul will sweat. The man-talk establishes Paul's affair with Ashleigh. As the writer goes deeper into character, Veronica will develop into a deeper person than Ashleigh. In a quick rewrite, the writer can use Snyder to frame Veronica's special spiritual qualities by using a dialogue line like: 'If I was lucky enough to have a wife like Mrs Watson, I wouldn't be messing about with girls like Ashleigh Bennett. How good was she with numbers?'

Scene 12 - Nob Hill Home: the characters are Veronica and Gwyn, an estate agent. This is an interesting twist. If Veronica shows Gwyn the note - Paul signing the house over - then Gwyn will have an excuse to hang out with Veronica. This is a great time to assess Veronica's character and her motives. If she loves the house, it means she has bought into the Cinderella dream. If she hates the house, Gwyn can help her sell it for big money to finance her return to graduate school. If the house has a heavy mortgage weighing it down - more secrets kept by nasty Paul - then Veronica must sell the house, creating even more need for a good estate agent. If there is a heavy mortgage, where did the money go?

Scene 13 - Interview Room: the characters are Paul, Snyder, and Anderson. This is a good time for Anderson to reveal his antipathy for rich men like Paul. Men born into wealth. Men who not only never had to work, but who also use their power to steal from the public. If the writer hangs onto the idea of corporate corruption, then Anderson can have photos of Paul that he pulled off a news website. If Anderson is smart, he will wait for evidence from Barbara, Paul's jealous sibling, who uses the corruption scandal to flush Paul from the executive cloakroom.

At the heart of Act Two, we find competition - for money, the house, and control of the business. Off to the side, Detective Anderson carries out his scapegoat sacrifice: Paul might be innocent of killing Ashleigh, but he is guilty of being rich. We still need to know more about the connection between Barbara and Detective Anderson. To find out how they connected, the writer will have to write more back story.

To keep the surface buzzing, the writer uses the barter ritual. Paul barters with Ashleigh to keep quiet about cooking the books at Phoenix Investments. Veronica barters with Paul to get the house. Barbara barters with Paul for control of the business. When the writer writes the sex scene between Gwyn and Veronica, the barter ritual will lurk in the subtext. We see Gwyn in action - she moves between lovers like Justine in the novel of the same name by Lawrence Durrell.

To write the Act Two rough draft, the writer expands on the scene-sequence used to develop the midpoint. After finishing the rough draft for Act Three, the writer will have time to work up the various subplots that have popped up. In this novel-in-progress, there is a subplot for each main character:

- Subplot 1 belongs to Paul. He is the main antagonist.
- Subplot 2 belongs to Barbara. She is Antagonist 2. Her subplot crosses Paul's each time they struggle for control of the company. Barbara is a shadowy character who will need some work (sketch, wardrobe, back story, dream) soon.
- Subplot 3 could belong to Gwyn or to Detective Anderson. Both are out for revenge. At this point in the writing, Anderson's revenge is clearer than Gwyn's.
- Subplot 4 belongs to the character who did not get Subplot 3. Gwyn, a walk-on with no agenda, has suddenly grown teeth as sharp as the Wicked Stepmother in Cinderella. As an estate agent, Gwyn could sell the Nob Hill mansion for Veronica, another barter ritual in progress.
- Subplot 5 belongs to the victim, Ashleigh Bennett.

The plot thickens in Act Two because your characters, who had no lives before you put them into your novel, are catching fire. You started out with stick figures and now here they are, cheating on each other, scrapping, fighting for their lifestyles just like mastodons versus great apes on the Darwinian Plain.

The scenes are moving faster now because the writer is approaching the climax. When you write your rough draft, it's better to keep moving. Don't stop to think. Don't stop to fix spelling and punctuation. A line-edit now will kill your story dead.

Because of Paul's deal with Veronica, we have an ethical question to solve. Will she help him? How badly does she need money? Can she get help from someone else? How about Barbara?

Weekends 44–49:
Writing your rough draft for Act Three

Act Three is the End.

There is no going back from here.

There is climax – the resolution that Aristotle called 'catharsis', where the audience gets purged, through the crafty use of symbols, of all rancid emotion.

There is the approach to the climax – a multi-step sequence that calls for your total focus.

There is the threshold-crossing from Act Two, which we explored when we crafted the rough draft for Act Two.

In Act Three, you bring back objects (gun, bullet, book, treasure, coffin, slipper) from the Plan B plotting section and you gather the characters that are still alive, still kicking, still seething with rage and lust and greed – characters with powerful motives and weighty agendas. And because Act Three is the end, you make use of echoes; those returning sounds that work like chords in this symphony of a novel. Echoes in a novel can glitter with the tinsel of romantic, Cinderella-ised happiness or they can fall with dead sounds, hollow and empty.

In the rough draft, you are a wild child flying free, arms flung wide, open to all things. As you keep writing, nose to the page, fingers tapping those keys, you mature into an artist, exalted by your creation. You write. You print out pages. You seek feedback from trusted friends who understand the pain and pleasure of the writing process. In the 'Writing State', achieved through writing practice, you might write even when you're not writing. When you started this novel, so many weekends ago, you went for speed. If you were writing with other writers, you felt competitive. If the writer sitting next to you wrote five pages, you tried for six. If the writer across the table waxed lyrical, you sweated to turn yourself into a poet.

Now that you are almost home, almost done with the Rough Draft, you will find that your writing wants to go deeper. The images that you dropped along the way want to repeat themselves. Now when you write, you go for torque – a slow and powerful gathering-together of all the elements of your story.

In Act Three, you move with relentless resolve towards resolution. You cap off minor characters. As the climax starts, you want the major characters either on your novel's stage, or waiting in the wings to come on. In Act Three, as you move towards resolution, you can keep the conflict going by letting your characters move at different speeds. Character A, for example, wants to rush forwards towards resolution, while Character B, working a different agenda, dawdles, stopping for a meal, a coffee, a bit of window-shopping.

To find the best strategy for Act Three, you look back at what you did for Acts One and Two. In writing Act One, you focused on the problem of characters onstage – getting them on, dressed, faces prepared and agendas pulsing – to drive your book through to Plot Point 1. In writing Act Two, you focused on ritual – teaching and training and the painful process of learning – as you deepened symbols and explored the past.

Now, when you write Act Three, you'll focus on echoes that resound – echoing images, echoing lines, echoing incidents – repetitions that replay themselves in your novel as you move, in the end, towards an effect not unlike a symphony.

In Act Three, you focus on resolution.

Sketching the fate of your protagonist

When he wrote *Tender Is the Night*, his novel about insanity and falling into ruin, F Scott Fitzgerald was writing from knowledge about the downward slide in his own life. Like his protagonist, Dr Richard Diver, Fitzgerald the writer was on his own personal downhill run to oblivion. The name 'Diver' symbolises the fall, the slide, the final dive.

All this becomes clear in Act Three, where Fitzgerald has chosen the Big X structure (see Figure 18) to represent not only the fall of Dr Richard Diver, but also the rise of Dr Diver's wife, Nicole – a mental patient who gets well. Trapped in his downhill slide on his leg of the Big X plot structure, Diver has a final meeting with Rosemary Hoyt, his lover from Book One. The year is 1930. Five years have passed since their First Encounter. And now they have this dialogue, where Dr Diver remembers how Rosemary looked in her negligée. And Rosemary says she will pretend that it is five years ago and she is 18 again.

The scene is the beach, a landmark brought forward from Act One. Dr Diver, trying to show off on an aquaplane towed behind a speedboat, cannot lift himself out of the water. And then his wife remembers that just last year on the Zugersee, her husband was able to lift a large man on his shoulders, and stand up on the speeding aquaplane. Panting for Rosemary, Dr Diver says that he could not have lifted a paper doll. And Rosemary remembers that her first drink was with Dr Diver. And Dr Diver mentions that he is going downhill, or so the rumour says.

The writing trick here is the point of view. Because Mrs Diver has the point of view, the writer shows us that it's her story now. And as her husband evokes the past by flirting with Rosemary, we watch a man dive deeper into ruin. At the end of Act Three, Dr Diver is about to make his last dive.

Act Three is the closing movement of your novel. Here, with the dramatic climax, you bring your action to a conclusion that satisfies the reader. If you're writing a love story, the lovers – having been split apart for much of Act Two – get together at last. If you follow Anne Tyler's lead in *The Accidental Tourist* and deepen the love story with a psychological rebirth of a reluctant, passive hero, you could wind up your story in London or Paris or Provence or Venice in the early morning, with sunlight and confetti.

In this section of the book, you need to refocus on the shape of your plot (see Figure 18) while you take one more run at the climax.

- In the Big X structure, the climax occurs when Protagonist 1 hits bottom. Good examples of the Big X are *Tender Is the Night* and *Leaving Las Vegas*. Both novels have generated feature films.
- In the dramatic structure of the rising line, the climax occurs with the sound of trumpets. Cinderella tries on the glass slipper and crosses the threshold from Lower World to Upper World.
- In the Heroic Cycle of Departure, Initiation, and Return, there could be two climaxes: one when the protagonist crosses that last threshold, and the other when s/he returns to the starting place. The shepherd boy-hero of Coelho's *The Alchemist* returns to Spain to find gold buried under the same tree from which he started.
- In the Mythic Journey of Cage, Escape, Quest, Dragon, and Home, the climax occurs when the hero meets the dragon. Gogol Ganguli discovers his wife's affair. Her mask falls, revealing a devouring dragon.

Because you have written the climax, spinning your words down the page, your main task in Act Three is to build an approach to the climax. You have subplots to manage, characters to orchestrate,

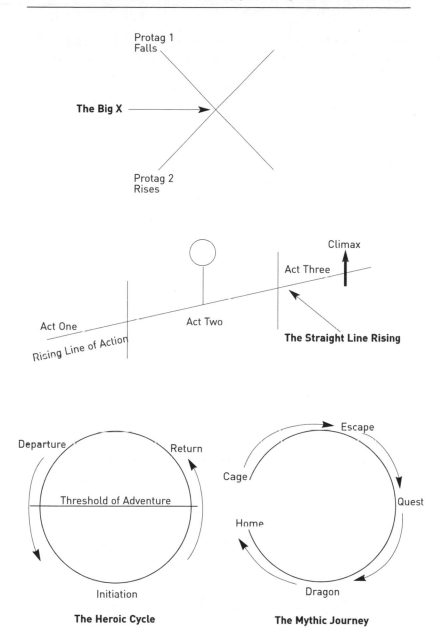

FIGURE 18: STRUCTURES FOR YOUR STORY: THE BIG X, THE STRAIGHT LINE RISING, THE HEROIC CYCLE, AND THE MYTHIC JOURNEY

motives to recheck for plausibility. A look at Tyler's Act Three in *The Accidental Tourist* offers some great strategies for your work. At Plot Point 2, Rose's wedding, we watched Macon think about turning away from Muriel. Macon is a systems guy. For him, action – made passive by multiple deflections – is always preceded not just by thought, but by weighty analysis. He is a writer, after all.

Getting help from other writers

Rain opens Act Three of *The Accidental Tourist*. It's almost a year after the rain of Chapter 1, when Sarah, in the closed setting of the car, asked Macon for a divorce, beginning the separation that continues as we start Act Three. Macon is living with Muriel, who was introduced in the middle of Act One in a memorable First Encounter. But repetition can mean change: Muriel has left her job at Meow Bow, and her passport photos tell Macon that she's ready, as suggested in Chapter 7, to fly with him to romantic Paris. On the phone with her mum, Muriel recalls her training of Edward (the ritual strategy which brought her close to Macon) as she chats about a current dog-training project.

Muriel has changed, but when the phone rings in Winnipeg, Macon finds that Sarah, who wants to move back into their old house, is much the same. At the end of Chapter 18, Macon goes home, too.

When Sarah moves back to the house, she brings the place alive. With his mistress around, Edward the dog chills out. So Macon is thinking about replacing Muriel with Sarah, the same way in which he replaced Sarah with Muriel earlier, at the midpoint, when they shared their secret wounds. But Muriel, a female in touch with the cosmos (and also with her own economic needs), jumps on him about Sarah and marriage. Her energy drives him away, and by the middle of Act Three, he's back with Sarah. This return to the rituals of the past has a comforting feel to Macon, and perhaps to us. It doesn't last, because Sarah's still on her power trip, dumping on Macon with more verve than she used in Chapter 1.

In Paris, Tyler turns Sarah into a witch doctor, drugging Macon on pain pills while she takes over his work. For Macon, the systems guy who gains his identity from work, this is the last straw. In a major action, he drops the pain pill without a long analysis preceding the action. He's leaving Sarah. He's going back to Muriel. Dropping the pill – a simple action of opening the fingers, tilting the palm, and letting go – marks the climax of Act Three for *The Accidental Tourist*.

You want this same thrill of triumph, brought about through cathartic change, in your Act Three. Macon Leary, a protagonist gritting his teeth over his back pain, is Tyler's substitute for the tough-guy hero of action films. This is a good strategy to follow: Give your protagonist a psychological wound, bury it deep, and then use the novel to heal your character. Macon has an interior wound left by the death of his son; he also has an exterior wound: an attack of Bad Back that brings Sarah to the rescue with a pain pill. Gritting his teeth, Macon exits, carrying his leather travel bag. Like Ike McCaslin, William Faulkner's hero in *The Bear* who leaves gun and compass at the edge of the wilderness so that he can meet the bear unencumbered by the trappings of civilisation, Macon Leary leaves his leather travel bag on a curb in Paris so he can make it to the taxi to pick Muriel up and start a new life. Unencumbered, Macon has made a fundamental decision to change his life dramatically.

Guidelines for writing your rough draft for Act Three

Read through your work – not just the rough-draft material, but also the character work (sketches, back story, dreams, wardrobe items) and the work you did on objects. Jot notes as you read, preparing you for the rough draft of Act Three.

When you start writing, use characters and objects to evoke the past. For example, in Act Three of *Jane Eyre*, a letter surfaces in the library of Jane's cousin, a parson named St John Rivers. The letter comes from the past; from Jane's uncle, John Eyre, who has left her an inheritance – enough money to set her free and enable her to locate Mr Rochester. In Act Three of *The Great Gatsby*, the protagonist is dead (killed by an assassin) and an old man named Mr Gatz arrives for the funeral. Mr. Gatz is the father of Jimmy Gatz, also known as Jay Gatsby, who lies dead in his coffin at West Egg. Like his son Jimmy/Jay, Mr Gatz comes from Out West, set in capital letters to separate it from the East, where Gatsby died trying to get accepted. Mr Gatz and Nick the Narrator and a party animal named Owl Eyes are the only people at Gatsby's funeral. Owl Eyes carries the object – the spectacles that give him his name – that evokes the image of the egg-like eyes of Dr T J Eckleberg, which look out at the Valley of Ashes in Act One.

Make sure that you know the fate of each character in Act Three. Does your protagonist live or die? Does your antagonist live or die? Does your helper live or die? If you are writing crime fiction, your sleuth's job is to execute or incarcerate the killer at the climax. At the climax of *Gorky Park*, by Martin Cruz Smith, the killer, a rich American named John Osborne, kills five people: two agents of the Russian KGB and three agents of the American FBI. Osborne, a fur breeder, has taken money and assistance from both agencies. Before the climax starts, as the sleuth enters the killing ground, he comes upon two other victims. They are in full view, left there by the killer as a message: he means business; he will kill again. Seven victim-bodies are piled up in Act Three, more than enough to justify an execution, but there are six more bodies in the back story.

To open the book, the writer uses three victim-corpses discovered by a policeman in the snow and ice of Gorky Park. And a quarter of a century earlier, in the back story, the killer executed three German officers in Leningrad because they laughed at him, covering him with scorn. It happened like this: before he became a killer, he was an idealistic young American exercising his altruism through a relief programme that distributed food from America to the citizens of Leningrad. The German officers laughed at him because they knew that the good citizens of Leningrad had turned to cannibalism to survive. Compared to the weight of the tons of flesh from the Russian dead, the food from America was insignificant.

Add three more victims for a total of 13 corpses, and the writer justifies the sleuth's execution of the killer in Act Three.

Get basic with Fate. In *Gorky Park*, the killer dies. The sleuth lives. The heroine, a Cinderella *femme fatale* from Siberia, also lives.

Once you know the fate of each character, develop a list of scenes for Act Three. The first scene on the list is Plot Point 2, which marks the end of Act Two and the beginning of Act Three. One of the smartest uses of Plot Point 2 is the wedding of Rose and Julian in *The Accidental Tourist*. If you recall, Julian's subplot begins in Act One, when he is 'treed' by Edward, and then it joins Rose's subplot when Julian has dinner at the Leary House. The wedding at the end of Act Two, a climax to the Julian-Rose subplot, brings our three major characters together – Macon the protagonist, Sarah the antagonist, and Muriel the helper – setting up a sexual triad (Macon has had sexual relations with both of these women) and highlighting the choice that the protagonist must make at the end of Act Three: Will he choose his wife, Sarah? Or will he choose his lover, Muriel?

Your two other obligatory scenes are the climax and a 'wrap-up' scene that contains a final image to help your readers remember your novel long after they have finished reading. The final image in *The Great Gatsby* is the green light that blinks at the end of Daisy's dock in East Egg. The final image in *The Accidental Tourist* shows Macon and Muriel in the taxi in Paris with the sudden sunlight hitting the raindrops on the windshield, turning them into confetti. The final image in *Gorky Park* shows the sleuth bleeding in the snow in rural New Jersey, watching the *femme fatale* walk away, muttering about needing a pair of fur boots. The final image in *Moby-Dick* shows Ishmael the Narrator riding Queequeg's coffin up through a spinning vortex, away from the Pequod, the dead captain, and the drowned crew – rising 'like Ixion', Melville writes, popping to the surface, where he is rescued by one of the nine ships so that he can live to tell the tale. The wrap-up scene should follow closely on the tail of the climax. The climax needs to be choreographed: Melville takes three days and three chapters for the climax in *Moby-Dick*; Martin Cruz Smith orchestrates the killer's killings, building motivation for the execution of the killer in *Gorky Park*; in *The Accidental Tourist*, Anne Tyler brings Sarah back to drug Macon with pain pills, forcing him to give up the pill (the sacred object) in the same way that a knight errant would give up a secret potion before taking his wounded body out from the Castle of Spells. You need to design an approach to the climax in the same way as you would build a staircase into a building.

The approach to the climax should start back in Act One, move through Act Two, and lead the reader through Act Three at a quickening pace to arrive at the climax. As we have mentioned, Tyler sets up Macon's decision – wife or lover; Sarah or Muriel – in the first scene, when Sarah asks for a divorce. Macon hires Muriel at Plot Point 1, in the same chapter where Julian meets Rose to start the Julian-Rose subplot that ends with the wedding at Plot Point 2. At the midpoint, halfway between Plot Points 1 and 2, Muriel and Macon share their wounds and Muriel takes Macon into her bed. They are together until Sarah comes to the wedding.

In *Gorky Park*, the sleuth follows a trail of dead bodies and sable fur from the opening scene in Gorky Park, where three victims lay buried in snow, all the way to the killer's sable farm in rural New Jersey, where the climax takes place. The three dead victims are young people in their 20s. One is an American; two are Russians from Siberia. The Russians worked at a fur factory in Siberia, where they met the killer, who promised to get them to America if they would smuggle out six sables. The young American threatened to expose the killer. The killer kills all three, then uses his skinning knife to cut off their fingertips and so delay identification of the bodies. Tracking the sable hairs left by the two dead Russians, the sleuth nails the killer. On the way, he loses his best friend, makes a new friend, falls in love, and has a near-death experience that makes for fine reading.

In *The Great Gatsby*, Fitzgerald uses cars (wrecked roadster, hearse, white car, blue car, and yellow car) to lay out his approach to the climax. In *Moby-Dick*, Melville uses the harpoon and related objects from the whale hunt to write his way to Ahab's line that echoes Shakespeare: 'Thus, I give up the spear.'

Watch those unhappy endings

Real-life scenario: A writer in a fiction seminar draws her novel on the board. The story is about a woman around the writer's age and of similar temperament who loses her husband in a car accident. As she reaches the dramatic climax, the writer pauses: 'My heroine dies here,' she announces. 'She kills herself.'

A 'downer' ending brings a groan from the group.

As a strategy, the writing teacher advises the writer to plug into Greek mythology. Read some Bulfinch, the teacher says, and come back next week with a different ending – something that smacks of redemption. She comes back with the story of Laodamia and Protesilaus, a warrior killed by Hector at the battle of Troy. 'When Laodamia heard about her husband's death,' the writer says, 'she asked the gods for a boon. She wanted three hours to talk to him and they said okay. Mercury brought him back to the upper world. When he died a second time, Laodamia died with him. Isn't it beautiful?'

Dipping into Greek mythology gave the writer a better ending for her story. The death of her protagonist, which reunited her with her husband, now made story sense. Be careful of those downer endings.

Exercises

1. Warm up
Use this startline: 'The shape of Act Three looks (feels) like...' (writing time: 10 minutes).

2. Climax
Using the down-the-page technique, write your climax in ten minutes. No stopping to think.

3. Approach to the climax
Following the climax-writing, write an approach to the climax in 20

minutes. *Tip*: Use numbers and named scenes; also, add action using strong verbs – Muriel leaves her job; Sarah phones Macon.

4. Threshold-crossing
Using the location-change as your key, write the threshold-crossing scene that moves your protagonist across the barrier from Act Two to Act Three. How much time has passed? What motive drives the character across?

5. Chain of events
Following the form used in the Guidelines above, create a chain of events connecting Plot Point 1 with your climax, and your climax with the wrap-up scene. Make sure that each event has a large action that connects to the earlier parts of the book.

6. List of scenes
Make a list of scenes for Act Three. Include pieces of scenes, bits of scenes, snippets. If a scene is finished, write 'Done' in red pencil near your entry. If a scene is unfinished, write 'Still to write' or 'More to come'. When your list is done, examine it for holes in the plot. Can an old scene be expanded to cover the hole? Do you need a new scene? If there are scenes you can cut now, do so.

7. Write the scenes
In timed writings of 15–20 minutes, write the scenes from your scene-list. By now you should be able to write full scenes, integrating the parts as you go. Your goal is 3–4 scenes per weekend.

8. Saving your work
Print out your scenes for Act Three. File the new pages in your folder.

Getting help from other writers

Once, when a writer of our acquaintance sent a final draft to an editor, the manuscript came back with all the dreams deleted. They were lyrical dreams, the writer remembers, packed with symbols and touched with the mysterious blend of dreamtime and shadowy shivers of eroticism. The writer had worked hard; the dreams were well-written, and the proud writer stayed miffed about the deletion of dreams all through the final copy-edit and the proof stage, and he was still miffed until he saw the manuscript turned into a book with a handsome cover, a product for the marketplace, and then, reading it over, searching for the holes he had patched after cutting those dreams, he realised that his editor, once again, had been right.

The dreams, though beautiful, had been excess baggage. In novel-writing, in this day and age, you cut the excess and save a tree. If the writing is good, you can save what you cut in a special folder, for use in another novel.

The novel-in-progress: *Trophy Wives*

When Veronica jerks open the French doors, she sees Paul sitting behind his big man-desk. The desk that belonged to his father. She does not see Gwyn, who hits her on the back of the head with a gun. She wakes up handcuffed to a high-backed leather chair to see Gwyn kissing Paul. Her stomach twists; she feels nausea. She must have passed out, because when she wakes up again, they are arguing. Something about money, numbers, Ashleigh's death.

Veronica says:'He knows you did it.'

'Who knows who did what?'

'Detective Anderson. He knows you killed Ashleigh.'

Gwyn gets nervous, stands up, waves the gun around. Paul reaches for the gun. Gwyn steps back, crying, hysterical. Outside the window, the sound of sirens. Brakes screeching, car doors slamming, the sound of men's voices. Gwyn moves to the window, aiming the gun outside. Paul grabs the gun. 'I'm clear,' he says. 'And you…'

Gwyn turns. The muzzle of the gun presses into Paul. There is a loud explosion. Veronica struggles with the handcuffs. A voice calls from the hallway:'Drop it.' Gwyn swings around. Her face is hard. The gun muzzle wavers, then points at Veronica. The gun explodes again and Veronica feels herself falling. As she falls, she sees Gwyn spurting blood from her throat and she remembers the time they spent together and it was all a lie.

Detective Anderson rushes into the room. He puts a finger on Gwyn's throat. He does the same with Paul. He walks on his knees to Veronica.

'Are you okay?'

'Yes.'

'I got here as quick as I could.'

'Yes,' she says. 'Thank you.'

'Your husband, he wants to say goodbye.'

Veronica's hands are free, but she's having trouble moving. She stares at Paul. His eyelids flutter. He holds out one hand. The fingers clutch. He utters a small scream, like a child. And then he is gone.

Detective Anderson picks Veronica up. Her arms tighten around his neck. She feels so small and he feels so strong. He is old enough to be her father. He carries her to an ambulance where he lays her on the stretcher.

'Thank you, Detective.'

'You'll be okay, Mrs Watson.'

From the ambulance, Veronica watches him walk about 20 feet away. His back is to her. He stops. He pulls out his mobile phone. Veronica closes her eyes.

1. Barbara's Office – Day
Barbara answers the phone.
The caller is Detective Anderson.
Her smile shows that she is happy.

2. Hospital Room
Detective Anderson walks into the room.
He sits in the chair by Veronica's bed.
They talk about the death of Paul.
He takes her statement.

3. Barbara's Boardroom
She sits at the head of the table.
She talks of change.
Men in suits nod and smile.

4. Barbara's Office
Veronica sits in a chair.
She signs papers.
Barbara offers to send money.
They shake hands.

5. Coffee Shop
Across the street from Barbara's office, Veronica sips a coffee.
She watches as the Silver Maybach pulls up.
Barbara walks out the front door of the office.
The side door opens and Detective Anderson helps Barbara into the car.

The writing in this section focuses on the end of Act Three. There is death and there is blood and the writer has reached the climax by writing – not by talking about it, not by thinking about it. There is action. There is retribution. The bad guy dies. The good girl lives. Only by writing your way to the climax do you feel the fates of your characters. And when you know who lives and who dies and who gets exiled, then you wedge the book in between the beginning and the end.

In *Trophy Wives*, we have three corpses – Ashleigh, Paul, and Gwyn – and three survivors: Veronica, Barbara, and Anderson. Because the dialogue is sparse, the writer could use an action to suggest Veronica's future. What if, for example, she removed an envelope from her handbag, and what if she set the envelope beside a new copy of *Jane Eyre*? And what if there was money inside the envelope? And what if she takes a taxi to a pleasant old-fashioned house in an older section of town? And what if the taxi passes by a university campus? And what if Veronica sighs and leans back against the car seat, closing her eyes?

Where to go from here

A year of weekends is almost over. The only thing left is a big and exciting decision: Where do you go from here? The writing has taught you a lot. You now know the highs and lows of novel-writing. You have a substantial manuscript that needs work. You have a story and some characters that have come alive. In the next three weekends, we have provided suggestions to guide you to further writing adventures. Depending on where you are with your manuscript – how much is fiction, how much your real life – you can now choose to work with this material in at least three directions: personal memoir, film script, or a rewrite of the novel you started 49 weekends ago.

Turn the page and find the pathway for your next writing journey.

part 7 Weekends 50–52:

Tapping the Power of Your Manuscript

By Weekend 49, the end of your writing journey, you have a pile of a manuscript, enough to make you proud. You have 200 pages, 300 pages, perhaps more. You have chapters and scenes and a rousing climax. You have passages of exposition that are perfect and you have descriptions that make you proud of your hard work. You have lists of characters, places, scenes, and objects. You have diagrams of your plot, sketches of key scenes, storyboards, and scene-profiles.

If your novel is finished – if you are satisfied that there is nothing you can do to make it better – then it's time to test the marketplace. Find an agent who can place your book with a publisher. But if your book still needs work, and if the manuscript contains problems – not enough action, no antagonist, more than one protagonist, too much autobiography, too many flashbacks – then you have three pathways to consider:

1. Write a personal memoir.
2. Rewrite your novel, starting with story.
3. Write a screenplay for a feature film.

Let's take these pathways one at a time.

Weekend 50:

The Weekend Novelist writes a memoir

If you are like most first-time novelists, you wrote something of yourself into your manuscript. Don't fret about it. Life is both precious and too short, and the urge to leave something behind, something to be remembered by, is only natural. Before he became famous with *Ulysses* (1922), James Joyce drew from his own life to write *A Portrait of the Artist as a Young Man*. Ernest Hemingway drew from his life as an expatriate in Cuba to write *Islands in the Stream*, a tale of an ageing writer fighting Nazis in World War II. Writing about yourself is natural – not sinful or self-indulgent – and now that you have finished a rough draft, you can page back through the manuscript and take notes. If you encounter stories and people and objects from your real life as you read, you might consider turning those real-life details into a personal memoir. Gather the memories into a list. Give each memory a name – First Date, First Day at School, Last Birthday Party, My Dad the Pious Prison Warden – and an approximate date that locates the memory in time. How much memoir have you already written? How much more do you need to write?

Using the list as a starting place, write for several weeks in your memoir journal, or on your trusty laptop. For a warm-up, use a start-line beginning with 'I remember':

'I remember that day…'
'I remember the time when…'
'I remember my first teacher…'
'I remember the day my mother told me…'
'I remember the day I fell down and there was blood on the pavement and…'

Write non-stop for three or four weekends, until you have 50–100 pages of memories, and then read them over, trying not to be critical, to find the patterns in your writing. What ideas have surfaced? What threads keep repeating?

Pattern in a memoir can be a period of time (the year you got engaged, that summer between school and college, that winter you got sick and almost died) or a series of memories linked together by place, person, object, or ceremony. A writer in one of our memoir workshops started writing about birthdays. She began with her last birthday, blowing out the candles, opening presents, writing about friends and relatives and the moment of suspense when her ex-husband crashed the party. She felt so good when she read what she had written (writing about things long buried is often therapeutic) that she built an entire memoir on birthdays: the guests, the presents, the songs, the cake and candles, the accidents, the intruders who crashed the party. Her dialogue got better, the people became more real, and the action of blowing out the candles took on heft and substance: 'As you lean over the cake, your mind targeted on those wavering candles, you grip the edge of the table with both hands. Your neck is tight, your head tilted back. You bend your knees, bringing your chest down, getting your lungs closer to the target. Your nose twitches and you smell cigarette smoke. This is a no-smoking household, so the cigarette is on the patio, and the French doors must be open. You remember closing the doors. The smell of smoke gags you, makes you want to vomit. The smell comes from Camels. Camels, the cigarettes of your ex-husband. Husband named Johnny, a handsome boy who smoked to keep the weight off. Off with the weight, he would say, firing up a Camel cigarette, and now he's out there, on the patio, robed in smoke.'

The writer writes in the second person – 'you', not 'I' – keeping her memories at a safe distance. Near the end of the passage, she starts a sentence or fragment with the last word of the previous sentence or fragment: 'The smell comes from Camels. Camels, the cigarettes of...' This is a rhetorical device called anadiplosis. We call it 'chaining' and we use the device to introduce writers to rhythm and repetition. The Camel cigarette is an object; the object attaches to the person, swathing the writer's husband in foul-smelling smoke, making him more real on the page. She divorced him, and now he's back, an intruder into the closed circle of the birthday party – friends and family only. She's feeling the power even through the 'you' pronoun; writing about this kind of power-packed memory could be the breakthrough that will keep you working away at your memories, until you write enough to mark a pathway to structure.

The best structure for the personal memoir is the Mythic Journey; the same plotting device you worked with during Weekends 3–4 of this book, when you started writing your novel. In novel-writing, you do your plotting early, before you commit to long paragraphs of prose, while you chart a path for your protagonist. In memoir-writing, you are the protagonist, and you write to sort through the material to see what comes up before you grab for structure.

The novel is fiction and the people are characters. In contrast, the memoir is real stuff remembered, and the people are called 'inhabitants'. Inhabitants in your memoir will match up with inhabitants in other memoirs: parents, siblings, grandparents, aunts, uncles, cousins, friends, teachers, bosses, colleagues, and enemies. In a novel you have one main antagonist and several minor antagonists. In a memoir, your antagonist figure is the Terrible Parent (two good examples are Lauren Slater's mother in her memoir *Lying* and Frank McCourt's father in *Angela's Ashes*) or, if the Terrible One is not a parent, you might have the Terrible Teacher, the Terrible Sibling, the Terrible Friend.

You can write about yourself, your life, your birthdays, how it was for you blowing out candles. You can write about the cars in your life, starting with the first car: 'The first car they bought was a Ford Galaxy, used, with white leather seats and white sidewall tires and...' You can write about a good friend who died, or you can write about a parent who took on the role of the jailer who kept you in a cage. Because the cage starts the Mythic Journey sequence of Cage, Escape, Quest, Dragon, and Home, writing about the parent-as-jailer pulls you closer to structure.

Case study: Writer A

A writer in one of our memoir workshops kept writing about her father, a businessman in the American Midwest who planted flowers in intricate patterns and who organised a girls' softball team. The pretext for the team, the stated purpose, was to get his overweight daughter away from the television and onto the athletic field. The real purpose, buried in the subtext, was Dad's love of the game. He had played semi-pro baseball, had made it as far as the Try-Outs. But he wasn't quite good enough for the big time.

This writer – let's call her Writer A – wrote with a super-formal prose style, always calculated, always precise, of measured sentences and empty polysyllabic nouns chosen with great care. She salted her prose with useless '-ly' adverbs like effectively and woefully and mercilessly and basically. Adverbs slowed down her already draggy prose, but to slow it down even more, she packed together compound verbs like 'should have been assumed', 'would have seemed to be', and 'might have been considered to have been contemplated'.

Slow, anguished prose that encloses the writer like a suit of armour suggests a writer mired in fear. Fear of being discovered. Fear of discovery. Fear of that special memory buried back there.

Writer A was hiding behind Armoured Prose – a straitjacket made of Plexiglas that choked her throat when she read, that kept her secret memory locked down tight while she forced herself to write about dear old dad, who made her play baseball when she loved tennis. Listening to Writer A read her Armoured Prose put the whole workshop on edge, and then to sleep.

After writing about her father for many anguished weeks, Writer A's memory-bank coughed up Terrible Dan, a blue-collar hoodlum who attracted Writer A because he was dangerous, because her friends were afraid of him, because he was attracted to her and made it clear with money and favours. Terrible Dan was three years older than Writer A. He became her first lover. He initiated her into the underworld of drugs and sado-masochism. When she tried to break it off, he became her first stalker.

Terrible Dan woke up the workshop. Writer A's writing got better, the '-ly' adverbs dropping away and the weak verbs becoming strong verbs. And when Writer A stepped back, away from the writing, she saw how she could use the Mythic Journey.

Writer A starts in a cage. Her father is a strict and orderly man. He is the jailer. She escapes the cage with the help of Terrible Dan, a dark force who brings energy into her bland middle-class life. Terrible Dan comes from a broken home. He smokes, drinks, does drugs. As he pulls Writer A into his murky world, she feels herself dissolving. The choice she makes – to get away from Terrible Dan – sends her on the quest for tools and wisdom. He is the Dragon. Before she can confront him, however, Writer A must grow up, shed her silly ideas, and recognise her Dad as the helper.

Once she saw the shape of her story, Writer A used the Mythic Journey to finish her memoir. When she started, she had no intention of writing about Terrible Dan; but finishing the memoir was a cathartic experience for her. When she left the workshop, she said she would seek a publisher.

The shape of the book

The Weekend Novelist Writes a Memoir has a three-part structure. Part I is writing your memories in your memoir journal. You can use a notebook or a laptop, but you will write more good stuff if you keep to the discipline of timed writing to distract the attention of the internal editor. In the journal, you write free, roaming the fields of memory – no editing, no grammar worries.

Part II is 'The Structure of Memoir'. Structure, whether you are writing a novel or building a bridge or writing a sonnet or a memoir, is an arrangement of parts. The key to the structure of the novel is the dramatic scene. The key to the structure of the memoir is the memoir moment. When you construct a memoir moment, you go deep into memory, writing as if you were playing music. First, you set the theme of the moment. Then you develop two or three variations on that theme. Then you fashion a recapitulation, where you create echoes by repeating – you guessed it – words and phrases from the section where you set the theme. Finally, you develop a smooth segue to the next moment.

Some memoir moments spring from the memory data bank. Others must be coaxed. If you're writing a memoir, you'll need 20-30 memoir moments. Because the memoir moment is like music, you will find more rhythm in your words and writing the memoir will move away from information towards beauty.

When Writer A discovered Terrible Dan, she was writing a memoir moment about softball: 'The place is Kenmore, Kansas, the yellow grass ball field of Kenmore City Park and the season is summer and the team is playing a ball game against a team of rich girls from Kansas City. My dad paces, his face sweaty, his fingers curling, then uncurling. My mom sits with my brother and sister on the wooden bleachers. My dad gives me thumbs up as I walk to the batter's box. I feel sweat under my arms and thick oily sweat on my forehead and the salt taste of sweat on my tongue as the pitcher, a beautiful rich Amazon named Sheila, fires her famous fast ball. I focus on the ball coming at me bigger and bigger and my foot slides towards the ball, and the bat swings itself, pulling my arms through the swing, and I see the stitches rotating and the fear fills my throat because the count is two strikes against me and three balls and because Sheila the pitcher has struck me out for nine straight times only today I'm not hitting for Daddy but I am hitting for me and my lungs making a huffing sound as the wood slaps the leather ball and a cry from my team-mates and a sharp cracking sound and the ball zooms back at Sheila who dodges the ball whipping past her nose and a thrill in my heart as toes dig dirt and the wind cool on my face and first base so fat so close so dusty white and Sheila slipping, falling, hitting the dirt on the mound the ball slipping past the girl at second base and they are chanting for me from the sidelines, Go, Girl, Go, and…'

This long sentence extends the normal breath line. The technique, sometimes called 'stream-of-consciousness', comes from a Greek rhetorical device called polysyndeton, where Writer A stops using full stops, but instead writes 'and' where the full stops might have gone. Because of the beat of the 'and', the writing gets more rhythmic. There is a sense of release. For a moment, on the page, the writer feels free.

The long sentence from Writer A marks her transition from bad writer to better writer, from dull writer to interesting writer, and from Daddy's Girl to Player Who Cares. Learning to write the long-long sentence is one of the techniques you'll learn in Part III, called 'The Language of Memoir'.

In 'The Language of Memoir', you will learn writing techniques that will carry you through the rest of your life. You have already learned about anadiplosis (chaining end-words to first words). You have felt the release of the long-long sentence in polysyndeton. To balance the long-long sentence, you write short, using a device called asyndeton. Where polysyndeton has multiple connectors, asyndeton erases the connectors. An example frequently used by rhetoricians is Caesar's line: 'I came. I saw. I conquered.' Writer A might write: 'She pitched her wonder ball. I smacked it back. She grabbed for it. I sprinted for First. She tripped. Fell. Dust rose up.' Without connectors, we write shorter sentences. Writing short changes the rhythm. When the rhythm sings, you have more fun.

When you reach the end of the memoir book, you will have 200–300 pages written: memories, memoir moments, chronologies, a list of objects, descriptions of photos and houses and rooms, a roster of your inhabitants, dialogues with your inhabitants. You will have a stack of structural diagrams, showing how you gained control over the material. If you are like most writers, you will have formed a memoir-writing group. A group is a great place to share and find support. And the techniques you learn by writing a memoir will stay with you for the rest of your days.

Exercises you can try now

1. Make a list of memories.
2. Look at old photos and write about them.
3. Read some memoirs. Suggestions follow.

Suggested reading list – memoirs

William Styron, driven mad by depression, climbed out of the darkness and found the ladder to Greater Fame by writing *Darkness Visible: A Memoir of Madness*. Another memoir of madness – *The Noonday Demon: An Atlas of Depression* – recently won an American National Book Award.

The subject for memoir can be the writer (e.g. *My Life as a Dog*, *The Liar's Club*). If you're writing about people, your subject can be someone famous, as in A E Hotchner's *Papa Hemingway* or *Willa Cather: A Memoir*, by Elizabeth Shipley Sergeant. Or the subject can be someone unknown, like Frank McCourt's mother, the now-famous Angela of *Angela's Ashes*. If you're doing a slice from a life, you follow a thread that creates a theme that ignites the writing, as Lauren Slater did in *Lying*. To date, Slater has published four memoirs with four topics from her life: epilepsy, Prozac, rebirth, and motherhood. She is a fine stylist. To locate memoirs on the World Wide Web, just Google the word 'memoir'.

Weekend 51:
The Weekend Novelist rewrites the novel

Your rough draft is done. It is 250–300 pages long. It has half a dozen major characters. It has key scenes and a rousing climax. You feel good about much of the writing, but you know that the manuscript needs work. You try to rewrite, starting with the first sentence on page 1, using time-honoured techniques learned at school when you worked on the school newspaper. Blue-pencil, they called it back then, or line-editing.

You go line-by-line, sentence-by-sentence, word-by-word. You cross out, you make marginal notes. You replace words and you polish up those metaphors. As you work the sentences, however, you feel the story changing. Like a tectonic plate, the plot slips out from under you and there you are, waltzing through a subplot, when you realise that you have just switched the point of view. That point-of-view switch makes you wonder if this is a pattern in your writing – switching the point of view – so you stop line-editing and you spend some time tracking the point-of-view switches throughout the manuscript.

There are so many switches in the point of view that you take notes. And then you convert the notes into a master list, and when the master list bulges with information, you pack all the point-of-view switches into a grid. The grid reveals pattern: every time you switched the point of view, there was a shift from plot to subplot, or from one subplot to another. So you make another grid, this one on subplots. You count three major subplots and two minor sub-plots. Seems like a lot, until you remember that *Jane Eyre* had five subplots and that *The Great Gatsby* had six. Thinking about *Jane Eyre* reminds you that you, too, are writing a rags-to-riches story. So you track down your copy of *Jane Eyre* and then you develop a character grid that shows, not only the breakdown for plot and sub-plot, but also role, object, and fate:

Name	Role	Archetype	Plot/ Subplot	Object	Core Story
Jane	Protag	Cinderella	Plot	Letter	Rags to Riches
Mr R	Antag 1	Prince	SP1	Cloak	Queen Replacement
Bertha	Antag 2	Wicked Stepmother	SP2	Fire	Revenge Quest
Mason	Antag 3	Messenger	SP3	Overcoat	Revenge Quest 2
Aunt Reed	Antag 4	Wicked Stepmother	SP4	Silk	Scapegoat Sacrifice
St John Rivers	Antag 5	Suitor	SP5	Bible/Letter	King Replacement

TABLE 8: A SNAPSHOT OF LAYERS IN *JANE EYRE*

Take a moment to peruse the grid based on *Jane Eyre*. The grid is a snapshot of layers in the novel. The plot, which runs on the surface of the novel, occupies the top row of the grid. The subplots stack up under the plot. The plot follows the path of the protagonist; each subplot follows the story of another character: antagonist, helper, etc. In *Jane Eyre*, Subplot 1 belongs to the antagonist, Mr Rochester. He has Subplot 1, even though he does not enter the story until Act Two, when his horse slips on the icy causeway and dumps him onto the ice, where he is rescued by Jane. This grid shows the other four antagonists – Bertha Mason Rochester; Bertha's brother, Richard Mason; nasty Aunt Reed; and Jane's pious cousin, St John Rivers, who wants to marry Cousin Jane and whisk her away to India, where she could do good works and convert the heathen.

The *Jane Eyre* grid gives you an insight: there is another way to rewrite besides fierce line-editing. So you stop line-editing – you can go back to that task at any time – while you read through the manuscript. Remembering your work when you prepared characters and plot, you make lists. You already have a list of subplots and switches in the point of view. Now you list characters, scenes, settings, and objects. You make notes as you read: 'Character A meets Character B. This scene is a First Encounter. The setting is the Las Vegas Strip, the time close to midnight. The object is money. The scene is number 15. Where are we in the structure? Feels close to Plot Point 1.'

Jotting down some basic information will give you control over your details for setting: time, place, lighting, and temperature. Temperature in your setting adds the reality of sensory perception. If it's hot in your story, the characters sweat. If it's cold, they shiver, huddled in their blankets. The novel-form is rife with paradox. You can have a plot without a single subplot but you cannot have a subplot without a plot, and if you don't pack in at least two subplots, you cannot write a novel. Because you need a few good objects, you must overload the manuscript with more objects than you need, but you won't know, until you start to rewrite, which objects will grow into symbols and which objects will shrink back to normal, everyday concrete nouns. Because place is so important, you play it safe by writing good, solid descriptions for every scene. Descriptions lock down place, and locking down place stabilises the characters by giving them a place to stand, sit, sleep, smoke, drive around town, get dressed, eat, smell, breathe. When you make your list of settings for the rewrite, you might realise that you're not using that particular scene – it takes the story in the wrong direction – so you cut that piece of description and grit your teeth against the pain. Because dialogue is an efficient way to get to know your characters, you write more than enough dialogue for two novels, and then when you rewrite, you chop half of it out. Ouch.

Tips for rewriting your novel

What kind of story are you writing here? Is it Rags to Riches? Is it a Grail Quest pulled forwards to the 21st century? Is it Coming of Age? Is it Revenge?

Manage your time. If you rebuild the story before you work on the language, then you'll have an efficient rewrite. If, however, you choose to dive into the words before the story is solid, you'll waste time and suffer major heartache.

Lock the plot to your protagonist – and remember that one protagonist is better than two or even three or four or seven. You are not writing *ER* here: this is your first novel. Jane Eyre, the orphan girl with a sturdy heart, needs no help driving her plot all the way to the climax. Using your list of scenes, track the plot from the opening page to the last page.

Attach a subplot to each major character. If you have only one major character besides your protagonist, you'll need at least one more. If you have ten major characters, you will have the makings of ten subplots, and sorting them out will take work. If you don't sort them out, your rewrite will be like rewriting *War and Peace* and *One Hundred Years of Solitude* combined. Number the subplots starting at Subplot 1. Line them up in a grid and feel the depth. Then count the number of scenes in each subplot. To do good work, a subplot needs a minimum of three scenes. Each subplot tells the story of one particular character. Each subplot needs a climax. If you have ten subplots peaking, your novel will get explosive; if you have ten subplots, you have some cutting to do.

Find models for your subplots in novels that have passed the time-test. Mr Rochester's subplot, for example, peaks at the end of Act Two, when he confesses to Jane, telling her about Bertha. He follows his confession by offering a slimy deal, in which Jane would become his mistress instead of his second wife. There is a second climax offstage, unseen by the reader, when Mr Rochester gets hurt trying to save Bertha after she sets fire to Thornfield. (In a recent film adaptation of *Jane Eyre*, the director shows the fire, Bertha falling, and Rochester getting hurt.)

Get to know your major characters by working each subplot from entry point to exit point. Which subplots are strong enough to reach the climax? Mr Rochester's subplot has 'legs'. It lasts all the way to the end. The lovers get married. Jane has a baby. And Mr Rochester gets his eyesight back. Aunt Reed's subplot, on the other hand, ends in the middle of Act Two, when Jane watches her die.

Nouns, verbs, word-pictures, style, and Operation Ratio

With the subplots nailed down and the objects cinching up the story, you can start working on the style – but don't do it sentence by sentence. Instead, develop a plan by doing some analysis. The tool we use for language analysis is called Operation Ratio. It works like this: We circle the nouns in a passage and divide them into two groups: concrete and abstract. Concrete nouns like harpoon and hoof and bell and perfume are known through sensory perception. Abstract nouns like love and administration and construction and predilection are known through the mind. Because the language of fiction is word-pictures, you want lots of concrete nouns and a mere handful of abstract nouns.

Operation Ratio is an awareness exercise for the left lobe of the brain. Don't just read your words; pay close attention, not only to what the words mean, but also to their bulk, their weight, their power. The highest ratio of concrete nouns to abstract nouns that we have seen occurs in *Justine*, part of Lawrence Durrell's *Alexandria Quartet*. The ratio is 20:1, concrete to abstract; you could learn from his word-pictures. The ratio in passages from *Jane Eyre* is 8:1. Anything less than an 8:1 ratio and you will have trouble writing word-pictures.

After analysing your nouns – and comparing your ratios to the ratios of your favourite writers – run Operation Ratio to find the ratio of weak verbs (subjunctives, passives, infinitives, and interiors) to strong verbs. Strong verbs express action: The boy hit the ball. Weak verbs slow the action down: The boy should have been considered to have been having trouble hitting the ball because he had thought that he had always been accustomed to being eliminated by this particular pitcher. (Verb-analysis: 'should have been considered' combines the passive voice with the subjunctive; 'to have been' is an infinitive; 'had thought' is an interior verb used in the past perfect, which warps time.)

Other interior verbs that shatter word-pictures are: know, assume, understand, allege, wonder, opine, consider, etc. If you don't feel the weakness in these weak verbs, you should write essays instead of novels. If, however, you love the feel of strong verbs, then you should take verb-selection to the next level. Hit, for example, is a generic verb – it's like run and dance and eat – and when you go for style (because, as a weekend novelist, you are the style, and the style is you), you must make stylistic choices. To make a stylistic choice, you have to work on the verb-slot in the sentence, changing the verb until you feel the words coming in a rush. For example:

The boy smacked the ball.
The boy drove the ball.
The boy whacked the ball.
The boy arced the ball.
The boy hammered the ball.
The boy shattered the ball.
The boy caught the ball in the dead centre of his bat, the sweet spot, and he felt the hum of victory zip from the wood to his fingers, his palms, his wrists, his forearms, and he took off for first base, toes digging in and dirt flying, boosted by the shouts from the stands.

Operation Ratio makes us aware of our language; awareness of language makes us better writers. This is one writing exercise you can try at home, when you are weary, when you've had a bad day, and when you are certain that your manuscript is useless. You have lost all hope of ever becoming a writer, so you grab a red biro. You circle your nouns. Your brain whirs. You don't remember writing that noun. Or that one. Or that. Who wrote those nouns? Using another colour – red for nouns, blue for verbs – you circle your verbs. And because you have done the work on language, your analytical brain sees a pattern, and the pattern leads you to a ten-minute rewrite loaded with concrete nouns and strong verbs, and if you keep rewriting like this, using your left brain to define pattern and your creative, child-like right brain to play, to have fun with both style and story, then you will finish this novel and readers will feel the energy, and they will stand in line at the bookshop, and they will order your novels online from Amazon.com and Powells.com, but don't give up your real job, because there is material there for the next novel.

Exercises

1. Read the manuscript and make lists. Character list. Object list. Scenes and settings and subplots.

2. Make a decision about subplots. This is your first novel. How many subplots can you manage? How many does your story need? How many subplots have three or more scenes? How many subplots start in Act One and end in Act Three?

3. Cut what you don't need. Cut characters. Cut subplots. Cut unnecessary scenes. Cut exposition. Cut narration. Cut dialogue. Cutting makes room for rewriting. After you cut, there is less to rewrite.

4. Perform Operation Ratio on 10–15 paragraphs in key locations: plot points, turning points, climaxes, mini-climaxes, and threshold-crossings.

5. With the truth of noun and verb ratios staring you in the face, set your timer and do some editing. When the timer rings, stop editing and rewrite.

Weekend 52:

The Weekend Novelist writes a screenplay

Turning your rough draft into a screenplay is a reductive process. Using the techniques in this book, you will have to squeeze the manuscript down and then extract the story elements (scene heading, action, dialogue, etc.) that make a screenplay. Squeezing takes work, sweat, discipline, tenacity, and all your writing muscle. At the end of the reduction process, you'll have no bulgy narration left and no puffy exposition taking up space. Your action will be clear, your dialogue sharp. Because of the strictures of the screenplay form, your pages will display more white space. And, alas, some of your characters will have abandoned the project.

Let's look at the numbers. The reading audience for your first novel could be 10,000 for the hardback, and another 90,000 in paperback. If your novel strikes a cultural chord, and becomes the summer beach book like Dan Brown's *The Da Vinci Code*, it could be read by millions.

Your film script, on the other hand, will be read by a handful of industry insiders: agents, directors, producers, and bankable actors. You're writing a 'spec' script. The word 'spec' is short for 'speculative', which means you are gambling – using your time and your money to develop a script before you sell it. You build it strong and you build it beautiful, and you aim at the marketplace in the hope that some buyer will turn it into a film. Your first step in scriptwriting is a story told with a list of scenes. No problem for a weekend novelist; you have been numbering your scenes since Weekend 29, when you launched your rough draft.

The scene list, with its numbers and named scenes, is a compression tool that helps you squeeze your story down. Consider this: *The English Patient* in novel form runs to page 301. The shooting script of *The English Patient* runs to 121 pages and contains 218 numbered scenes. The finished script of *Leaving Las Vegas*, printed in book form and a must-read for any aspiring novelist-turned-screenwriter, runs to 105 pages, while the paperback novel runs to page 189. The number of pages is a measuring device: in most films, one page of script equals one minute of screen time.

Perform this easy test: open a novel and stand it up on your desk, so that the pages are visible. Alongside the novel, prop a film script. Back away a couple of steps and what do you see? The novel is mostly black type. The film script is thin lines of black type separated by chunks of white space. One page of a paperback novel can hold 300–400 words. One page of a film script might hold 150–200 words.

Because you have worked your material through the weekend process, you have had several chances to feel the power of compression. We started out with compression on Weekend 1 with the plot diagram, a compression device that reduced your story down to one sheet of paper. We followed the diagram with writing down the page, where you hugged the left-hand margin, forming a column of prose. In a screenplay format, that column moves to the centre of the page. We followed writing down the page with the grid. You learned about character grids and scene grids and grids for plotting the sections of your novel.

Story

Story, in its most basic form, is a competition for a resource-base. For example, Cinderella wants the castle. To gain access to the castle, she must become Princess. To become Princess, she must win the heart of the Prince. To win the heart of the Prince, she must attend the royal ball. She cannot attend the royal ball because she is a slave-girl with nothing to wear. Cinderella's slave-master is the Wicked Stepmother, one of the best villains in the history of storytelling, a nasty woman who wants the castle for one of her evil daughters. The castle is the visible resource-base. The competition in this story is between Cinderella and her Wicked Stepmother, who keeps her locked up.

With this basic competition - protagonist vs. antagonist - in mind, rework your story for the screenplay. Let's look at some other examples. Jay Gatsby, a male Cinderella figure, wants East Egg, an enclave of the rich. He wants not only to live there, but also to be accepted by the East Eggians. In dramatic terms, East Egg is a closed circle, a citadel of the rich, and Gatsby is the archetypal intruder. The guardian of the threshold at East Egg is Tommy Buchanan, husband of Daisy. Daisy, who wears white, fell in love with Gatsby in Louisville during the war. The resource-base is East Egg. Gatsby is the protagonist; Tommy is the antagonist. Because they are equally matched, Daisy seizes control. She will decide Gatsby's fate. She will choose what happens to her Louisville Lover. If she chooses him, she will have to leave East Egg. So Daisy chooses Tommy and Gatsby loses, and the novel, published in 1925, continues to sell today.

While Gatsby intrudes into East Egg, Jane Eyre penetrates the closed circle of Thornfield Hall, an English country house, where she struggles with her lover-antagonist, Mr Edward Fairfax Rochester. Jane is a 19th-century British Cinderella and she wants safety and warmth and comfort. Jane's competition with Mr Rochester is a lesson in balance for all storytellers. He has money; she has standards. He gets drunk; she saves him from death by fire because she does not drink. He invites her to become his mistress; she not only says no, but she leaves Thornfield behind and spends the night on the deadly, fog-bound heath. Thornfield Hall is the resource-base in *Jane Eyre*. When Jane discovers that her beloved Thornfield conceals the secret wife – Bertha Mason Rochester, the real Mrs Rochester – Jane rejects Thornfield and all that it means to her.

Squeezing the story in *Trophy Wives*

If you are writing a rags-to-riches story with a Cinderella protagonist (Gatsby, Jane, the Julia Roberts character in *Pretty Woman*), you can use wealth-symbolism (money, big house, enclave) as the resource-base. In *Trophy Wives*, our novel-in-progress, the Cinderella figure is Veronica, the mixed-race Indian girl who meets the handsome prince in the rainswept car park. The resource-base in *Trophy Wives* is the family business, Phoenix Investments – the machine that produces the money to keep the big Nob Hill house running. Let's compress the rough draft, which runs to 221 pages in manuscript form, with a list that runs down the page:

Veronica marries Paul.
He is rich.
She is poor.
Paul has a mistress, Ashleigh, who cooks the books at Phoenix Investments. Ashleigh wants to marry Paul, have his babies.
Gwyn, Paul's lover before Ashleigh, wants to marry Paul and be rich.
Barbara, Paul's older sister, wants control of Phoenix Investments.
Barbara has a secret lover, Detective Anderson.

With six characters competing for the resource-base, you add murder, and evil ripples through the character list. Once Ashleigh dies, Veronica is alone with three characters who want her dead – Barbara, Gwyn, and Anderson – and her conniving husband, Paul, who betrayed their love with a rival female. Her only hope for survival is to turn herself into a detective. But she still needs help. One of the biggest decisions you have to make in screenwriting is the genre. For example, when you drop a murder into your story, the genre becomes a mystery. Without the murder, the story on film is a 'drama'. Add a policeman like Anderson, and there is no doubt: you're writing a mystery. If you have read *The Weekend Novelist Writes a Mystery*, you probably remember the four character roles: Killer, Sleuth, Victim, and Catalyst. So let's assign roles to the characters in *Trophy Wives*:

Killer: Gwyn
Sleuth: Veronica
Victim: Ashleigh
Victim 2:   Paul
Catalyst: Barbara
Catalyst Helper: Anderson

In a mystery tale, the catalyst character makes things happen. One of the best example is Caspar Gutman, the fat man in *The Maltese Falcon*, who orchestrates the action by sending his thugs out to do the work. In *Trophy Wives*, the catalyst role shifts our attention to Barbara Watson, Paul's older sister, and the plot takes on another level. What if Barbara wants Veronica dead too? What if Barbara sends Gwyn to kill Veronica? What if she sends Anderson to kill Gwyn? And, since Veronica needs a helper, what if Anderson has a change of heart? What if he is a wounded hero who is tired of corruption? What if he meets Veronica, is touched by her innocence, and feels something go 'click' inside his heart? How much killing will it take to clean Anderson's tarnished shield?

Writing the screenplay: *Trophy Wives*

As you continue to play with roles and motives, you can get acquainted with the structure of a screenplay. Screenplays are short, the form is both rigid and helpful, and there is fancy screenwriting software to help you convert your prose to the film-script format.

One type of software, Final Draft, sets up the page as a template, and then offers seven story elements, one for each part of the screenplay: Scene Heading, Shot, Action, Character, Dialogue, Parenthetical, and Transition. On the page, the elements control the space:

Scene Heading identifies the scene: EXT. A RAINSWEPT CAR PARK – DAY

Shot applies focus: Close on the SHOPPING BAG. Rain-soaked.

Action is action: Veronica drops the shopping.

Character identifies dialogue speaker: VERONICA.

Dialogue is what the character says: Thank you.

Parentheticals cue the actor: (shaking her head)

Transitions like CUT TO signal jump-cuts to the next scene heading.

Because you already have a list of scenes, you can test the power of the screenplay software by entering your Scene 1 onto Page 1. If you were the writer of *Trophy Wives*, you could start with Veronica in her black funeral dress standing at the door of the Nob Hill house, or you could start with the First Encounter in the rainswept car park.

EXT. CAR PARK IN THE RAIN — DAY

Veronica Dane, 25, drops a bag of shopping on her way to the car, a battered Honda with rust spots. We hear the sound of glass breaking. She looks up to see Paul Watson stepping out of a Porsche. He wears Mephisto shoes and a Burberry raincoat.

Squatting down, Paul helps Veronica carry her groceries to the Honda.

VERONICA
Thank you.

PAUL
No problem. Are you going to be okay?

VERONICA
As soon as I get these things home.

SOUND of the starter grinding, but the Honda refuses to start. Veronica looks out of the window to see the Porsche alongside her car, Paul getting out. She winds down her window. Paul shows her an expensive mobile phone.

PAUL
If you give me your car dealer's number, I'll get some help out here.

VERONICA
(shaking her head)
I can't. There's no way. There's no dealer and I...

PAUL
Hey. Don't cry, okay?

CUT TO: INT. COFFEE SHOP – DAY

Veronica sits huddled in her raincoat, watching Paul at the counter of the coffee shop, smiling as he chats with the waitress, a stunning blonde. Reaching into her rucksack, Veronica pulls out a vintage hardback copy of *Jane Eyre*. The book, a treasure, is held together with two rubber bands. She's reading as Paul approaches.

PAUL
Your tea, madame.

Veronica closes the book, takes a deep breath, and forces a smile.

END OF SCREENPLAY.

In this opening scene, Paul seems like a good guy because he rescues Veronica. His heroic action in the rainswept car park tricks her into thinking that he will protect her from the hardness of the world. He does not come on heavy like Mr Rochester, and that leaves Act One for courtship and marriage, with two turning-point scenes. In the middle of Act One, Veronica sees Paul with Ashleigh, as she reveals what she wants. At the end of Act One, which could be a wedding scene, Veronica responds to a kindness from Barbara.

When the subplots start to 'cook' in your script, you can push a button and tell your software to collect together all the scenes featuring Character X. You can print out those scenes and analyse the subplot of Character X. As you analyse, check for objects like wardrobe items (e.g. the Breitling watch that Paul inherited from his dad), vehicles, buildings, rooms, and dialogue lines that echo through the story.

Keep pushing events that lead to the climax. What if Veronica takes the role of sleuth? What if Paul tries to protect Gwyn? What if Gwyn plans on killing Veronica next? What if Paul tries to stop her? And what if Gwyn kills Paul and then goes for Veronica, who then has to defend herself?

Exercises

1. Identify the resource-base in your story.
2. Transform your main characters into archetypes.
3. Using your list of scenes, enter the first ten scenes into your favourite screenwriting software programme.
4. Using the software, isolate the subplots.
5. Keep writing to the end.